COMPARATIVE AND INTERNATIONAL EDUCATION SERIES

Volume 3

Human Rights and Educa

COMPARATIVE AND INTERNATIONAL EDUCATION

NOTICE TO READERS

Dear Reader

An invitation to publish in and recommend the placing of a standing order to volumes published in this valuable series.

If your library is not already a standing/continuation order customer to this series, may we recommend that you place a standing/continuation order to receive immediately upon publication all new volumes. Should you find that these volumes no longer serve your needs, your order can be cancelled at any time without notice.

The Editors and the Publisher will be glad to receive suggestions or outlines or suitable titles, reviews or symposia for editorial consideration: if found acceptable, rapid publication is guaranteed.

ROBERT MAXWELL
Publisher at Pergamon Press

Human Rights and Education

Edited by

Norma Bernstein Tarrow
California State University,
Long Beach, USA.

PERGAMON PRESS
OXFORD · NEW YORK · BEIJING · FRANKFURT
SÃO PAULO · SYDNEY · TOKYO · TORONTO

U.K.	Pergamon Press, Headington Hill Hall, Oxford OX3 0BW, England
U.S.A.	Pergamon Press, Maxwell House, Fairview Park, Elmsford, New York 10523, U.S.A.
PEOPLE'S REPUBLIC OF CHINA	Pergamon Press, Room 4037, Qianmen Hotel, Beijing, People's Republic of China
FEDERAL REPUBLIC OF GERMANY	Pergamon Press, Hammerweg 6, D-6242 Kronberg, Federal Republic of Germany
BRAZIL	Pergamon Editora, Rua Eça de Queiros, 346, CEP 04011, Paraiso, São Paulo, Brazil
AUSTRALIA	Pergamon Press Australia, P.O. Box 544, Potts Point, N.S.W. 2011, Australia
JAPAN	Pergamon Press, 8th Floor, Matsuoka Central Building, 1-7-1 Nishishinjuku, Shinjuku-ku, Tokyo 160, Japan
CANADA	Pergamon Press Canada, Suite No. 271, 253 College Street, Toronto, Ontario, Canada, M5T 1R5

Copyright © 1987 Pergamon Books Ltd.

First edition 1987

Library of Congress Cataloging-in-Publication Data
Human rights and education.
(Comparative and international education series; v. 3)
Includes index.
1. Right to education. 2. Human rights—Study and teaching. 3. Comparative education. I. Tarrow, Norma Bernstein. II. Series.
LC213.H86 1987 370.19 87-10392

British Library Cataloguing in Publication Data
Human rights and education.——(Comparative and international education; v. 3).
1. Civil rights——Study and teaching
I. Bernstein-Tarrow, Norma II. Series
323.4'07 JC571

ISBN 0-08-033887-9 (Hard cover)
ISBN 0-08-033415-6 (Flexicover)

Printed in Great Britain by The Whitefriars Press Ltd., Tonbridge

Introduction to the Series

The Comparative and International Education Series is dedicated to inquiry and analysis on educational issues in an interdisciplinary cross-national framework. As education affects larger populations and educational issues are increasingly complex and, at the same time, international in scope, this series presents research and analysis aimed at understanding contemporary educational issues. The series brings the best scholarship to topics which have direct relevance to educators, policy makers and scholars, in a format that stresses the international links among educational issues. Comparative education not only focuses on the development of educational systems and policies around the world, but also stresses the relevance of an international understanding of the particular problems and dilemmas that face educational systems in individual countries.

Interdisciplinarity is a hallmark of comparative education and this series will feature studies based on a variety of disciplinary, methodological and ideological underpinnings. Our concern is for relevance and the best in scholarship.

The series will combine careful monographic studies that will help policy makers and others obtain a needed depth for enlightened analysis with wider-ranging volumes that may be useful to educators and students in a variety of contexts. Books in the series will reflect on policy and practice in a range of educational settings from pre-primary to post-secondary. In addition, we are concerned with non-formal education and with the societal impact of educational policies and practices. In short, the scope of the Comparative and International Education Series is interdisciplinary and contemporary.

I wish to thank a distinguished editorial advisory board including:

Professor Suma Chitnis, Tata University of Social Sciences, Bombay, India.

Professor Kazayuki Kitamura, Research Institute on Higher Education, Hiroshima University, Japan.

Professor Gail P. Kelly, State University of New York at Buffalo, USA.

Dean Thomas LaBelle, University of Pittsburgh, USA.

Dr S. Gopinathan, Institute of Education, Singapore.

Professor Guy Neave, Institute of Education, London.

PHILIP G. ALTBACH

Contents

Prologue

The Western Region of the US International and Comparative Education Society is to be congratulated on its initiative in preparing this book. Its publication is very timely because of its two themes—education as a human right and education for human rights—are the subject of considerable debate all over the world.

In addition to their traditional role of transmitting knowledge and values, education systems are being pressed to respond to a new range of aspirations and to a wide variety of economic, political, social and cultural developments whose roots lie outside the education system.

It has been claimed that the twenty-one countries that make up the Council of Europe represent two-thirds of the world's parliamentary democracies. But, probably as a result of the economic recession, there has been a disturbing increase in challenges to democratic values in Western Europe in the past few years through the growth of intolerance, xenophobia, violence and terrorism.

Governments and public figures have expressed concern that many young people leave school after ten or more years of compulsory education, without the basic knowledge and skills to make informed political decisions. This bodes ill for the future of democracy, and national authorities and international organizations like the Council of Europe have intensified their efforts to ensure that young people are guaranteed their right to education and that education systems equip them with the knowledge, skills and attitudes that they will need if they are to take an active part in the operation of democratic institutions.

The highest political body of the Council of Europe, the Committee of Ministers, has recommended that "throughout their school career, all young people should learn about human rights as part of their preparation for life in a pluralistic democracy." The development of human rights education has become one of the Council of Europe's priorities, and the Council is working with teachers, specialists and non-governmental organizations to answer such questions as: how can education systems help to make young people aware of their common heritage of freedom and the rule of law? How can they further an active commitment to human rights and the principles of pluralistic democracy? And how can they encourage a respect for others and the special qualities of other cultures? The promotion of intercultural understanding is of crucial importance because so many countries have become multicultural societies through migration and immigration.

Human rights education is much wider than just teaching about human rights or learning legal texts and procedures by heart. It should permeate the whole of school life—the ethos and organization of the school, as well as the content of the formal curriculum. It should lead to an understanding of, and sympathy for, the concepts of democracy, justice, equality, freedom, solidarity, peace, dignity, and rights and responsibilities. It should also lead to the acquisition of certain basic skills, in particular:

—skills associated with language development, such as written and oral expression and the ability to discuss and listen;
—skills involving judgments—the collection and analysis of material from various sources, the detection of prejudice and bias (including the mass media), and the ability to arrive at fair and balanced conclusions;
—social skills, including the recognition and acceptance of differences and the ability to form positive and non-oppressive personal relationships;
—action skills such as solving conflict in a non-violent way, taking responsibility, participating in group decisions, and understanding and using the mechanisms for the protection of human rights that exist at local, national, European and world levels.

Given the diversity of national education systems, the content of human rights education varies from country to country and, in some cases, even from school to school. Nevertheless there should be a common core consisting of:

—the main categories of human rights, duties, obligations and responsibilities. In human rights education, the idea of rights should be matched by that of responsibilities and duties to other individuals, to the community and to humanity as a whole;
—the various forms of injustice, inequality and discrimination, including racism and sexism;
—people, movements and key events in the historical and continuing struggle for human rights;
—the main international declarations and conventions on human rights, e.g., the Universal Declaration of Human Rights and the European Convention for the Protection of Human Rights and Fundamental Freedoms.

Many educators argue that the climate and organization of a school are important factors in the social and political education of its pupils, and some aspects of human rights education will, therefore, stem from the ethos of the school rather than be taught directly.

Extracurricular activities too can give pupils an opportunity to use and develop their interpersonal and planning skills, to learn and practice participation, and to acquire a sense of responsibility and cooperation. Such activities can range from school clubs and cooperatives to contacts with organizations working for human rights in the community, e.g., Amnesty International and the Minority Rights Group.

As human rights education involves the domain of political activity, it can be sensitive and, at times, even controversial. However, as was pointed out by the Council of Europe's Symposium on Human Rights Education in Schools in Western Europe, in Vienna in 1983, "the dangers of not preparing the next generation to assume their role in society are much greater than the risks involved in a balanced human rights education."

MAITLAND STOBART
Deputy Director of Education, Culture and Sport
Council of Europe

PART 1

Education as a Human Right

CHAPTER 1

Human Rights and Education: An Overview

Douglas Ray
University of Western Ontario

Norma Bernstein Tarrow
California State University, Long Beach

Introduction

This is a book about human rights and education and the relationship between the two. It is dedicated to the proposition that human rights are held equally by all persons simply by virtue of being human; that they go beyond the basic rights of life and liberty to include cultural, economic, social and political rights essential for the maintenance of human dignity. The book is written by educators and reflects a conviction that education is not only encompassed within the concept of human rights, but is the ultimate sanction and guarantee of all the others. It is responsible for informing people of their responsibilities and their rights and should build public awareness that oppressive laws and inappropriate traditions may be reformed. Thus, it offers a dual perspective—of education *as* a human right and education *about* human rights.

This book is directed at educators, policymakers, and advanced students in such areas as comparative and international education, educational foundations, sociology, political science and public policy. It is based on the premise that a unique contribution can be made by identifying educational rights addressed by various international agreements and analyzing case studies representing various regions, political systems, and levels of development where progress has been made towards implementation of these rights. The authors have taken the position that, imperfect as these agreements may be, they are still the best available statements of international goals and the most appropriate basis for analyses and comparisons of such progress. Rights are neither achieved easily nor uniformly, and thus, the authors have taken the further position that it is facile yet counterproductive to focus on violations. While well aware of many negative instances, the writers have, therefore, taken a positive approach in examining representative cases where major problems are being met with some degree of success that have implications for other nations and for the future.

3

Part 1 examines different aspects of the right to education. Included are rights of access and equality of opportunity without regard to race, religion, ethnic group, socioeconomic class, gender, or geographic location. The right to universal literacy, to preservation of language and culture, to political education, to education for multicultural understanding, to technical and vocational education, to political education, and to education to meet special needs on a lifelong basis are examined. Ways of achieving some balance among the rights of parents and children, as well as students and teachers, are also considered. Progress towards the implementation of these rights is assessed in terms of the criteria established by international agreements.

Part 2 examines education about human rights. This includes knowledge of and respect for human rights—a kind of civic education that may extend from primary level to the training of professionals, such as lawyers, law enforcement personnel, and teachers. Included are aspects of curriculum and teacher preparation to assure effective human rights education. The best guarantee of human rights is an educated public that is aware of its rights. Thus, education about human rights is, after all, seen as the ultimate sanction of human rights—including the right to education.

Some Basic Assumptions[1]

In each of the subsequent chapters, the focus on a particular educational right is a positive one, with each author illustrating the rights implementation in selected societies from various parts of the world. Because of their specificity of focus, none of these chapters directly addresses the most basic notions about the nature of human rights in general. Yet, such unstated notions undergird the central issues treated throughout the book. It is therefore incumbent upon us to identify a number of such concepts so the reader might more readily recognize these implied assumptions. The concepts explored are those concerning (1) how rights are defined and (2) conditions affecting the setting of standards and implementation.

Rights Defined

Different societies define rights in terms of their own historical experience, their value systems, and the political and economic realities of modern life. In each chapter, the authors have devoted considerable attention to these issues. In addition, this section will examine some unstated assumptions that should be noted regarding the adjectives used to describe rights, their dialectical nature and the rationales used in their support.

[1] We are indebted to all the authors of this volume for their suggestions and critiques of various versions of this chapter—and, most of all, to R. Murray Thomas for his major contribution to this section.

Rights to groups and groups of rights

A right is a privilege or opportunity to which an individual is entitled simply by virtue of being a member of the group to which that right applies. The group that deserves the particular right is typically identified by an adjective that accompanies the word "right." Thus, a *human right* is a privilege belonging to all *Homo sapiens*; *children's rights* are entitlements that apply to those *Homo sapiens* who are below a given age level; *Brazilian citizen's rights* are privileges owed to everyone who qualifies for citizenship in Brazil; and *students' rights* are prerogatives of all those who fit the designation "student." The aspect of life to which a right applies can also be indicated by an adjective, as in such terms as political rights, nautical rights, and educational rights. Both of these types of adjectives—those designating groups and those designating aspects of life—appear in this book. The entire volume is about rights in one aspect of life—education, while individual chapters concern different groups identified by their ethnicity, gender, religion, type of handicap, and the like.

Rights: privilege and responsibility

Often, a right is simply a privilege which people are free to adopt or not while others involve obligations for certain segments of the population in certain situations. For instance, the right to vote does not oblige Canadian citizens to do so while in Australia, by contrast, a penalty is exacted on citizens who do not vote. Various other rights are partly an opportunity to participate or not, but the laws of most modern societies regarding the right to education, at least officially, mandate schooling through a specified age or grade, assigning certain responsibilities for conformance to both parents and students.

In brief, rights are usually both related to a particular aspect of life and are privileges people acquire because of their membership in a particular group. In some cases people are free to decide whether or not to avail themselves of these rights. In other cases they are, at least officially, obligated to exercise the rights—and they can expect to suffer negative sanctions if they fail to do so.

Rights from a dialectical perspective

In defining rights, one must take into account the complications created by dialectical perspectives. Certain rights can be seen as the converse or reciprocal of other rights with which they are in conflict. In the world's current population-growth crisis, the right of parents to bear as many children as they want can conflict with the right of the state to prevent population increases from outstripping the ability of the society to house and feed all its members adequately. The right of criminals to humane treatment and to the assumption of innocence until proven guilty can conflict with the right of the victims of crime to be safe from future criminal attacks. The right of free speech conflicts with the right to protection from slander. And in the realm of education, whenever the number of openings to advanced educational institutions is limited, the right of everyone to have equal access to schooling conflicts with the right of the more apt students to receive admission preference. Sometimes the factors contributing to the conflict over rights are more complex than the above paired examples imply. Thus, not only can teacher's rights conflict with students' rights, but they can conflict also with administrators' rights, parents' rights, and the rights of the general public. Finally, all societies deal with the conflict between the rights of the individual and those of the group. As will be discussed later, the weight given to either side, and the balance established between sides, differs in different political systems and has implications for the interpretation of various agreements.

There are at least two ways that this dialectical perspective can contribute to an understanding of this book. First, as the authors of the chapters have described struggles over educational rights in selected nations, they have not always specified the dialectical pairs of rights that are in contention. Rather, they often focus only on the rights being sought by one group—such as the rights of an ethnic group or the rights of the handicapped. The authors' assumption is that the reader will automatically recognize potential converse rights which may be claimed by another group or groups competing for rights. Thus, we are suggesting at this point that readers be alert to identifying what the unmentioned reciprocal or converse rights may be as each chapter presents evidence of the struggle and progress towards implementation of particular educational rights.

The second way a dialectical perspective can aid understanding is related to the first. It concerns the matter of being forthright about one's motives. People who are struggling to attain or retain a particular right are not always willing to be open and honest in their intentions, because the right they are claiming is unpopular. Thus, while in earlier times, privilege could usually be openly claimed on the basis of status (such as social class, ethnic or racial group, caste, nationality, gender, or religion) such a rationale is generally unacceptable to current prevailing world opinion. This does not mean that people have given up trying to win privilege on such bases. Rather, it means that they do not openly argue their case on such grounds but offer nobler reasons for their claims. Therefore, readers are likely to find the events described throughout this book more comprehensible if they are aware of hidden desires of claimants of educational rights.

Rationales in support of rights

If one claims a right, yet no one else believes the right is deserved, then in actuality one does not have that right at all. Unless others accept a claim as valid, or at least enforceable, one will be prevented from exercising it. This observation appears to be governed by the principle that a claim becomes a right in reality only in proportion to the number of people of influence who accept that claim and abide by it. To this end, advocates of rights typically adduce rationales that are intended to convince people of influence that a proposed right is truly deserved by citing various authorities. What types of authority are usually cited?

Perhaps the simplest approach is to assert that the validity of the right is so apparent that it requires no proof. It is assumed that, anyone in his or her right mind would recognize the truth of the matter, as in Jefferson's famous words:

> We hold these truths to be self-evident,—that all men are created equal; that they are endowed by their Creator with certain unalienable rights; that among these are life, liberty, and the pursuit of happiness (*US Declaration of Independence, 1776*).

A second sort of appeal—and one obliquely included in Jefferson's assertion—is to authority. For example, evidence that the right has been granted by The Almighty is found either in direct statements in the holy scriptures or in the interpretations provided by priests, pastors, imams, gurus, or the like. Support for a claim to a right may also be offered as the opinion of a secular authority—a jurist, philosopher, king, president, official or legislative body. For children, parents or teachers often serve as adequate authorities for assuring the propriety of a right. Widespread popular belief represents another source of authority. If a great many people agree that a claim to a right is valid, then the claim must be true. This sort of rationale is founded on the assumption that the majority is always right. There may also be an appeal to tradition or custom. If the claimed privilege has been generally accepted over a period of many years, then it obviously has stood the test of time and thereby qualifies as an authentic right. The conviction that a claim is valid can also be strengthened by casting it in legal form—as in a written agreement among nations, in a government's constitution, or in a law or regulation passed by a local body. The force of conviction is further increased whenever negative sanctions are provided for people who violate the right.

Rather than citing authorities, supporters of a right often attempt to gain support by appealing to people's sympathies. This approach often involves asking people to empathize with the plight of those for whom the right is being sought. The wording of a rationale in support of a right can also influence the extent to which people will accept the claim as proper. An example is Jefferson's including in his assertion the term "unalienable," implying that there is no possible way that such a right could be removed. Other phrases intended to foster conviction include: *God-given right, inherent right, entitlement, undeniable right, irrefutable right*, and *immutable right*.

In summary, then, proponents of a particular right may use any variety of arguments to convince others that their claim is just. The educational rights discussed in this volume have depended on such modes of appeal for their acceptance.

With the foregoing observations about the nature of rights in hand, we next consider the question of why human rights become of general concern at particular points in history.

Conditions Affecting the Setting of Standards and Implementation

This chapter, as well as subsequent ones, identifies numerous human rights agreements that have been endorsed by official representatives of nearly all nations of the world.[2] A significant feature of these agreements is that they are all products of the past four decades. Admittedly, there have been landmark declarations of rights at earlier times in world history—the *Magna Carta* in 1215, documents associated with the American and French revolutions in the eighteenth century, the *Covenant of the League of Nations* in the early twentieth century, and others. However, never before in history have so many governments, representing so many people, committed themselves to promoting so many kinds of human rights as has been the case since World War II. We are living at a time when concern for human rights—including educational rights—has reached new heights. Why, then, has this occurred? Or, to cast the question in broader terms, what conditions influence the establishment of a right, and how have such conditions coalesced at this juncture of history to produce such great interest in human rights? Answering this query in any detail is far beyond the scope of this chapter. However, we can offer some illustrative speculation about the matter in order to indicate the direction such analysis might take. In so doing, we may alert the reader to types of conditions, described in subsequent chapters, that affect the exercise of various sorts of educational rights in each of the societies described. Any such analysis must separate verbal commitment from the actual implementation of a right in daily life—because the factors influencing verbal support and actual implementation may be similar but are by no means identical.

[2] Summaries of education provisions of most of the related international human rights documents are contained in the three appendices: 1: United Nations Documents, 2: UNESCO Documents, and 3: Regional Documents.

Verbal Commitment: Standard-Setting Documents

What, then were the conditions that contributed to such international concern with human rights? In the mid twentieth century, most of the world's people had just emerged from some measure of participation in World War II. It was a war which the victors had fought under a rallying cry of rights, including such rights as political self-determination and freedom from ethnic and religious persecution. The United Nations was formed as a body to promote these rights in a peaceful, lawful manner. Peoples who had suffered in the past from various forms of colonial domination enthusiastically embraced the notion that in the world's new political climate they might enjoy opportunities never before available to them. In addition to these attitudinal factors, the advances in transportation and communication technology in the twentieth century also contributed to the scope of endorsement of rights declarations. By mid-century, people in every region of the earth could be immediately informed of events occurring in all other parts of the world and thereby could participate in monitoring violations of rights. Such unprecedented worldwide exposure of political activities served to exert pressure on political leaders to avoid appearing to be bigoted, prejudiced, imperialistic, and exploitative, so that—whatever their true motives or opinions—they were obliged to commit their governments to the support of the rights described in the series of agreements that have evolved over the past four decades.

Consider the commitment embodied in the very *Charter of the United Nations* which placed the traditional concept of national sovereignty into a framework of interdependence and international responsibility for the guarantee of human rights:

> The United Nations shall promote . . . universal respect for and observance of, human rights and fundamental freedoms for all without distinction as to race, sex, language, or religion (*United Nations Charter, 1945. Chapter IX, Art. 55*).

Recognition of global responsibility for education as a fundamental human right was thus acknowledged in the Charter as well as in the Constitution of the agency charged with the specific responsibilities of education and promoting human rights—the United Nations Educational, Scientific and Cultural Organization (UNESCO).

> The purpose of the organization is to contribute to peace and security by promoting collaboration among the nations through education, science and culture in order to further universal respect for justice, for the rule of law, and for the human rights and fundamental freedoms which are affirmed for the peoples of the world, without distinction of

race, language or religion by the Charter of the United Nations (*Constitution of UNESCO, 1945, Art. 1*).

International idealism received a further stimulus on December 10, 1948, when the General Assembly of the United Nations approved, without opposition, the *Universal Declaration of Human Rights*. The Declaration affirmed so-called "old rights"—such as life, liberty and security (Art. 2), protection from inhuman punishment (Art. 5), and equality before the law (Art. 7) that were traditional in various eighteenth- and nineteenth-century constitutions and legislation. It proclaimed, as well, "new" rights in economic, social and cultural areas essential to human dignity—such as the right to participate in the cultural life of the community (Art. 27) and the right to education (Art. 26).

Among other things, the Declaration proclaimed that free universal schooling should be extended through the primary grades everywhere in the world—as a human right. It also declared that secondary and higher education should be accessible on the basis of merit rather than wealth or station, with access to specialized and technical programs, in every part of the world—as a human right. The rights of parents to choose the type of education appropriate for their children was also affirmed. Perhaps most audacious, the quality of education was also addressed:

> Education shall be directed to the full development of the human personality and to the strengthening of respect for human rights and fundamental freedoms. It shall promote understanding, tolerance and further the activities of the United Nations for the maintenance of peace (*Universal Declaration of Human Rights, 1948, Art. 26*).

Thus, from its start, the United Nations enunciated its concerns both about education *as* a human right and education *about* human rights. These proposals were made when few nations had primary education that was free and compulsory; more often it was not available to all. Access to secondary and higher education was even more limited. Nevertheless, the Universal Declaration enunciated a set of ideals that legitimized education as a priority for development and harmony in many parts of the world. Its clauses have been reaffirmed, amplified and made more specific by later United Nations documents that deal with specific rights (such as education, employment, and expression) or with the rights of particular groups (such as women, children, disabled persons, or refugees).

The 1959 *Declaration of the Rights of the Child* recalled the Universal Declaration and set out ten principles to protect the young. In regard to education, it called for equal opportunity and access to free and compulsory elementary education for all. Such education should promote general culture and develop individual abilities and responsibility. The importance of the parent's role and of opportunities for play and recreation were stressed.

Both of the declarations referred to above are technically resolutions of the General Assembly of the United Nations, which do not require ratification by member states. They do not specify any enforcement procedures but merely call for member states to observe and promote their principles. Approved as standard-setting resolutions, they were intended to influence national constitutions, policies and practices related to the protection and expansion of human rights (Buergenthal and Torney, 1976).

Such international agreements are frequently criticized for describing an ideal rather than reality—losing sight of the fact that they were viewed as standard-setting rather than descriptive, inspirational and aspirational rather than reportorial—directing attention beyond the dust at our feet to the stars in the skies. Setting standards remains a function of persuasion rather than enforcement. There are UNESCO recommendations (which are also not binding), regional agreements (binding on contracting states), and numerous expert conferences, public relations campaigns and scholarly works. All of these attempt to accomplish their aims by gradually moving toward a global consensus on certain aspects of human rights. The force of international law applies only to treaties, conventions and covenants, which will be discussed in the next section.

Implementation of Rights Agreements

Let us consider next, the implementation of declared rights. Events in recent years have shown that implementation has fallen far short of the widespread verbal commitment to rights. Almost daily, the news media report outright violations—or certainly, neglect—of the variety of rights, including educational rights. What factors affect the actual implementation of international agreements?

Economic and social factors

Some of the conditions that contribute to such violations are obvious. One is economic. Although every present-day government has committed itself to universal basic education for its populace, in some countries millions of children never attend school because funds are lacking to pay for buildings, staff, and supplies. Economic factors also combine with long-standing intergroup competition, prejudice, and mistrust to frustrate the implementation of rights. For instance, people in the upper social classes may fear that their superior position will be threatened if people in lower social strata are furnished favorable educational opportunities. Likewise, members of a religious or ethnic group may be unwilling in practice to accord equal rights to those outside their group.

Legal status

A further condition influencing the implementation of rights is the legal status of a right. As the basis for all future agreements, the Universal Declaration has become so influential that Humphrey (1984, p. 73) describes it as part of customary international law, which means that it is binding on all states (a position that does not share universal acceptance.) This renowned legal and human rights expert points out that the criteria for determining what is part of the customary law of nations are met by the Universal Declaration in the following ways:

- It is cited for interpretation of the UN Charter;
- Subsequent resolutions, recommendations, declarations, conventions, and covenants are based on it;
- Treaties, national constitutions and legislation have been derived from it; and
- There has been international condemnation of those who have violated its principles.

  ". . . if the principles set forth in the Declaration are now part of the customary law of nations—and there can be little doubt that they are— they are binding on all states . . . whether they voted for the Declaration or not" (Humphrey, 1984, p. 73).

It must be remembered that while few Third World nations were directly involved in the framing of the Declaration, many of them *were* directly involved in writing and signing many subsequent documents based on its principles. These include the *International Bill of Rights (1966)* and the *Proclamation of Teheran (1968)*. The Bill of Rights is comprised of two important covenants derived from the Universal Declaration and opened for ratification in 1966. Although they are international treaties, binding their signators under stipulated conditions, because only eighty-three nations (1984) have endorsed the *International Covenant of Economic, Social and Cultural Rights* and only eighty the *International Covenant on Civic and Political Rights*, these documents remain imperfect protections of human rights. The former calls for education directed to strengthening the respect for human rights and fundamental freedoms and mandates free, universal primary education with secondary education increasingly accessible. The latter proclaims the rights of ethnic, religious or linguistic minorities "to enjoy their own culture, to profess and practice their own religions, or to use their own language."

The Teheran Proclamation stated that the Universal Declaration "constitutes an obligation for the members of the international community." It further called on all states to conform to various other human rights agreements, protested apartheid and other forms of racial discrimination and called for international action to eradicate illiteracy and discrimination against women, and for protection of the family and of the child. (*Proclamation of Teheran, 1968.*) This proclamation of twenty-nine resolutions, which were adopted by the representatives of eighty-four states gave new direction to subsequent work in the area of human rights.

Interpretation

The level and quality of implementation of human rights agreements is also a function of interpretation, and the history of human rights has continuously been ruffled not only by the differing perspectives of Eastern and Western nations, as well as developing and industrialized societies, but also by the different emphasis on "individual" as opposed to "group" rights. In Western capitalist countries, interpretations tend to focus on individual liberties, but rights in socialist states are considered neither inherent in the individual nor inalienable. In such settings, society takes precedence over the individual and responsibility over privilege. And in regard to human rights, law provides few restraints on those in power (Kartashkin, 1982; Mower, 1980; Szymanski, 1984). Nevertheless, it is an over-simplification to associate individual or group rights exclusively with certain nations, for both categories are studied, addressed, and implemented to some degree everywhere, subject to local procedures.

In addition, some of the agreements approved in the early years of the United Nations are criticized for reflecting a particular cultural perspective (e.g., "Western oriented"). Such labels have been used by cultural nationalists both to justify violations and to advocate wholesale rejection of the human rights movement (Coomaraswamy, 1982). This type of skeptical relativism is the greatest threat to the protection of human rights and one which could lead to a denial of the recognition of the common values which transcend cultural differences between early and present members of the international community (Valticos, 1979).

Effectiveness of machinery to deal with violations

Unfortunately, rights are also denied or infringed in many parts of the world. Violations of human rights take many forms—from the deliberate (e.g., apartheid) to the less obvious (e.g., exploiting certain groups, such as women). This suggests the necessity for looking at actual practice in addition to the existence of national laws reflecting international standards concerning human rights. Those governments accused of violating human rights often have a penchant for redefining rights in such a way as to bring themselves into compliance (Orwin and Pangle, 1984). For example, detainment of Soviet dissident educators and scientists can be perceived as a clear violation of Article 12.2 of the *International Covenant on Civil and Political*

Rights, but an alternative perspective states that the right of emigration may be superceded by actions to protect the public good.

Clearly, the most consistent example of human rights violations is presented by the case of South Africa. In 1952, the question of apartheid was raised in the United Nations. South Africa challenged the authority of the Assembly to deal with, or even discuss, a matter within its domestic jurisdiction—resulting in the Assembly's justification of its action on the basis of Article 56 of the *United Nations Charter*. The Assembly called on all Member States to bring their domestic policies into compliance with the obligations under the Charter. Since then, the abolition of racist domination and exploitation in South Africa, in the field of education, as well as all other aspects of life, have become primary concerns of the entire United Nations system of organizations and of the international community as a whole. Various documents have addressed the issues of apartheid, including the *International Convention on the Suppression and Punishment of the Crime of Apartheid (1973)*. Apartheid has been decreed a crime against humanity, and measures to prosecute and punish those responsible for acts of apartheid have been demanded. The overall ineffectiveness of these efforts highlights one of the major problems in the area of human rights—the ineffectiveness of enforcement mechanisms.

The last four decades have witnessed the adoption of numerous "legally binding" conventions and covenants, as well as the establishment of various commissions charged with enforcement—both at world and regional organization levels. The reality, however, is that these commissions have been able to do little more than hear appeals. Pervading pessimism is reflected even in the words of one of the framers of the Declaration:

> . . . if the adoption of the Declaration is one of the greatest achieve-
> ments of the UN, the inability of the organization to respond effectively
> to . . . appeals is one of its greatest failures (Humphrey, 1984, p. 71).

A more optimistic view contends that by compelling governments to justify their actions, exposing situations of non-conformance, and creating an educated public, eventually a different international environment, more conducive to full implementation of international human rights, will be established.

The Chapters That Follow

Each chapter of Part 1 entitled *Education as a Human Right*, deals with one of the components implied by the right to education. Since existing international documents presuppose substantive agreement among peoples, these documents are considered the yardsticks to assess the implementation of the various constituent rights. Analysis and comparison of the cases of two or more nations provide some positive examples of progress towards implementation.

Chapter 2: Rights of Access and Equal Opportunity: Focus on Sub-Saharan Africa

Chapter 3: The Right to Education Free From Discrimination: The Cases of India and Saudi Arabia

Chapter 4: Exceptional Abilities and Educational Rights: Concern for the Handicapped and Gifted in Britain, China, and Indonesia

Chapter 5: The Right to Literacy

Chapter 6: The Right to Education for Multicultural Development: Canada and Israel

Chapter 7: The Right to Education for Employment and Mobility: Norway and Yugoslavia

Chapter 8: The Right to Lifelong Education in Kenya and the United States With Special Reference to Adult Education

Chapter 9: The Rights of Parents, Students and Teachers in Canada and the Philippines

Chapter 10: The Right to a Political Education

Each author, using a personal style within a common theoretical and structural framework, has provided information about each of the rights and countries discussed to help the reader understand:

- What direction has been taken or solutions attempted towards implementation of the right being considered?
- What are the problems encountered in implementation in view of traditions, cultural factors, political and economic factors, etc., which may hinder implementation?
- What direction has been taken or solutions attempt towards implementation of the right being considered?
- What progress has been made and what measures of success achieved?
- What are future plans and prospects in regard to implementation of the right being considered?

Part 2 examines *Education about Human Rights including*:

Chapter 11: Human Rights Education in Schools

Chapter 12: Education About Human Rights: Teacher Preparation

Synthesis and Conclusions

The concluding chapter by Judith Torney-Purta contains a synthesis of the material in the preceding chapters organized around six thematic questions relating to human rights:

- Education for whom?
- Education with what goals and content?
- Education responsible to what social, cultural, political, or economic context?
- Education organized within what decision making structure?
- Education judged by what criteria of overall success?

An agenda for further work by comparative educators including policy research, social and behavioral research, and curriculum research is also suggested. The implications she extrapolates provide a fitting conclusion to this work and an optimistic introduction to a new era of consciousness of the interrelationship between education and human rights.

Throughout the book, each chapter invites some type of comparison, with examples which are often representative of many other nations in particular ways. Representation of different political ideologies, levels of development and geographical regions was also a consideration in the selection of case studies. In addition, each case is an integral part of the experience and knowledge of the scholars who presented preliminary versions of these chapters at the western regional meeting of the Comparative and International Education Society at California State University, Long Beach in November 1985. The versions that follow benefitted greatly from the constructive criticism of conference participants and subsequent extended dialogue with their fellow authors.

References

Buergenthal, T. and Torney, J. (1976) *International human rights and international education*. Washington, DC: National Commission for UNESCO.
Coomaraswamy, R. (1982) A third world view of human rights. *UNESCO Courier*, August/September, pp. 49–50.
Humphrey, J. (1984) *Human rights and the United Nations: A great adventure*. Dobbs Ferry, NJ: Transnational.
Kartashkin, C. (1982) The socialist countries and human rights. In K. Vasek (Ed.), *The international dimensions of human rights* (Vol. 2). English edition edited by P. Alston. Westport, CT: Greenwood Press.
Mower, A., Jr. (1980) Human rights in the Soviet Union. In J. L. Nelson and V. M. Green (Eds.), *International human rights: Contemporary issues* (pp. 199–227). Stanfordville, NY: Human Rights Publishing Group.
Orwin, C. and Pangle, T. (1984) The philosophical foundation of human rights. In M. F. Plattner (Ed.), *Human rights in our time* (pp. 1–22). Boulder, CO: Westview.
Szymanski, A. (1984) *Human rights in the Soviet Union*. London: Zed.
Valticos, N. (1979) The role of the ILO: Present action and future perspectives. In B. G. Ramcharan (Ed.), *Human rights: Thirty years after the universal declaration* (pp. 211–232). The Hague: Martinus Nijhoff.

CHAPTER 2

Rights of Access and Equal Opportunity: Focus on Sub-Saharan Africa

William M. Rideout, Jr.

Introduction

In considering the relationship between human rights of access and equal opportunity in education, it is important to keep in mind that human rights are often defined on both moral and/or legal bases. *Moral rights* are ". . . inherent and inalienable rights due to man simply because of being man," while *legal rights* "are established according to the law-creating process of societies, both national and international" (Levin, 1982, p. 11). Therefore, even though most nations recognize human rights, these rights are, as Levin notes, "sometimes limited or eliminated (by) legislation or by arbitrary means and are often widely violated by states in spite of their status as legal rights" (p. 12).

While there are indeed serious problems regarding compliance, as pointed out in Chapter 1, there is also often an unwillingness by national officials to recognize or acknowledge lack of compliance because both nationally and internationally the state *has* affirmed the *right* to access and equal opportunity in education and ergo *is* in legal compliance. Thus in dealing with human rights, we are repeatedly faced with a pervasive dichotomy between policy and practice—between what should be (and perhaps legalistically exists) and what *is* in terms of practice and reality. Whether serving as a means of avoiding the obligation to comply, or a self-mollifying delusion that the goal has been achieved, or a conviction that since it has been legally promulgated the application must subsequently and inevitably follow, such legalistic tunnel-vision is a major impediment to evaluating accurately (and ultimately to the actual achievement) of rights of access and equal opportunity in education. Since lack of compliance legalistically is rare, e.g. South Africa, while lack of compliance in implementation of accepted legal pronouncements remains pervasive, the focus of the chapter will be on the actual rather than the conceptual.

The "right" to education is, at the same time, an obligation. As Professor Huberman of the University of Geneva has pointed out (1979), "There is no right *not* to be educated, should a child or his parents so choose" (p. 58).

However, whereas the right is fundamental at the primary level, it becomes increasingly qualified thereafter; it is to be "available to all" at the secondary level and "accessible to all on the basis of merit" in higher education (see Chapter 1). Quite clearly, as has been acknowledged by UNESCO, the availability of education beyond primary schooling is most probably contingent upon the economic abilities of countries to meet those costs (Mialaret, 1979). What remains unsaid is that the wherewithall needed to achieve even the fundamental right to primary education is also obviously influenced by a nation's poverty and there are, as will be noted, serious questions as to whether or not primary schooling can be provided to all children in all developing countries within the limited time lines to which most aspire. As Martin (1980) wrote in a study on regional disparities in Cameroon, ". . . the majority of adults are and will remain illiterate, since education is aimed primarily at the younger generation; and . . . the enrollment of all children of school age is still a remote goal . . ." (pp. 26–27). Although legally *and* morally committed to education, the goal cannot be achieved given existing conditions—a situation typically pervasive in many developing countries and especially in Africa.

The tendency has been toward broadly emphasizing the human right to education, but making increasingly specific recommendations on its implementation with regard to children. From a legal point of view, the position that all humans have a right to education is not compromised; from a practical point of view, the emphasis is on realizing the child's right to education through the completion of grades 1 through 4, which is the major determinant of who will become literate. This approach also determines who will suffer from the results of inequality of access and lack of equal opportunity in education—i.e., those preponderantly likely to live with the burdens of illiteracy throughout their lives. Although certainly an oversimplification, it is basically true that education for children up to the age of 15+ is schooling while education for adults is some form of literacy training. In effect, therefore, this chapter will focus on children's access and their right to education within the context of schooling as exemplified in Sub-Saharan Africa.

And what is education? If it is the process by which humans have for generations transmitted to their descendants the acts, thoughts and feelings of their culture, including their artifacts (Kneller, 1965), then this process of learning one's first culture, i.e., enculturation, has obviously been successfully accomplished historically or unschooled cultures would have ceased to exist. Access and right to education within this educational model were never issues.

On the other hand, if by education we mean the process employed in modern societies, or the developed societies of the First and Second Worlds and the modernizing (largely urban) sectors of the Third world, then we are just as obviously referring essentially to instruction and learning occurring within a formal national, provincial or local educational system, private or public. While access in the developed countries is at or near 100 percent at the primary level because of enforced compulsory education (the duration of which is specified by national or provincial laws) in the developing countries, the access at this level (as represented by the proportion of the age group enrolled in primary schools) drops to under 50 percent for some of those in the least developed category.

This contemporary model of education, i.e., schooling, seeks to prepare the child to live not only in his immediate world but to live in the world beyond his daily experience and thus it provides broader national as well as international viewpoints. This then serves as a mechanism for learning a second culture, or acculturation (Siegel, 1974), which almost invariably means the process of learning a modern culture including science, technology and a world view. The result, as rather succinctly put by Lerner in his concept of "empathy", is the ability to put oneself in another person's shoes (Lerner, 1964).

Even when functioning within developed cultures which originally participated in spawning the modern mode of education, schooling is often berated because of important and pervasive external and internal inefficiencies. Nevertheless, schooling *per se* in these societies has increasingly become a major (if not *the* major) enculturator and that process is occurring to some extent even though the acculturation components of the school's curricula (those which will provide access to participation in the changing social, political and economic sectors) are being castigated for their inadequacies (Spindler, 1965, 1974 and 1982). Thus, even inadequate schooling in developed countries is probably performing at least a minimal level of enculturation, though failing to meet satisfactorily their societies' desired acculturation standards. However, in many developing countries traditional enculturation processes have atrophied and the schooling process, never considered a vehicle for enculturation, is still not participating in that process and is also failing to acculturate as well.

While there are running debates on the extent to which various traditional enculturation processes are working, fears are very often being expressed by many of those employing these age-old transmission patterns that they are not as effective as they used to be or should be—that children are losing their cultural birthrights. On the other hand, there is an internationally held concensus that a common "schooling" experience for a specified period of time (almost obligatorily assuming a minimal level of common knowledge transfer and acquisition during those years) is essential for the betterment of mankind individually as well as collectively. Furthermore, those deprived of such a minimum cannot be fulfilled and responsible members of the world community. Yet illiteracy figures for 1985 showing 889 million illiterates in the world (of whom 60 percent are women), are indicative of the failure, overwhelmingly in the Third World, to achieve the right to primary education (UNESCO, 1985). Therefore, many children in developing countries are ultimately being deprived of adequate education either in terms of enculturation or acculturation. Consequently they are unprepared to perform in either environment—they have mastered neither the prescribed local nor the prescribed national/international standards. In a summary statement on cultural transmission, Cameroonian journalist David Ndachi Tagne (1985) wrote:

> "Some people think that the little interest which is given to the promotion of creativity among our youth comes from the fact that what they do create lacks in consistency and is not integrated into traditional Cameroonian culture. We cannot but be cultural hybrids and nothing can be done (to correct the present malaise) if we don't take into account the western influence on our lives and on our world view" (p. 13).

The analysis of cultural transmission failure, especially in developing countries, is extremely important, and will also be addressed in part in Chapters 3, the Right to Education Free from Discrimination, and 6, the Right to Education for Multicultural Development. This chapter focuses on issues related to the enculturation/acculturation roles of education in the school context.

Greater emphasis is placed on acculturation which in UNESCO publications has been characterized as education in the new sense typical of modern societies, where it is essentially instruction imparted through educational systems responding to national needs and aspirations (Mialaret, 1979).

Education: The Goal and the Reality

By resolution 31/169, the United Nations General Assembly in 1979 proclaimed the International Year of the Child. Among other things, the desire of that action was to provide an opportunity to promote more aggressively the goals of Articles 3 and 4 of the *Convention Against Discrimination in Education* (1960)[1] which called for free and compulsory primary education, secondary education accessible to all, and higher education accessible on the basis of individual capacity. These lofty aims, which were later accorded international legal status in Article 13 of the *International Covenant on Economic, Social and Cultural Rights* (1966), expanded on the *Declaration of the Rights of the Child* adopted 20 years earlier.

Schools were supposed to do in the developing countries what they did in the developed—provide the child with both enculturation and acculturation

---

[1] See the Appendixes for summary of this and other relevant international documents.

so that he could participate ". . . on an equal footing in the universal dialogue between cultures" (Mialaret, 1979, p. 13).

This chapter focuses on the Sub-Saharan African region where, following over a decade of magnificent achievement in educational access and equity during the 1960s and 1970s, the region, in general, appears to have reached a point where many states have ceased to be able to expand the proportion of children being admitted even (or perhaps especially) at the primary school level. Instead, serious doubts are being expressed as to whether or not universal primary education (UPE), originally targeted for accomplishment in 1970, will be achieved by 1990, 2000 or even during the lifetimes of today's children. Since access and equity must first be achieved in primary schools in order ultimately to pervade the rest of the educational structure, this chapter also concentrates on the status of access and equity at the primary level.

Access

Concern about access to education is, like the right to education, a relatively recent phenomenon.

Although Prussia was the first country to introduce compulsory primary education in 1793, neither France nor England achieved compulsory free and secular primary education until the 1880s, and the school-leaving age in France, set at 12 in 1880, was not raised to 14 until 1936 (Le Thanh Khoi, 1979). Yet with nothing like a comparable economic base to support the costs of universal primary education (UPE), newly independent countries in the post World War II period were beginning to proclaim national education goals for their own populations which were similar to, or in excess of, those which developed European countries had taken over one hundred years to achieve. Moreover, African countries which were signatories to the UNESCO Addis Ababa Conference of 1961, established UPE as a regional goal set to be accomplished within a decade (Ahmed and Coombs, 1975). This effort proved impossible to accomplish then and, as noted by a Cameroonian journalist, ". . . remains a dead letter, if one dares to say so" (Radany, 1986, p. 19).

Enrollment accomplishments

The initial rates of growth in educational systems in Africa throughout the 1960s were extremely impressive and education was popularly equated with "schooling" (Coombs, 1968). Between 1960 and 1975 the number of pupils in primary schools rose by 128 percent in Africa. Table 2.1 illustrates the advances made by major geographical regions and/or groupings of countries by levels of economic development.

Despite the progress, Table 2.1 illustrates that the enrollment ratios in the less developed regions as of 1975 were about two-thirds those of the more

TABLE 2.1. *Enrollment Ratios by Age Group, Both Sexes (percentages)*

Region	Age group 6–11				Age group 12–17				Age group 18–23			
	1960	1965	1970	1975	1960	1965	1970	1975	1960	1965	1970	1975
MDR[1]	91	92	93	94	73	79	82	84	15.2	24.6	26.5	30.0
LDR[1]	46	54	58	62	22	28	32	35	3.4	5.0	7.0	8.7
Africa	33	40	44	51	17	22	26	31	1.9	2.7	4.1	5.8
Latin America	59	65	73	78	36	43	50	57	6.3	9.1	13.1	19.7
East Asia[2]	95	97	98	99	68	73	75	83	7.9	11.2	14.6	19.8
South Asia	48	56	58	61	19	26	29	31	3.3	5.0	6.4	6.9
25 LDCs[3]	13	19	22	28	9	12	14	17	0.7	1.1	1.8	2.7
Sahel countries[4]	9	15	17	19	5	9	12	13	0.5	1.1	1.9	2.6

1. More Developed Regions and Less Developed Regions. This grouping follows that used by the United Nations and is established according to fertility levels. Following this criterion, the MDRs include the following: Japan, Europe, northern America, Temperate South America (Argentina, Chile and Uruguay), Australia and New Zealand.
2. Includes Japan, the Republic of Korea, Mongolia and Hong Kong.
3. These countries, classified by the United Nations as the 'Least Developed Countries', are: Afghanistan, Benin, Bhutan, Botswana, Burundi, Chad, Ethiopia, Guinea, Haiti, Lao People's Democratic Republic, Lesotho, Malawi, Maldives, Mali, Nepal, Niger, Rwanda, Sikkim, Somalia, Sudan, Uganda, United Republic of Tanzania, Upper Volta, Western Samoa and Yemen Arab Republic.
4. These countries are: Chad, Mali, Mauritania, Niger, Senegal and Upper Volta.

Source: A. M. Huberman, The Present Situation and Future Prospects. In Gaston Mialaret (Ed.), *The Child's Right to Education.* 1979, p. 64.

developed for the ages 6–11, two-fifths for the age group 12–17, and less than one-third for the age group 18–23 years.

Moreover, as this 15 year period evolved, the growth rate gradually slowed down; it fell per annum by 6.6 per cent between 1960 and 1965 to 4.4 percent between 1965 and 1970, and then to 3.8 percent between 1970 and 1975 (Le Thanh Khoi, 1979). Moreover, by 1985, in the 25 Least Developed Countries (LDC), there was growing concern that the rate of primary school enrollment might have slipped below the rate of population growth.

Economic factors

Although the proportion of public education expenditures as a percentage of gross national product (GNP) and national budget has increased steadily for all regions of the world, it is very impressively evident that the contributions of the less developed regions (LDRs) have risen more rapidly and now nearly match those of the more developed regions (MDRs) (World Bank, 1980). Moreover, in many of the LDCs the annual proportion of the national budget being devoted to education ranges from 20 to 30 percent. While these proportions are evidence of commitment, that commitment cannot compensate for the vast differences in the total amounts of money involved. Accenting the dimensions of the gap between American wealth and African poverty, Eagleberger and McHenry (1985) reported that an average African's income is less than one-thirtieth of the average American's and that Africa must support 400 million people on an economy that produces no more than the state of Illinois.

Primary education costs in Africa, on the basis of per student year as a percent of per capita GNP, are about twice as much as in other developing areas; secondary education costs are 4 to 5 times as much and higher education costs 5 to 10 times as much (World Bank, 1981).

In short, poverty is a pervasive and profoundly debilitating factor; it is not, unfortunately, the only one plaguing the achievement of access and equal opportunity.

Population growth

Obviously, a critical determinant for success and quality is the sharp increase in the school age population in LDCs attributable to rapidly declining child mortality and continued high birth rates. Increasingly, the LDCs are faced with struggling just to maintain the existing proportions of school age children enrolled rather than trying to expand education to include larger shares of the school age population (World Bank, 1984). The Population Division of the United Nations has estimated that for the LDCs to maintain their enrollment ratios of 1975 for the age group 6–11 years, the enrollment of pupils would have to be increased by 30 percent between 1975 and 1985. At the same time the rate of increase in developed regions would be at 3 percent. "If that forecast were extended to the year 2000, the required increase in enrollment in the LDCs for the age group 6–11 years would be 73 percent, *just to keep pace with population growth* and maintain the 1975 enrollment ratios" (Huberman, 1979, p. 68). Africa, with the world's highest birth rate, will have doubled its population by the year 2000 and will have a myriad of problems, other than those of education, to deal with as well (Poats, 1984).

> "As most developing countries want to improve their schools quantitatively and qualitatively, they will have to generate more national savings or curtail other investments in, for example, power and transport. If a country is unwilling or unable to make these sacrifices, spending must be spread over a larger group of school children (to the detriment of the quality of education); otherwise a growing number of children have to be excluded" (World Bank, 1984, pp. 84–85).

Retention and literacy

If it is argued that becoming literate requires completing the fourth grade (an index often used in international studies), it is important to determine what proportion of those attending primary school actually remain long enough in the system to achieve this goal. A serious question arises about the significance of access if children enrolled in primary education leave the system prior to the fifth year. Moreover, UNESCO calculations completed for their 1977 conference on "Development of School Enrollment", showed how many out of 100 primary school children enrolled in the first year, in fact, gave up prior to starting the fifth year (see Table 2.2). Given that on the average it was found that 55 percent of the children gave up before starting the fifth year, the question must be asked, what did they learn which benefitted their well-being if they left the educational system prior to achieving permanent literacy? What in fact, was access to primary education worth for those children—and their families and societies—if they only attended grades 1, 2, 3 and/or 4 but stopped their schooling at a pre-literate stage?

Availability of schools

While there are a number of significant reasons for quitting school, one of them, which is directly related to access, is the failure of governments to provide complete systems. Many children successfully complete a grade which, if it is the last grade offered at the school they were attending, means that their schooling has ended. While this is a problem in both rural and urban areas, it is profoundly more serious in the rural areas as is illustrated by Table 2.3.

TABLE 2.2. *Percentage Rates of First Grade Students Leaving School by the Start of Grade 5 Between 1970–1975*

Region	Girls	Boys
Eastern Africa	54	56
Middle Africa	39	49
Northern Africa	83	89
Western Africa	61	62
Middle America	45	47
Temperate South America	68	63
Tropical South America	36	36
South East Asia	49	52
South Middle Asia	31	39
South West Asia	72	77

Source: International Conference on Education XXXVIth Session, *Development of School Enrolment: World and Regional Statistical Trends and Projections, 1960–2000*, (doc. ED/BIE/CONFINTED/36/4/Ref. 2), Annex III ("Apparent Cohorts by Region"), pp. 83–84. (These figures include pupils who repeat classes and they are not strictly comparable since some countries have introduced the system whereby pupils are annually promoted to the next grade automatically.

TABLE 2.3. *Rural–Urban Comparisons of Incomplete Schools in Selected Developing Countries*

Country	Complete urban schools as a percentage of all urban schools	Complete rural schools as a percentage of all rural schools
Africa		
Chad	68	47
Gabon	89	59
Gambia	47	45
Togo	98	67
Zambia	81	43
Asia		
Jordan	75	79
Lao People's Democratic Republic	60	11
Socialist Republic of Viet Nam	100	37
South America		
Argentina (1970)	94	79
Ecuador	88	43

Source: *Unesco Statistical Yearbook, 1972*, pp. 131–8.

Equity

Efforts to expand and equalize educational opportunities face a variety of constraints, including physical[2] and human[3] constraints. All of these may make construction of schools, delivery of supplies to schools, provision of qualified teachers and supervision and control of schools extremely difficult.

Learning environments

Equal opportunity in schooling is also inhibited, as was insinuated earlier, by the way in which the education budget is expended. Schools are too often characterized by a lack of books and classroom supplies, increasing student–teacher ratios beyond levels often already considered excessive, jamming two to three times as many students into a classroom as it was designed to accommodate, failing to provide basic maintenance for school facilities, which consequently are unable to provide the learning environments and conditions for which they were originally constructed, etc. The dimensions of the gap between the amount spent per primary school pupil varies enormously between high and low income countries; Bolivia, El Salvador, Malawi and Ivory Coast, for example, spent less than $2 a year on classroom materials, for each child at primary school.

Quality and relevance

In addition to expanding access to education, concerns about the quality dimensions of education have received growing attention with the added caution that emphasis should not only be on *performance* as it has customarily been defined and judged, but quality must also be concerned with the *relevance* of what is taught and learned in terms of the learners' present and future needs and prospects (Coombs, 1985). Are students learning anything of value beyond what permits them to continue with more schooling if they are successful?

Reaction against miseducation outcomes was poignantly expressed in the interior of Senegal during the past few years, when government supported

---

[2] Physical constraints include geographic and demographic factors such as extreme distances, low density and/or isolated populations, poor communications and harsh environments.
[3] Human constraints include powerful cultural and sociopolitical influences; such as vested interests of diverse and influential groups, resistance to providing equal education for women, religious inhibitions, and (even where capital, per se, is not a restricting factor, such as in many of the Organization of Petroleum Exporting Countries (OPEC) often a lack of the analytical, managerial and professional capabilities needed to design and implement expansion and equalization of education. There are also populations who may not wish to send their children to schools because to do so deprives families of a source of labor and income and promotes alienation.

primary schools were closed because parents withdrew their children and placed them in 2 or 3 year Koranic schools instead. There they (basically boys) learn the fundamental tenets of Islam, moral values and rudiments of Arabic. They learn how cultured people in their traditional societies should behave, i.e., they are more thoroughly enculturated. They learn little of what might be called the curriculum of nation-building and acculturation. Once their schooling is finished, a few might go on to more advanced religious studies, but, as was always intended, the vast majority will prepare for adult roles in their society by working with their elders. Based on what they have learned, they know which adults in the society provide the best role models for them to follow.

Parents willingly explained their reasons for such drastic action as withdrawing their children from schools. The formal schooling to which they had access was, for the most part, preparing their children to leave home to become thieves and prostitutes in the cities; the parents were no longer willing to accept the inferior quality nor those outcomes as either desirable or inevitable (Rideout, 1985). They had judged formal schooling (those elements of it to which their children were both exposed and restricted) to be not only a waste of time and not worth the effort and investment required given the occupational options their children were experiencing, but also a harmful acculturation exposure which promoted their debasement rather than their advancement. They felt the Koranic school experience to be more relevant and more valuable for their children. Here the concept of relevance pertains not only to the relationship between the national life and culture and the external world (referred to as "authenticity and modernity" by the Conference of African Ministers of Education, 1976), but also to the more specific and perhaps particularistic needs of different clientele within the country—the rurally based, religious, and ethnic groups.

Mismanagement

For the purposes of this chapter we focus on three aspects of mismanagement: overcentralized, deliberate (malicious) and unintentional (non-malicious). The latter includes the spectrum of bungling, often bureaucratically induced, which mislocates schools; which puts the water source for a school downhill from the buildings when there is no pump, no electricity and no reason why the two couldn't have been switched; where schools do not receive books until the end of the academic year even though they are available in the country; and where teachers' paychecks are in arrears even though the funds are available in the capital city.

On the other hand, there is the malicious mismanagement which ranges from petty larceny—stealing gasoline from school inspectors' vehicles, using government property for personal profit, "misplacing" funds allocated for school maintenance—to grand theft on a national scale which so debilitates the economy that all sectors, and especially the service sectors, nearly cease to function.[4] Since education, along with military and the civil service, is usually among the largest national budgetary allocations, it is inevitable that education suffers profoundly from corruption—especially since the other two leading budget items are nearly sacrosanct. Zaire is a nation where not only has thievery at the top[5] debilitated the nation's resources, but discouraged ". . . honest or hard work among the subordinates, who, understandably, match the boss' grand larceny with petit larceny of their own" (Kestin, 1986, p. 106).

A facit of mismanagement traditionally classified as inadequate "absorptive capacity" deserves special attention and reconsideration. Derived from economics, it has denoted the inability of a country to use efficiently developmental inputs either made available from donors or already at its disposal. However, it appears that there is increasingly another phenomenon now occurring in many developing countries, and especially in Africa; where central governments, in spite of inflated bureaucracies, are indeed unable to absorb new inputs, but where their own local governments could absorb these inputs with alacrity and efficiency.

At the central level, the process of decision-making is one of reviewing, commenting, and passing proposals to the next higher level without any resolution whatsoever until a bloated dossier finally surfaces on a Minister's desk.[6] This incapacity at the central government level may have nothing to do with the real absorptive capacity existing at the proposed implementation site where the proposal may have originated but where it will never have a chance of being realized. Thus, it is suggested that analyses of mismanagement should also evaluate the third focus mentioned earlier—central as opposed to local absorptive capacity—and it is also suggested that it is the former which, in the field of education, is overwhelmingly the greater barrier to progress. Here children's rights are being very effectively thwarted through incompetent overcentralization in which no one is "to blame" and no one is held "accountable". The sense of commitment has been dulled and the sense of urgency lost by bureaucracies insulated from local pressures, needs, and demands.

[4] These latter cases, the most obvious of which is Sub-Saharan Africa have included, among others, Zaire, Nigeria, Liberia, Uganda and the Central African Empire, and reconfirm the old African saying that "the fish stinks from the head".
[5] Irwin Blumenthal, a West German installed by the International Monetary Fund to manage Zaire's banks, found Mobutu using the national treasury as a private checking account from which he made transfers to Europe in $5 million accounts.
[6] There is an excellent chance that the Minister will never read the original proposal which has been repeatedly reviewed by officials in a chain of command made up of some or many who may not have done their work thoroughly or may never have been competent to evaluate the content. The Minister, furthermore, has so many demands accumulating in his office (individual personnel requests which may be interspersed with multi-million dollar projects, all of which receive basically the same treatment) that a significant number of dossiers become outdated, defunct or lost; thus it is not uncommon for decisions to be made by lack of decision and passage of time.

The sum total of the three types of mismanagement listed above are, obviously, unknown; their combined impact is, however, readily apparent in developing countries and is devastating to education and especially to equality and access—the areas of most basic popular concern.

Internal mismanagement, as reviewed above, has reached a point in many developing countries where it is a major contributor to national insolvency and certainly to the perpetuation of educational inequality.

Lack of qualified teachers

Certainly one of the greatest constraints on equal opportunity in education has been, and is, the lack of qualified teachers, yet in more than half of the countries in Sub-Saharan Africa 50 percent or more of the teaching staff lack formal training and do not meet the standards the countries themselves require (World Bank, 1981). While there is a repeated appeal for equal distribution of qualified teachers among the schools, given a situation where so few are qualified within a country or region, it becomes a "qualified teachers' market"; redistributing them nationwide on some parity formula becomes extremely difficult.

Ironically, education is itself a reason (or excuse) very often given by teachers for refusing to accept rural assignments or, if assigned to a rural area, for expending every effort to get transferred back to the cities as quickly as possible. Teachers complain, accurately, that at rural assignments they are condemning their own children to inferior educations, for these teachers know better than most, that rural schools are indeed inferior—they have the fewest textbooks, the least equipment and training materials—in addition to a disproportionate percentage of unqualified teachers. In rural Swaziland, where a very adequate road system serves a small country and permits travel to an "urban center" from anywhere in the nation within a few hours, in 1984 it was not uncommon to have Peace Corps Volunteers listed among those faculty members in rural secondary schools with greatest longevity after the volunteers had completed a 3 year assignment (Rideout, 1985).

Regionalism

An intriguing phenomenon, patently apparent in many parts of Africa especially, is the powerful and pervasive regional disparities which derive from socio-historical factors and which continue to influence national development profoundly. For example, where disproportionately intensive European penetration occurred during the colonial period, various parts of the continent had access to schooling whereas other regions, or what are now different parts of the same country, had none—and in many wanted none.[7] Today, however, the former "have-not" regions remain overwhelmingly in that same position in terms of both access and equality (Carron and Ta Ngoc Chau, 1980; Coleman and Ngokwey, 1983).

Cameroon is one case in point where the difference in access to education and the level of educational equality within those "have" regions forms an arc extending inland from the Atlantic Ocean for approximately 250–300 kilometres. From within that arc came 95.5 percent of candidates for the baccalaureat in 1969 while the remainder of the country, constituting some two-thirds of the national territory and 51 percent of the population, supplied just 4.5 percent of the candidates (Martin, 1980). While national policies since independence have sought to rectify this imbalance and provide comparable opportunity to the remainder of the country, the results have been that while the deprived regions have advanced, the favored regions have also and generally at a more rapid rate so that the "haves" now have proportionately even greater access and educational equality than the "have nots" (Rideout, 1985).

A somewhat different situation exists in Zaire where two of the major tribes, the Baluba and the Bakongo, disproportionately constitute the educated elite within the country (Rideout *et al.*, 1969; Coleman and Ngokwey, 1983).

Religion

Significantly, the educationally advanced regions along the coast of Cameroon continue on into Nigeria with roughly the same sized zone of "educationally privileged" extending from the coast inland for approximately the same distance. Obviously, the increasing resistance to education, which was controlled by Christian missionaries, played a role in inhibiting penetration into an interior which was increasingly Moslem dominated. Moreover, distance from the coast generally meant weaker colonial presence and control, which gave traditional leaders greater opportunities to resist and deflect foreign domination. Even in the mid-1970s, the enrollment ratios powerfully reflected the continued differences so that at the primary school level the rate dropped from 150 per thousand in the non-Muslim southern parts of Nigeria and Cameroon to 30 and 58 respectively in the northern Muslim dominated parts of both countries. By 1985, the northern regions of Cameroon still had slightly less than 30 percent of children ages 6–11 in school while, in the southern regions, it approximated 85 percent. The same phenomenon to a lesser degree occurs in Chad

---

[7] This was due to such factors as proximity to the ocean or major traditional arteries of communication and transportation, successes in evangelization, acquiescence or a positive response by Africans to the Europeans' technological and scientific prowess, and the African's use of the foreign presence for local and/or regional political purposes.

where enrollment in the Christian dominated south is at 75 per thousand and drops to 11 in the Muslim north.[8]

Health and environment

In the context of access and equal opportunity health conditions are also important.

A growing series of studies, especially in Latin America, are showing that lower socioeconomic status preschool age children perform substantially worse in tests of cognitive development than children from higher income groups. In summarizing these findings, Selowsky (1981) identifies malnutrition, lack of sanitation, low levels of psychological stimulation and other environmental deficits surrounding children in poverty, not in destitution, as contributing factors to their inferior performances. Not only do young children suffer most from undernourishment, but girls suffer significantly more often from it than do boys (World Bank, 1980).

International attention has, during the past decade, especially focused on Africa where there has been a breakdown between people's needs and their environmental support systems which has dramatically increased destitution, malnutrition and actual starvation. While drought has intermittently plagued much of the continent since the late 1960s, the World Bank (1985) claimed that the drought has only triggered adverse trends previously established; "namely, a rapidly growing population and the widespread denudation of the vegetative cover, leading to erosion, soil and water loss, desertification, and lowered crop yields" (p. 72). Conditions are observably worsening and the sustainability of long-term development patterns in the region are being seriously questioned. Moreover, all indexes of destitution, from the number of refugees to the number of those dying from malnutrition, are rising and the United Nations has estimated that "40 percent of African children under the age of five go through a period of malnutrition severe enough to cause mental or physical damage affecting their growth" (Lamb, 1984, p. 32).

When the continent of Africa is faced with the prospect of having millions of children who have suffered from malnutrition, will access and equality, if and when provided, simply offer an enhanced opportunity to fail? Or might schools in fact serve a remedial function to help these rural populations ultimately achieve a more improved well-being than could otherwise have been expected? Questions such as these will become increasingly pertinent as, year after year, growing numbers of these damaged children become part of the population profile.

Most of the present school systems in Africa, basically employing only the former colonial languages, are functioning poorly with access stabilizing;

---

[8] In this case, however, religious factors are comingled with racial/tribal factors (Martin, 1980).

and with equality, as measured by dropout and wastage rates, deplorable. Such schools for the most part, are not preparing children for available adult roles in their existing societies; rather they are preparing a few children to move into government positions, the modernizing sectors, and urban areas. The perpetuation of colonial style school systems which endorse this orientation in independent states is increasingly dysfunctional.

While strongly endorsing primary education in languages which the children most fully command, we acknowledge that the implementation of such a policy would, initially at least, be costly as well as difficult. Eventually this additional cost might be compensated for through factors such as higher primary school completion and lower repeater rates, and higher rates of life-long (and more proficient) literacy which would permit greater access to information, which in turn could improve standards of living and pro-ductivity—not to mention cultural enrichment and perhaps psychological benefits (Bamgbose, 1976). Nevertheless, it must also be noted that among Sub-Saharan Africa's nations only a few can claim linguistic homogeneity (Somalia, Swaziland, Rwanda, Burundi and Lesotho), although several others have a widely used indigenous language which appears to hold promise for serving as an acceptable language for educational instruction (e.g., Mali-Bambara, Tanzania-Swahili, Senegal-Wolof, Burkina Fasso-Mossi).

However, the majority of countries have no dominant culture acceptable nationwide from which an indigenous language of instruction would be readily accepted. Moreover, tribalism and/or regionalism have contributed to serious national crises, some of which have continued interminably in a number of states (e.g., Angola, Uganda, Ethiopia, Zimbabwe, Sudan, Chad). Especially inhibiting is the absolute number of languages which exist in many African states; for example, Zaire, Cameroon, Chad and Nigeria each has over 150 indigenous languages, many of which have not yet been reduced to writing. While language in written form is a *sine qua non* for literacy, it should be noted that most major African languages are already written and that impressive advances are being made in completing this task. While such efforts are continuing, there is no reason why existing written indigenous languages could not be used in school systems (Bamgbose, 1976). In short, the latter need not be delayed while the former is continuing.

Based on post-independence educational history in Africa, it appears that rural populations can most successfully compete with those in urban areas when education occurs in languages which the children use and control.

Summary and Recommendations

We have, in this chapter, examined a number of factors contributing to educational access and equity. Access, clearly, is related to such issues as poverty, population growth, retention, literacy, and availability of schools in both urban and rural areas.

While the education system in these countries have, as noted, many imperfections, they still constitute probably the most prominent evidence of their governments' concern for their respective citizens. Moreover, as demonstrated by the continuing popular demands for education, the majority of people still believe that schooling can help them to lead better lives. In short, the school remains the most important institution available to most governments for addressing their most critical problems. Schools have the potential to make a major contribution toward providing people with a chance to learn how to deal with survival issues—learning to live more successfully in their own social and physical environments prior to acculturation.

If we look at children enrolled in primary and secondary education and compare them with school-leavers or unschooled, and if we concentrate only on, and list the most consistent findings from, research in developing countries, we note that longer attendance at school is associated with:

". . . greater educational aspirations for one's children; more openness to agricultural innovation; frequency of book and newspaper reading and of radio-listening; membership in community organizations; higher rates of voting; belief in progress (e.g., belief that man will some day understand the cause of floods, droughts and epidemics); greater receptivity to birth-control measures; lower levels of prejudice and ethnocentrism; higher scores on intelligence tests which are relatively culture-free . . . , and on other tasks of verbal reasoning; a greater capacity, in general, . . . to empathize, to weigh alternatives" (Huberman, 1979, pp. 61–62).

Developing countries are seeking to have the opportunity to learn their first culture well in school, followed by acculturation (which, in a heterogeneous society, might very well be the national culture—if one has been identified), followed by a world view component (which would be the acculturation component in developed societies, but might more realistically be identified as "uniculture" or "world view culture" for many Third World countries). Thus, schools, instead of ignoring the particularistic first cultures in heterogeneous LDCs, would explore their first cultures and assist in their enrichment so that children would learn how to improve their well-being—living better lives within their everyday cultural environments—even if they did not continue on to acculturation and uniculture. Consequently, if half of the children continued to drop out of school by grade 3, before achieving permanent literacy, they could still have a better chance of improving their well-being because of the relevant and more thoroughly comprehended schooling experiences which had been provided them.

Given this type of school revision, the impact of even the limited educational experiences which a large proportion of LDC populations are, for economic reasons, going to continue to receive, could be far more profound.

When one analyzes what the World Bank considers the four main areas of human development—education, health, nutrition and fertility—it is fairly obvious that education serves as a cornerstone in the development process.

Conclusions and Implications

To accomplish their goals, African nations need help from the international community of financial and development institutions to save much of what they have achieved since independence. Without such help they face "'international desertification'—the disintegration of rural health services, basic education, training, agricultural extension, etc. (which) threatens to intensify poverty and inequity, (and thus) compounding the difficulty of reactivating development". However, such an undertaking between developed countries and Sub-Saharan African countries must be done within a partnership context. Poverty, which during the past decade has been aggravated by natural disasters, has made developmental progress difficult, if not impossible, for a significant number of African countries. If a combined commitment were to be made by the donor nations as well as by the nations suffering "institutional desertification" to accomplish universal primary education (among other basic social goals) that illusive objective, sought since the Addis Ababa Conference of 1961, could finally be realized.

However, while poverty constitutes a barrier to significant progress, other important factors must also be addressed. Thus, donor assistance in overcoming the poverty barrier would require a collaborative partnership with developing countries to achieve the following:

1. Modifications in managerial practices which would put an end to corruption, malicious mismanagement and as much of the non-malicious mismanagement as possible.
2. More rational allocations of the educational budget to encourage teachers and administrators to become more qualified and to have available the educational materials needed to make teaching effective.
3. Administrative measures which would permit popular participation in educational development so that the lack of absorptive capacity at the central government level would not block local initiative, will, and ability to progress.
4. Greater use of the results and findings of efforts to promote educational development over the past quarter century. There are grossly inadequate mechanisms for sharing research data and information on curriculum development innovations, educational reform efforts and

experiments, national programs to upgrade teachers and administrators, development of local textbooks and teaching materials, etc.

5. Inclusion in basic school curricula, of content dealing with problems of malnutrition, poverty and disease and methods to improve agriculture and to protect the environment.
6. Educational programs designed to study the outcomes from education in maternal, vehicular, and international language instruction.
7. Reductions in wastage, dropouts, and repetition rates within the educational structure.
8. Sexual equality in schooling.
9. Comparability between rural and urban schools.
10. The development of longitudinal approaches to education in non-academic streams so that post-schooling functional and/or literacy education programs could build more effectively on whatever schooling individuals might have received during their pre-adult years.
11. Rationally developed educational programs in LDCs progressing from enculturation to acculturation to "uniculturation".

While Sub-Saharan Africa, the only developing region identified by OECD as requiring extraordinary international assistance, does have especially critical needs, it is also suggested that any developing nation which has tried for over a quarter of a century to achieve UPE and to improve the well-being of its people through greater educational access and equity, and which obviously cannot succeed in this effort by the end of this century, should, if it desires to participate in a non-neo-colonial international effort such as the one recommended here, be included in a worldwide undertaking to accomplish this human rights goal. It appears increasingly evident that the time for this type of international commitment has arrived; humans should no longer be deprived of the right to educational access and equality, a basic human right, universally endorsed by the sovereign states and international organizations of the world.

References

Ahmed, M. and Coombs, P. H. (Eds.) (1975) *Education for rural development: Case studies for planners.* New York: Praeger.

Bamgbose, A. (Ed.) (1976) *Mother tongue education: The west African experience.* London: Hodder and Stoughton.

Carron, G. and Ta Ngoc Chau (Eds.) (1980) *Regional disparities in educational development: Diagnosis and policies for reduction.* Ghent: Imprimerie L. Vanmelle.

Coleman, J. S. and Ngokwey, N. (1983) Zaire: The state and the university. In R. M. Thomas (Ed.), *Politics and education: Cases from eleven nations* (pp. 55–78). Oxford: Pergamon.

Coombs, P. H. (1968) *The world education crisis: A systems analysis.* New York: Oxford University.

Coombs, P. H. (1985) *The world crisis in education: The view from the eighties.* New York: Oxford University.

Eagleburger, L. and McHenry, D. (1985) The United States cannot ignore hunger and poverty in Africa. *The International Herald Tribune,* Nov. 30–Dec. 1, p. 8.

Huberman, A. M. (1979) The present situation and future prospects. In G. Mialaret (Ed.), *The child's right to education* (pp. 57–75). Paris: Imprimerie des Presses Universitaires de France.

Kestin, H. (1985) God and man in Zaire. *Forbes*, Nov. 18, pp. 100–110.

Kneller, G. (1965) *Educational anthropology: An introduction*, New York: John Wiley & Sons.

Lamb, D. (1984) *The Africans*. New York: Vintage Books.

Lerner, D. (1964) *The passing of traditional society: Modernizing the middle east*. New York: The Free Press.

Le Thanh Khoi (1979) Action by the authorities. In G. Mialaret (Ed.), *The child's right to education* (pp. 173–188). Paris: Imprimerie des Presses Universitaires de France.

Levin, L. (1982) *Human rights: Questions and answers*. Paris: Imprimerie des Presses Universitaires de France.

Martin, J. (1980) Social differentiation and regional disparities: Educational development in Cameroon. In G. Carron and Ta Ngoc Chau (Eds.), *Disparities in educational development: Diagnosis and policies for reduction* (pp. 21–113). Ghent: Imprimerie L. Vanmelle.

Mialaret, G. (Ed.) (1979) *The child's right to education*. Paris: Imprimerie des Presses Universitaires de France.

Poats, R. (1984) Crisis and response in Africa. *OECD Observer*, Nov., 13, 26–29.

Radany, A. (1986) Les jeunes du tiersmonde dans le miroir du sous-developpement. [The youth of the third world in the mirror of underdevelopment] *Cameroon Tribune*, Feb. 8, No. 3496.

Rideout, W. M., Jr. (1985a) Cameroon: Regional, ethnic and religious influences on a post-colonial education system. In M. Thomas (Ed.), *Politics and education: Cases from eleven nations*, New York: Pergamon.

Rideout, W. M., Jr (1985b) Two promising educational reforms: A new identity for Senegal. In C. Brock and W. Tulasiewicz (Eds.), *Cultural identity and educational policy*. London: Croom-Helm.

Rideout, W. M., Jr. and Wilson, D. N. (1975) The politics of national planning: The case of Zaire. *Journal of the International Society of Educational Planners*, 1(3), 35–63.

Rideout, W. M., Jr., Wilson, D. N. and Young, M. C. (1969) *Survey of education in the democratic republic of the Congo*. Washington, DC, American Council on Education, the Overseas Liaison Committee.

Selowsky, M. (1981) Nutrition, health, and education: The economic significance of complementarities at early age. *Journal of development economics*, **9**, 331–46.

Siegel, B. J. (1974) Conceptual approaches to models for the educative process in American communities. In G. Spindler (Ed.), *Education and cultural process: Toward an anthropology of education* (pp. 43–50). New York: Holt, Rinehart & Winston.

Spindler, G. (Ed.) (1965) *Educational anthropology: An introduction*. New York: John Wiley & Sons.

Spindler, G. (Ed.) (1974) *Education and cultural process: Toward an anthropology of education*. New York: Holt, Rinehart and Winston.

Spindler, G. (Ed.) (1982) *Doing the ethnography of schooling: Educational anthropology in action*. New York: Holt, Rinehart and Winston.

Tagne, D. N. (1985) Jeunesse d'hier a aujourd'hui: Les jeunes face a la culture nationale. [Youth of yesterday and today: the young against the national culture] *Cameroon Tribune*, Feb. 8, No. 3496.

UNESCO (1985) The Challenge of Literacy. Paris: Author.

United Nations (1983) *Human rights: A compilation of international instruments*. New York: United Nations.

World Bank (1980) *World Bank development report, 1980*. New York: Oxford University Press.

World Bank (1981) *Accelerated development in sub-Saharan Africa: An agenda for action*. Washington, DC: Author.

World Bank (1984) *World Bank development report, 1984*. New York: Oxford University Press.

World Bank (1985) *World Bank annual report, 1985*. New York: Oxford University Press.

CHAPTER 3

The Right to Education Free From Discrimination: The Cases of India and Saudi Arabia

Ratna Ghosh and Aman Attieh[1]

Introduction

In the period following World War II, the United Nations and its organizations spearheaded the fostering of political, social, and educational rights of human beings in the world community. In so doing, the United Nations challenged communities to transcend differences manifested in gender, race, ethnicity, language, culture, religion, social class, national origin, etc.

Prevention of discrimination, in education, as well as other spheres, has been addressed by more international documents than any other aspect of human rights. Beginning with the *United Nations Charter (1945)*, the *UNESCO Constitution (1948)*, and the *International Bill of Rights (1966)*, the struggle has continued with various declarations, conventions and recommendations.[2]

This chapter examines the perception and application of the right to education free from discrimination in two Asian countries, namely India and Saudi Arabia. This right is viewed with special reference to education free from religious, racial/ethnic and gender discrimination within the context of the framework of standards set by the UN organizations. The notion of educational rights free from discrimination has been interpreted to mean that all individuals have a natural right to share, on an equal footing and without any discrimination, the educational resources, services and benefits available in their respective societies. The right to education free from discrimination is examined here under three broad classifications: educa-

[1] Although Aman Attieh's name is second, the two co-authors have contributed equally to this chapter.

[2] See Appendices for summaries of relevant documents, including: *Convention Against Discrimination in Education* (1960), *International Convention on the Elimination of All Forms of Racial Discrimination* (1965), *Convention on the Elimination of All Forms of Discrimination Against Women* (1981), *Declaration on the Elimination of All Forms of Intolerance and of Discrimination Based on Religion or Belief* (1981), *Universal Islamic Declaration of Human Rights* (1981), and UNESCO's *Second Medium Term Plan* (1984–1989).

37

tional access to all levels of the educational systems, educational programs in all fields and content areas, and outcome in terms of the wide range of career and professional advancement.

Rationale for Selecting India and Saudi Arabia

Although both are Third World countries, basic differences between India and Saudi Arabia regarding population composition, economic conditions, religious and cultural beliefs, political systems and ideological stances have prompted their selection as valuable case studies for their perspectives and implementation of human rights.

India is a land of a bewildering variety of religions, languages and people. It has a population of over 700 million whose inhabitants are descendants of several races. Although 1,652 mother-tongues were enumerated in the 1961 Census, Hindi is the official language and 14 other languages have been specified in the Constitution. The continued use of English has been authorized by Parliament. India is a secular country represented by several major religious communities but Hindus constitute about 80 percent of the population.

Saudi Arabia is largely a homogeneous country with regard to its native population. Ethnically, the people, whether sedentary or nomadic, are predominantly Arab. Small pockets of other ethnic groups exist but are assimilated into the culture through religion. There is a large alien population of different nationalities and creeds, both Arab and non-Arab, working as skilled technical and professional laborers who have sought economic opportunities and filled the national work force shortage created by the development process spurred by oil yields. All Saudi citizens function in one language, Arabic, which is the official national language. English is used with foreign employees, in labor transactions, in international trade, and in diplomacy. All Saudi citizens are Muslims, with 90 percent adhering to the Sunnī faith and 10 percent to the Shī'ite sect.

Economically, India and Saudi Arabia are at two opposite ends of the spectrum. India is considered to be one of the poorest nations in the world (despite high levels of industrialization) with a soaring population and per capita income of only $250 in 1981 (World Almanac, 1986). Saudi Arabia, in contrast, has enjoyed abundant wealth from incremental oil revenues which, when positioned against a sparse density population of approximately nine million, have given rise to a relatively high per capita income of $14,578 (World Almanac, 1986).

The two countries have different systems of government. India is a Sovereign Democratic Republic with a written constitution of a secular nature which is the legal basis for its parliamentary democracy and for guaranteeing equal rights to all citizens before the law, irrespective of religion, language, race or sex. Saudi Arabia is an Islamic theocracy, an absolute monarchy with no written constitution as such, but the prescriptions of Islamic jurisprudence, the *Sharī'ah*, serve as the "constitution" and form the basis for the government and the legal system. In the *Sharī'ah* all Muslims are equal, although women have differential status in certain respects. However, equality and non-discriminatory treatment between Muslims and non-Muslims is an alien notion (Ahmad, 1970) and, the *Sharī'ah* accords preferential standing and treatment to Muslims and less favorable status to non-Muslims, both spiritually and socially.

In the area of human rights as defined by United Nations standards, India and Saudi Arabia have played antithetical roles. India has been one of the earliest and staunchest supporters of the *International Bill of Human Rights*, and parts of its constitution cover the same premises as those found in the *Universal Declaration of Human Rights* (*Yearbook of Human Rights*, 1949). The eagerness of India's leaders to solve the problems of inequalities handed down from the past in the social system and colonial heritage has been demonstrated in India's efforts on human rights in a wide range of areas including political, social, economic, personal, status of women, employment and judicial precedents and cases (*Yearbook of Human Rights*, 1949–66, 1973–80). The involvement of Saudi Arabia in the human rights movement has been negligible and to date the government has not ratified the *International Bill of Human Rights*. Its position has been repeatedly justified by such statements as: "Islamic Law is so flexible that it does guarantee, in the Kingdom, human rights in conformity with the United Nations Universal Declaration of Human Rights" (*Yearbook of Human Rights*, 1955), a claim which is subject to controversy. Since then, Saudi Arabia has been silent on the subject on the international scene, but has displayed a flurry of activities with other Muslim countries which culminated in the proclamation and signing of the *Universal Islamic Declaration of Human Rights in 1981*. To what extent this declaration is binding remains to be tested. Earlier attempts made to draft a legally binding document specifying the basic rights of its subjects and the relationship between the governor and the people in the early 1950s and 1960s did not go beyond the stages of proposal and royal promise (Walpole *et al.*, 1971). All of these factors have significant implications on the right to education without discrimination in India and Saudi Arabia.

The case studies of India and Saudi Arabia indicate that the two countries view rights from somewhat different positions with resultant variances from the UN documents. Thus, part one of each case study provides a brief statement of the ideological context within which human rights are discussed, educational policies are adopted, and the realities of the school system operated in each country. Part two highlights the legislation and policy documents focusing on human rights and education as they relate to the categories of religion, race/ethnicity, and gender in each country. Part three proceeds with an analysis of what has been achieved and discrepancies in stated policy and actual practice in the context of their distinctive societies. Part four integrates the two cases vis-à-vis the standards provided by the International Documents on human and educational rights and concludes with a prognosis.

India

Ideological Context

Human rights in modern India cannot be examined appropriately without taking into account the socio-cultural and religious forces at play. While the influence of Islam has been significant, Hinduism has been the dominant religion, and the traditional Hindu world view has been operative for nearly two millenia. As such, it may be useful to briefly examine the intellectual and social foundations of traditional Hinduism in relation to the ideology of human rights.

Hinduism is based on doctrines such as *Maya*, *Karma* and *Dharma*.[3] It is risky to generalize about such a complex tradition, but for our purposes it should suffice to say that social reality is defined in terms of the concept of Dharma which emphasizes duties rather than rights.

The operational unit in Hindu society has usually been identified as caste. The traditional society was one of rigid hierarchy and extreme inequities in which the collectivity of caste (or kinship group) rather than the individual was the salient factor. Rights and duties were defined by membership in a particular kinship group or caste. There was no concept of individual rights. Consciousness of individuality manifested itself only at the spiritual level. The *Universal Declaration of Human Rights*, however, is based on an ideology designed to uphold individual rights as well as collective rights.

With the process of modernization, which began in India at the start of the nineteenth century, the lower segments of the population challenged Hindu orthodoxy and religious conservatism. The emergence of a new middle class started reorganizing society through wealth and educational attainment rather than on the basis of caste.

Modern India is based on the ideals of democratic socialism. The demand for independence (1947) and the adoption of fundamental rights in the Indian Constitution in 1949 *was* based on the belief that democracy cannot be established unless certain rights are assured to all citizens.

Policy

The Preamble of the *Indian Constitution* reflects the spirit of Article I of

---

[3] *Maya* refers to the conception of the universe in its phenomenal (illusory) aspect, or as relative existence. *Karma* refers to work and the results of work—the law of cause and effect in the moral world. It is related to the theory of transmigration of souls. *Dharma* literally means "that which upholds" and has therefore been interpreted as the essential constituent of any unit (individual, social, political, etc.) whose integrity it ensures.

the *Universal Declaration of Human Rights* that "All human beings are born free and equal in dignity and rights." It also mentions essential individual rights which have implications for education.

The right to education

The State is directed to strive for the right to education, make provision for free and compulsory primary education (Article 45), and promote the educational interests of Scheduled Castes and Tribes, and other weaker sections (including women).

Education is primarily the responsibility of the State Governments, but the Union Government has certain responsibilities specified in the Constitution on matters such as planning, higher education and promotion of education for weaker sections. Most states have enacted legislation for compulsory education. At the end of the sixth Five Year Plan (1985) primary education for ages 6–11 is free in all states, and for age group 11–14 it is free in all except Orissa, Uttar Pradesh and West Bengal. In these states, girls and members of Scheduled Castes and Tribes get free education, and incentives such as mid-day meals, free books and uniforms, are provided. At the secondary stage several states have free education for all children and those which do not make free education available to all, do so for girls, Scheduled Castes and Tribes. Thus, free education in all states is provided at the primary and secondary stages for girls, Scheduled Castes and Tribes.

Anti-discrimination and equality legislation

The prohibition of discrimination on grounds of religion, race, caste, sex or place of birth in Article 15:1 and 2, of the Constitution, implies an education free from discrimination. The Constitution also offers religious and linguistic minorities fundamental rights to conserve their culture, language and script as well as to establish and administer educational institutions of their choice (Article 30).

Groups included are defined more by linguistic boundaries than by ethnicity. Nowhere are ethnic groups mentioned in legislation, although the population is multi-ethnic and multicultural. All the equality clauses forbid discrimination on the basis of language. The government policy is to encourage the use of Hindi as the official language but also the development of all Indian languages, including classical, modern and tribal ones. The National Policy on Education has adopted a three-language formula whereby all children learn the mother-tongue, the regional language and a foreign language which may be English. While there is no explicit policy on multiculturalism, curricula content reflects the multicultural history and nature of Indian society.

Scheduled castes and scheduled tribes

Both of these terms are of recent origin. The name scheduled caste first came into vogue during British rule with the *Government of India Act* of 1939 when those castes which suffered great social disabilities due to "untouchability", and had no objection to their name being included, were put on a list or schedule. The Scheduled Castes have suffered from socio-religious disabilities associated with the caste system which consisted of a four-fold division of society according to occupations but based on the theory and practice of purity and pollution. The higher castes were associated with purity and the polluted "untouchables" were at the other end of the scale. Several theories have been advanced on the genesis of the caste system: some emphasize the religious aspect, some describe the functional division of society, others racial factors (Revankar, 1971). Although the category of scheduled castes is based on religion, caste status is closely associated with occupational status. Ritual status determines caste status on the basis of purity and pollution as aspects of religious ideology, yet social status differences are derived not from the religious elements but from social stratification of caste. It was inevitable that at independence, the traditionally discriminatory and exploitative power relations had to be changed in terms of human rights. The practice of untouchability is now an offense punishable by law.

Article 46 of the *Indian Constitution* states that the State shall promote with special care, the educational and economic interests of the Scheduled Castes and Schedules Tribes, and shall protect them from social injustice and all forms of exploitation.

Gender

As a percentage of the total population women constitute a larger group than any other minority. In recognition of this, the Constitution has adopted a wide variety of legislative action to counter injustices faced by the majority of women. In terms of the *UN Declaration on the Elimination of Discrimination Against Women (1967)*, which was ratified by India, the Indian Constitution does very well for women. Compared to the *US Bill of Rights* and subsequent Constitutional Amendments it has been pointed out that the Indian Constitution affords women "essentially more of, and certainly more explicitly, the rights afforded to men" (Katzenstein, 1982).

The *National Educational Policy* endorses a common curriculum for males and females in the belief that differences exhibited by men and women are the result of social conditioning and unequal social positions accorded to them in society. Although the Constitution states that there shall be no discrimination on grounds of gender, it further provides that nothing shall prevent the State from making any special provision for women and children

(Article 15:3). The State is permitted to discriminate in favor of women if that is deemed necessary.

Having looked at stated policy on education, including legislation and anti-discrimination clauses regarding religion, caste/tribe and gender, we may now examine the reality of current practices in India.

Practice

Any change in modern India must be measured against the pre-independence period and should delineate the traditional attitudes and practices against which educational and social changes are presumably examined. This is so, especially because regional differences are tremendous. It must also be recognized that constitutional safeguards alone are insufficient in changing unequal power relations and power polarization between socio-economically advantaged and disadvantaged groups, be they economically handicapped, the Scheduled Castes and Tribes or women.

Education in India before independence was categorically exclusive. Moreover, the idea that knowledge is sacred denied education to lower castes and women because they were considered ritually impure. So, in a land where knowledge is embodied as a goddess, Hindu women were traditionally forbidden to read the scriptures.

The right to education

Useful measures of achievement in terms of the right to education are literacy and enrollment levels. The contemporary picture, however, is not as good as one would expect after 39 years of independence. The literacy rate has risen from 16.6 percent in 1951 to 36.6 percent according to the 1981 census. But regional variations indicate a range of above 60 percent literacy in Kerala to below 20 percent in some states. Nearly 120 million in the functional age group of 15–35 are still illiterate (Bhandari, 1981).

Over the last three decades of planned development, rapid growth in facilities has attempted to provide access for minorities and girls. The number of educational institutions has more than doubled, while the number of teachers and students has multiplied many times. But despite the fact that 93 percent of the rural population have access to schools, nearly 30 percent of 6–14 year olds (60 million) do not go to school and 77 percent drop out. A large percentage of the dropouts are girls and Scheduled Caste and Tribe members. The main problems are socio-economic constraints which result in educational constraints. Poverty is a major cause for keeping children away from school.

Religion

While the majority is Hindu (82 percent), the population of India practices many religions. Muslims account for 11.21 percent of the people, whereas Christians (2.6 percent), Sikhs (1.89 percent), Buddhists (0.70 percent, Jains (0.47 percent), and others (0.41 percent) have much smaller minorities according to the 1971 Census. Data from surveys have led to assertions that Muslims are not responding adequately to the large increase in educational facilities in contemporary India. One reason given is that Muslims fail to respond to secular education, but it has been argued (Ahmed, 1981) that the educational backwardness of Muslims in independent India is due to the fact that only a small percentage of Muslims have tended to go into professions and services and it is only this group which is likely to exploit educational opportunities for their children. Since independence and the creation of Pakistan, this group has been further reduced. Ahmed further points out that Muslims in India are stratified along two distinct axes. First is that of caste or caste-like groupings based on descent and racial origin. The second is one of occupational and political power. There is historical evidence that secular education was limited to the upper social stratum which also has political power and which is very small. Kamat (1981) asserts that although professing to be secular, the larger Hindu community, in fact, discriminates against Muslims in education and jobs. Muslims have also tended to exclude females from educational opportunities.

Language ethnicity

Regional language boundaries in India have been sources of controversy. The political implications of language, not only as a medium of communication but as an instrument for maintaining the existing occupational structure and the distribution of power and privilege in society, are obvious. Knowledge of English, through English-medium elite schools, maintains an elitist educational structure by facilitating the optimum use of higher educational opportunities and entry into the financially lucrative jobs in the private sector. There are no educational data according to language, but government policy regarding the use of regional languages for the prestigious Civil Service competitive exams is perhaps making a dent in changing the elitist structure.

The term Scheduled Tribes was retained in the *Constitution* for groups previously called Aboriginals and Hill Tribes and who up to 1819 were included with other Backward Classes.

Studies indicate that structural expansion in the provision of educational facilities has not resulted in comparable growth in educational achievement for scheduled castes and scheduled tribes who continue to be poorer and more illiterate than the general population. They go into lower paid, lower status jobs and are largely rural based. Poverty is a major factor in their poor performance, repeated failure, and drop-out rates in school. Although the Government has a scheme of scholarships for them, these are often inadequate for their needs. They tend to cluster in inferior educational institutions; thus, due to inadequate basic qualifications the provision of reserved employment is underutilized. Legislation and education are not by themselves enough to liquidate "untouchability" because the groups lack economic and political power.

Gender

In 1951 female literacy was 7.9 percent as compared to a male literacy rate of 25 percent. In 1981 only 24.8 percent women were literate as compared to 47.7 percent men. While more boys were enrolled in elementary classes in 1979–1980 than in 1968–1969, there is no comparable percentage increase in girls' enrollment between 1968–1969 and 1979–1980 at the primary level, and only a 10 percent increase at the upper elementary level. In 1979–1980 girls constituted 35 percent of the total elementary population. Drop out rates for girls are higher than for boys and two-thirds of this wastage occurs in grade one (India, Ministry of Education, 1981). Only about one quarter of all girls enrolled in class one complete primary school.

In a traditional and heterogeneous country like India dimensions of culture, religion, region and class have a significant impact on the education of girls. These variables are critical in defining social norms and values relating to women's roles which affect their education. Disparities regarding attitudes to women's roles exist not only between urban and rural areas, but also among different regions. The religious communities respond according to variations in their socio-cultural traditions. Communities (both Hindu and Muslim) which have historically practiced *purdah* (or seclusion) and therefore sex-segregation, have had low education rates among their females. The related concept of female virtue and honor views the education of girls as risky and has its impact in terms of fear of co-educational schools and male teachers, early withdrawal from schools and early marriages, especially in rural areas. It is felt that girls do not need to go to school to learn to be wives and mothers. In any case, girls are "lost" to the family after marriage, and in the absence of social security in old age, parents give preferential treatment to boys. They prefer to invest in boys' education because they have greater claim to their incomes.

Class is an important determinant of educational opportunities for girls. In the upper middle class there is no distinction in educational opportunities for boys and girls. The gap between male and female enrollment in India is narrowing much more rapidly at the tertiary level than in the primary and secondary levels, unlike in Western countries.

Despite policy, equality of treatment in the curriculum is not a reality. Content analysis of school textbooks indicate stereotyping of males and females and a patriarchal and male favored bias which conditions males for leadership and women for servitude (Kalia, 1982). The curriculum accords high status to women exclusively for being ideal mothers and wives, thus promoting an ideology which is restrictive.

Although women technically have equal access to any field of study, a constellation of variables limits their access, opportunities and aspirations to those fields of study (particularly technological ones) which have rapidly increasing job opportunities in a modernizing and developing society. The educational system has special social and economic consequences on the lives of men and women. Economic power is usually accepted as a most influential factor in determining power and status. Yet, only 11.8 percent of the total female population of 15–59 years is in the work force as compared to 52.51 percent of men in the same age group. In 1971, 94 percent of women workers were in the unorganized sector where they are subject to exploitation. With little or no education, they lack confidence and are unaware of their rights. Even in professional fields women tend to cluster in lower status positions (19 percent are doctors while 95 percent are nurses). Although 17 percent are at the tertiary level, only 12.5 percent are in university graduate degree programs. In management positions, a very small number of women from the upper-middle class are in good positions (India, Ministry of Education, 1974).

Saudi Arabia

Ideological Context

Any study of Saudi Arabia has to take note of the world view of Islam, as well as the traditional value system of the society and customary practices of the nomads. Saudi Arabia today is deeply rooted in Islam which is a system of belief and an ideology. These are based on a divine revelation of Truths bestowed from the Omnipotent, Omnipresent, Allāh, who made them known unto the people through a messenger, the Prophet Muhammad. These Truths, once in oral tradition form, were gathered into an orthographic script, the Qur'ān which is considered by all Muslims as holy, absolute and universal, eternally valid and applicable to all people at all times.

Islam is far more than a heritage or a creed; it is a way of life (Hitti, 1970). It ordains all affairs dealing with religious tenets and obligations, civic responsibilities, government, economics, transactions among individuals, group relations, morality and conduct, family life, personal status, dress code, eating habits, sexual intercourse, legislation as well as human rights and education.

Islamic law or the *Sharī'ah* is the basis of the legal system of Saudi Arabia. It is incumbent that all Muslims (and the non-Muslim communities at large) adhere to the law.

The concept of human rights and equality has been an integral part of Islamic thought since the religion originated. Islam maintains that "all people are equal in virtue of being His (Allāh's) creatures" (Ahmad, 1970). This, however, merely means that everyone regardless of sex, race or creed has the right to become a Muslim, it does not mean that Muslims and non-Muslims alike have the same rights (Ahmad, 1970). Thus, such as they are practiced, human rights in the Islamic *'Ummah* are regarded not as being dictated by virtue of one's birth right, but as exclusive rights of Muslims. In conjunction with those rights, every Muslim has certain responsibilities and duties to him/herself, society, the Islamic community and above all to 'Allāh. The notion of equality is perceived in terms of the concept of comparable worth. All practicing Muslims, regardless of race, color, gender and occupation, are equal in status before the Divine. At the human level, parity of rights is not equated with possessing identical opportunities but is viewed in terms of assigning equivalent values to different functions and opportunities. Thus, when considering human rights and equal opportunities by gender, it must be kept in mind that the differentiated roles and functions ascribed to each do not necessarily place men and women in a superior-subordinate position on a vertical structure, but rather on a horizontal complementary configuration.

Policy[4]

The right to education

Official statements in the pertinent literature of Saudi Arabia do not convey the same interpretation of the right to education devoid of all forms of discrimination that is maintained by the United Nations and its agencies. The first binding and all-inclusive official source that sets forth the foundations, goals, and orientation of Saudi education, entitled *The Educational Policy in the Kingdom of Saudi Arabia* of 1970, makes a general appeal and an impelling call for education. An analysis of its content, which encompasses a total of 236 principles, however, indicates that they do not clearly communicate that education is a human right in and of itself.

"Education, in all its forms, stages, organs and facilities, is geared to achieve Islamic objectives and is subject to the requirements and provisions of Islam. Education endeavors to reform the individual and develop the society morally, intellectually, socially and economically" (Principle 232). This intertwining of provisions for education with those for fostering religion undergirds all the other educational principles of this policy statement.

Notwithstanding, one may argue that the notion of education in Saudi Arabia is also associated with the notion of human rights, at least by implication. This argument rests on the fact that Principle 9, in contradistinction to all others, announces education as a right to a selective group (women) and guarantees them "the right to obtain education which suits

[4] Unless otherwise indicated, all references in this section on Policy are to *Educational Policy in the Kingdom of Saudi Arabia* (1970).

(their) nature." Since the educational rights of men are assumed, Principle 9 appears to ensure that Saudi Arabia's position approaches, at least in essence, that of the international organizations concerning the view that education is a human right of both sexes.

Policy statements indicate that there are also other common elements between Saudi Arabian educational policy and the international organizations' educational standards regarding education free from discrimination at all levels. "The period of schooling in the elementary stage is 6 years" (Principle 120). The State shall provide "educational opportunities to all children that have reached the required school age group," (Ministry of Planning, 1980, p. 241). "Schooling at this stage is free for all children reaching the required age" (Principle 121). "(The) authorities (have) set up necessary plans to accommodate all students reaching the age of elementary schooling . . ." (Principle 122). With reference to the higher levels, there is provision for an intermediate level of 3 years which affirms that "schooling in this stage is available as much as possible" to the graduates of the elementary stage (Principle 125). Provision is also made for a secondary level of 3 years: "Education in this stage is diversified and is available as much as possible to graduates of intermediate schools. . . . (The appropriate) authorities define conditions of enrollment for each type of secondary education in order to meet various needs and orient each student toward the field that suits him" (Principle 128).

Despite the convergence between Saudi Arabia and the UN agencies on the interpretation of the right to education providing equal educational access, points of divergence between the two become fairly pronounced when one considers the second part of this said provision: the right to education without any distinctions on the basis of gender, race, ethnicity and religion.

Religion

The right to education free from religious discrimination forces Saudi Arabia to part ways not only with the international organizations' standards but even with those of the *Universal Islamic Declaration of Human Rights (1981)*.

Educational and other policy statements of Saudi Arabia zealously profess the centrality of Islam in the society and in the goals and curricular activities of Saudi public schools. This policy deprives non-Muslim parents of their prerogative to opt for religious training that fosters the knowledge and practice of their faith for their children.

Race or ethnicity

As to the aspect of race, Saudi Arabia endorses an overt policy of racial non-discrimination. This non-discriminatory policy, nonetheless, is strictly applicable only to Saudi citizens who, as mentioned previously, belong to a varied racial and ethnic background, and are exclusively Muslim.

Gender

There is no uniform policy statement for all areas of education for the two sexes. Saudi Arabia officially subscribes to a de jure policy of institutional segregation and deliberate variegation in statements of educational objectives and curricular programs for the two sexes. There is for example, a separate policy statement of general objectives for males and another distinct statement for females that direct program implementation. The one for male students guarantees a wide array of possible subject matter and encourages them to embark on the study and research of as many areas of knowledge as can be envisioned within the confines of the Islamic religion. In contrast, the policy statement of educational goals for women is much more restrictive. When it is translated into actual training and instruction, the domestic sciences and the female dominated curriculum areas prevail.

In summary, Saudi Arabia's position towards human rights in education with regard to racial, ethnic, and religious minorities is one of requiring conformity. As long as minority children adapt to the Islamic ideal of conduct, they are ensured equal rights—male with male and female with female. Saudi Arabia does not recognize the merits of Western-type pluralism whether on the basis of gender, race, ethnicity or religion. Human rights and equality in education are practices within the framework of conformity to established norms.

Practice

Religion

The right to education free from religious discrimination does not exist in either policy or practice in Saudi educational institutions. Even though Saudi Arabia has made commitments to two inconsistent positions—the national position of serving only Islam and no other religion, and the principles of religious freedom and fair treatment of all religious groups as a signatory of the *Universal Islamic Declaration of Human Rights* and the *UNESCO Convention Against Discrimination in Education (1960)*, current conditions in the schools clearly indicate that practices representing the national position are dominant. First, the curriculum avidly teaches not only that Islam is the ideal and true religion, way of life and thought, but that it should be viewed through the particular rites to which Saudi Arabia adheres. Second, it commits omission biases in not teaching other religions including the Shi'ite Muslim faith to which 10 percent of its indigenous population belong. Third, references to other religions are often presented in the context of assault on their thought and tenets, ridicule of their rituals, and prejudice and defamation. Fourth, all school children who do not belong to the *Sunnī* faith (even those attending the three foreign educational institutions permitted by law) are not allowed to be openly involved in activities showing any group faith solidarity, let alone observe their faith publicly if they so desire.

Race

It is difficult to locate data assessing implementation in educational institutions of the non-racial discrimination policy Saudi Arabia professes. Unlike the case of gender, distributions of school statistics on the basis of race and ethnicity are not reported. Factors of race and ethnicity are set aside when other weightier variables such as Saudi nationality and religion come into play.

Gender

Currently, actual access to schooling and offerings of educational programs for both genders appear to be congruent with national educational policy. Open educational access free from gender discrimination at the elementary level is the general direction taken by the authorities despite the fact that Saudi Arabia has not yet adopted the provision of compulsory education.

Although girls' attendance has increased many-fold in recent times there is still a wide discrepancy in the enrollment ratios between genders at this primary level. While male enrollment ratios in 1979 represented 78.1 percent as compared to 50 percent for females, projected figures for boys in 1985, are 85 percent as compared to 55.3 percent for their female counterparts. This gender lag becomes even more acute when enrollments of girls of the appropriate age group living in the rural and desert areas are computed.

Achieving open access to schooling, however, is not a sufficient measure of non-discrimination in education. Lowering the dropout rate is also needed to attain universal education. Only about 50 percent of Saudi females who begin elementary school graduate 6 years later at the end of the primary cycle (Al-Bassām, 1983). Thus with respect to implementing the right to education through primary level to all children, Saudi Arabia is undoubtedly found wanting. However, judging from the rising pattern of enrollment—which has been more and more affected by the increasing migration trends from the rural and nomadic communities into the urban centers for better economic opportunities (Walpole *et al.*, 1971)—it appears that it is just a matter of time before Saudi Arabia will be able to fully implement the right of universal access to elementary education. If the same enrollment trends continue, Saudi Arabia will very likely achieve universal schooling by year 2020, with complete attendance for boys achieved 20 years earlier—bringing Saudi Arabia into compliance with international standards for open access to elementary education level—on the basis of separate facilities and differential curriculum for boys and girls.

Access to secondary education is, in principle, open to both genders. The academic standards and conditions that govern entry to this level are uniform to all boys and girls. Despite the official policy, there is a great disparity in enrollment figures between males and females, though the latter are evidencing stronger growth rates.

Failure to pass the primary school certificate is claimed as the main obstacle to access to secondary education. This may hold true in the case of boys. As for girls, there are actually a host of other equally hindering factors, chief among which are: (1) the long-standing tradition of early marriage, (2) catering to siblings and assisting in the house work, (3) the effects of the practice of female seclusion, (4) economic imperatives on the poor, particularly the nomadic families living on subsistence levels, and (5) parents reserving the value of education for sons and not daughters.

Entry requirements for higher education programs are uniform for all males and females. Overall, however, female participation in higher education is lagging behind that of males even though women are making headway.

In brief, then, a distinct possibility exists for men and women to attain, in the foreseeable future, equal rights and status with respect to actual participation at the three educational levels, primary, secondary and tertiary—within segregated systems and with different curricula.

Operationally, Saudi Arabia, consistent with its stated policy, implements a system of education that follows a gender-segregated model throughout. This duality is prominently reflected in the curriculum at all levels. Each of the two school systems—one for males and the other for females—endorses distinct variations in their instructional programs that are gender-related. The gender-based gap in the curriculum is narrowest at the elementary level where 13.64 percent of the weekly program of studies is devoted to the subject of home economics and female oriented crafts for the girls. Approximately the same proportion of the curriculum is assigned to male oriented crafts in the case of boys. At the secondary level, however, there are further differentiations in the area of non-general education between the two sexes. Females are restricted to two tracks, teacher training and vocational training, a misnomer for the domestic arts. Males have four tracks: vocational training, secondary industrial, secondary commercial, and secondary agriculture. At the university and higher institutes of learning, females experience additional access constraints to a variety of fields of study. Presently, they are barred from enrolling in engineering, geology, meteorology, sea sciences, agricultural sciences and pharmacy, among others.

The reinforcement of sex discrimination is equally conspicuous in the subject matter content that is common to both girls and boys, even though this is more prevalent at the elementary and intermediate levels. This preoccupation with "femaleness" and "maleness" themes in Islamic thought (Deaver, 1980) is repetitively depicted when teaching, for example, specific gender roles, female role models and male role models in Islam, the ideal attributes of women juxtaposed against those of men, the Islamic defense of these distinctive gender roles and attributes, the public image of men versus the private image of women and the visible contributions of men and imperceptible participation of females in the local histories. One has only to scan the assigned textbooks in subjects such as social studies, Arabic and religious studies for confirming evidence.

To summarize, on the basis of international agreements, critics focus on two main violations: (1) the promotion of inequality between the sexes and (2) the imposition of a monolithic view of the world through religious instruction.

Saudi officials claim that the gender dual model is arguably defensible in the light of the cultural, religious, and social contexts of their country. Pervasive sexual segregation has for many centuries been deeply ingrained in the society and legislated in the *Qur'ān*, posing insurmountable obstacles when changes are introduced regarding the role of women that run contrary to traditional values and conventions. The UN appeal to developing nations to promote equality of educational and job opportunities by ensuring the participation of women "on equal terms with men, in the political, social, economic and cultural life" for "the full and complete development of [their] country" (*Declaration on the Elimination of Discrimination against Women*, 1967, Preamble), is unworkable in such a society because of the specificities of the culture which dictate a legal, religious basis for sexual segregation. Instead of judging it as a violation of the precepts of human rights regarding sex equity, it might be more realistic to work within a model indigenous to a particular society to improve the conditions of its women. Given that men and women in Saudi Arabia constitute large separate subsocieties, the dual model of sex segregation has helped promote the education and employment of women. In the subsociety of women, where there are educational, social, entertainment, medical, banking, and other services exclusively for women, it has become imperative that educated females with certain skills and specializations be called upon to cater to the needs of women in the subsociety. This is increasingly taking place in Saudi Arabia.

By the same token, one can argue in defense of the religious imperatives set forth by the theocracy of the Saudi state. Since a given cultural or religious configuration is judged valid on its merit in terms of the consistent relations evident among its elements, such as the values and means it adopts in relation to the ends it expects to achieve, the Saudi model could be seen as valid for that country. It must be understood that the Saudi Arabian government bases its policy of discrimination against non-Muslims on the belief that it has unravelled the truth and the structure of reality of the world through Islam and views itself as a crusader whose mission is to carry out this message to other people on or outside Saudi soil.

Conclusion

The preceding case studies of India and Saudi Arabia have provided data and analyzed four facets of education free from discrimination. This has been depicted within the complex interrelationship between policy and practice and the even more complicated fabric of economic, social, religious, value and belief systems.

To begin with, India and Saudi Arabia demonstrate two distinct ideological perspectives making their views of human rights very different. This chapter has examined the contrasting stances and particular experiences of each country regarding religion, race and ethnicity, and gender.

The most significant distinction between the two countries is in the official position relating to human rights. Legislation and policy statements in India come much closer to the human rights principles in the UN documents. Saudi Arabia, on the other hand, has a completely different reference point based on the principles enunciated by Islam. India has ratified the *Universal Declaration of Human Rights* while Saudi Arabia has not but is a signatory of the *Universal Islamic Declaration of Human Rights*. Human rights legislation as applied to education in India is based on equal rights to all irrespective of religion, race, language and gender. The Saudi system is based on a monolithic view of religion, which distinguishes between Muslims and non-Muslims but gives equality to all Muslims irrespective of race and ethnicity, although women as a group have differential status.

Both countries still include a number of disadvantaged subordinate groups. Although India has been bold in its legislation and equality is ensured in educational access, program and outcome, it lags behind in achievement in all these aspects. Despite tremendous expansion of the educational system, the right to education is far from being realized. Availability of educational opportunities does not ensure its utilization. Poverty is an important factor affecting implementation of the right to elementary education. Inequality is the result of various socio-economic and cultural factors for disadvantaged groups such as Scheduled Castes and Tribes, and women. Similarly, Saudi Arabia registers a serious underrepresentation of several subordinate socio-economic and religious groups regarding access to schooling and in the work force, particularly in the higher skilled and professional jobs. Despite its high per capita income, the main disadvantaged citizens in Saudi Arabia continue to be the rural and bedouin communities and the

Shi'ites; the latter claim that they are discriminated against mainly in scholarships, promotions and appointments to public offices.

Accomplishments in both cases, however, are better appreciated if they are viewed from an appropriate point of reference. At independence in 1947, India inherited great educational disparities and data indicate that despite present inequalities, considerable gains have been made in the education of disadvantaged groups and particularly women. The beneficiaries of education and human rights legislation have been the middle and advanced castes in rural and urban areas (Kumar, 1985), and the small minority of urban middle-class and elite women who are beginning to go into a variety of fields in higher education. Due to legislation the caste system has undergone considerable change, and the recruitment of a small number of Scheduled Castes and Tribes persons into the prestigious civil service indicates a positive aspect of the progressive discrimination policy. As for Saudi Arabia, the sweeping educational reforms and modernizing processes of the 1960s, spearheaded by King Faisal and embodied in legislation, have resulted in greater representation of members of the bedouin and rural communities in the educational system and in employment in the public sector than ever before. Such reforms, manifested in their upgraded educational qualifications, have increasingly been earning the bedouin women certain positions in the intelligence service, and their male counterparts, enrollment in the national guard and the army.

With respect to gender, both countries suffer from disparities in access to and participation in the educational system. Despite the fact that India has had a much higher enrollment ratio for both sexes than Saudi Arabia, the enrollment rates of females in both countries, especially at the elementary level, are very similar, constituting approximately one third of the total enrollment, with Saudi Arabia showing a slight edge at the elementary level.

The discernible difference in effects between the two educational systems regarding gender related issues is in career outcomes, which are largely linked to the types of curricular offerings. As such, Indian women have equal rights with men to participate in the labor market, while there are limitations imposed on Saudi women due to differential treatment in these respects. Effects of such policies are more favorable to the former, as exhibited by their higher participation rate in the whole spectrum of occupations in the labor market, both public and private.

Nevertheless, it should be borne in mind that discriminatory effects of a segregated society like that of Saudi Arabia have brought forth, albeit by default, positive consequences to women. Segregation has relatively enhanced the occupational mobility of Saudi women at least in the areas where they are free to function, in that they have helped diminish the sex biased occupational distributions defined as "women's work" versus "men's work" that are rampant in desegregated societies, a direction towards which India seems to be moving. Thus the concentration, overall, of one sex at certain levels in the occupational structure is not found in Saudi Arabia as it is in India. Within each of the men's and women's spheres, the gamut of occupations from the highest positions to the lowest is filled by members of its respective sex.

In India the UN principles cannot be totally implemented at this time. Failure to achieve the right to education free from discrimination is largely rooted in economic incapacity where poverty is correlated with disadvantaged groups and the preferential treatment of males. The fact that equality of opportunity in modern India co-exists with inequality of conditions is because what characterizes the liberal interpretation of human rights is the separation of different systems in society—social from economic, economic from political, and educational from social, economic and political.

For Saudi Arabia, the difficulty in the total application of human rights, UN style, stems from a totally different understanding of key concepts that have a bearing on the human rights configuration. One such concept is the different outlook towards gender status and rights. Saudi Arabia does not view the concepts of differentiation it holds towards Muslim men and Muslim women as discrimination against women or preferential treatment for men. The UN orchestrators of human rights documents, on the other hand, find difficulty equating differentiation with equality. A second concept is that of labor. The dichotomous notion of the industrialized West—which consists in giving more value to labor that has direct renumeration and to undervalue work that is not wage earning—is foreign to Saudi Arabia, though with the modernization process such an imported concept is gradually gaining ground. Saudi Arabia's traditional economy recognized two types of value for work and roles performed by members of its community, both of equal importance: material value and moral value. The hierarchical differentiations of labor given in the literature on economic development labeled as "work", i.e. work in the public domain, performed by men, and "support work" or work in the private domain, performed by women, cannot be appreciated in Saudi Arabia, where both kinds are considered work, with no superior-inferior value attached to either. A concrete example is the very prestigious and almost sacred role that is assigned by Islam to mothers and wives in the privacy of the household. As such, Saudi Arabia finds difficulty accepting the allegation that it practices discrimination against women. A third concept is related to the principle of religious tolerance, which presupposes the coexistence of diverse religious groups on an equal footing, a position which Saudi Arabia cannot accept, on the basis of its understanding of Islam as the only and true religion.

If legislation were the only measure, India's record in education and human rights would be very impressive indeed. The above data indicate that legislation is not a guarantee of equality. The strategies adopted to achieve the goals are crucial but they are incapacitated by factors such as poverty and social discrimination. Nevertheless, legislation is undoubtedly an important factor in the elimination of inequalities and discrimination because it creates a greater awareness of inequalities as well as indicating a commitment to the principles reflected in the various UN documents. It is in view of the commitment, not only in statistical outcomes, that success is fully measured.

The prospect for India fully implementing the UN standards are brighter with economic development, and socio-cultural value and attitude change. For Saudi Arabia changes towards UN standards would mean radical change in ideology and cultural practice which is unlikely to take place.

References

Ahmad, M. K. (1970) Human rights between theory and practice in the Islamic and Western civilizations. In Al-Azhar Academy of Islamic Reseach (Eds.), *The Fourth Conference of the Academy of Islamic Research* (pp. 875–880). Cairo: General Organization for Government Printing Offices.

Ahmed, I. (1981) Muslim education backwardness. *Economic and Political Weekly*, Sept. 5, pp. 1457–65.

Al-Bassām, M. (1983) *Al-Rusūb wa al-Tasarrub fī al-Marhalah al-'Ibtidā'iyyah li-l-Banāt fī al-Mamlakah al-'Arabiyyah al-Sa'ūdiyyah wa 'Alāqatuhumā bi-Khuttatay al-Tanmiyah.* [Repetition and dropout rates of girls in primary education in the Kingdom of Saudi Arabia and their relation to the two development plans]. Unpublished Master's Thesis, King Saud University, Riyahd, Saudi Arabia.

Bhandari, R. K. (1981) Crisis in education in India. *New Frontiers in Education.* **14**(3), 74–81.

Deaver, S. (1980) The contemporary Saudi woman. In E. Bourguignon (Ed.) *A world of women* (pp. 19–42). New York: Praeger.

Hitti, P. K. (1970) *Islam: a way of life.* Southbend, IN.: Regnery—Gateway.

India. Ministry of Education (1981) *India: A reference manual.* New Delhi: Author.

India. Ministry of Education. Department of Social Welfare (1974) *Committee on the status of women in India report: Towards equality.* New Delhi: Author.

Kalia, N. N. (1982) Images of men and women in Indian textbooks. In G. P. Kelly and C. M. Elliot (Eds.), *Women's education in the Third World: Comparative perspectives.* (pp. 173–187). Albany: State University of New York Press.

Kamat, A. R. (1981) Literacy and education of Muslims. *Economic and political weekly*, June 6, pp. 1031–33.

Katzenstein, M. F. (1982) Toward equality? Cause and consequence of the political prominence of women in India. *Asian Survey,* **18**(5), 473–486.

Revankar, R. (1971) *The Indian Constitution.* Cranbury, N. J.: Associated University Presses.

Walpole, N. C., Bastos, A. J., Eisele, F. R., Herrick, A. B., John, H. J. and Weiland, T. K. (1971) *Area Handbook for Saudi Arabia.* Washington, DC: The American University.

World almanac and book of facts (1986) New York: Newspaper Enterprise Association Inc.

Yearbook of Human Rights (1949–66, 1973–80) New York: United Nations.

CHAPTER 4

Exceptional Abilities and Educational Rights: Concern for the Handicapped and Gifted in Britain, China and Indonesia

R. Murray Thomas
University of California, Santa Barbara

The purpose of this chapter is to investigate the question: How do societies differ in the way they define and provide educational rights for their handicapped and for their unusually talented members?

The mode of analysis consists, first, of offering four propositions related to educational rights for exceptional people. Then the propositions are illustrated with examples from Great Britain, the People's Republic of China, and Indonesia. However, before introducing the propositions, we may profit from (1) reviewing statements from international declarations regarding rights for the handicapped and talented and (2) identifying characteristics of the three illustrative nations that influence how their societies address issues of rights for the exceptional.

Human Rights Declarations[1]

The most widely accepted proposals about human rights are those issued by the United Nations, with the most basic of these proposals being the *Universal Declaration of Human Rights* adopted by the United Nations in 1948. Article 26 of the declaration states that "Everyone has the right to education. Education shall be free, at least in the elementary and fundamental stages" (*Human rights*, 1983, p. 3). Although we could assume that this broadscale commitment is intended to apply to the handicapped as well as to the average person, the document speaks of no special provisions that might be needed to meet the particular learning needs of the handicapped or gifted. More than a decade passed before specific mention was made of rights for handicapped children. The fifth principle of the *Declaration of the Rights of the Child* in 1959 stated that "The child who is physically, mentally, or socially handicapped shall be given the special treatment, education, and care required by his particular condition." And in 1971, the United Nations issued a *Declaration of the Rights of Mentally Retarded Persons* which included an obligation to provide the mentally retarded with educational opportunities (*Human rights*, 1983, p. 141). But not until the 1975 *Declaration of the Rights of Disabled Persons* was such a provision extended to all disabled people, who were then said to deserve "education, vocational training and rehabilitation, aid, counselling, placement services and other services which will enable them to develop their capabilities and skills to the maximum and will hasten the process of their social integration or reintegration" (*Human rights*, 1983, p. 142).[1]

The chronology of the foregoing declarations reflects the typical sequence of educational provisions in individual societies throughout the world—the educational needs of the average are cared for well ahead of the educational needs of the handicapped. In contrast to educational rights for the handicapped, educational rights for highly talented people are rarely if ever mentioned in human rights documents. However, most societies provide special educational opportunities for the gifted without formally declaring that such people deserve exceptional treatment.

The Three Illustrative Nations

The term *Great Britain*, as used throughout the chapter, means the United Kingdom—England, Northern Ireland, Wales, and Scotland (even though educational practices in Scotland differ in some respects from practices in the other three regions). The People's Republic of China is Mainland China, the vast area controlled by the Chinese Communist Government, since 1949. Indonesia is the Southeast Asian island nation that was known as the Dutch East Indies before its people gained independent political status during the period 1945–1949.

In population, China ranks first in the world, with its one billion inhabitants accounting for one-fourth of the total number of people on earth. Indonesia ranks fifth, with over 160 million people who live on 900 of the 3,000 islands that compose the archipelago. Great Britain's population at 56 million ranks 14th in the world and is less than 6 percent the size of China's and about one-third the size of Indonesia's.

Politically the three nations operate under different systems. Great Britain is nominally a kingdom, with the ostensible ruler achieving his or her position by hereditary succession. However, in practice the country is governed as a bicameral parliamentary democracy, with the elected members of parliament representing multiple political parties that contend for control of governmental affairs. Indonesia is likewise a parliamentary democracy under an elected president, with multiple political parties competing for control of the parliament. In recent times, however, the Golkar party, sponsored by the present administration and dominated by the nation's military and civil-service establishment, has been able to wield

---

[1] See Appendices for summaries of relevant documents.

control over the government. In the People's Republic of China the only effective political organization is the Communist Party, which establishes policies governing the country's political and economic affairs.

In regard to occupational structure, the two Asian nations have much in common. Their populations are mainly rural, engaged in agriculture. In China 80 percent of the people are peasants, while in Indonesia 70 percent engage in farming and fishing. Great Britain, on the other hand, is highly industrialized, with less than 2 percent of the nation's working force engaged in agriculture and with over one-third of the population living in cities larger than 200,000 (*Britain*, 1985, p. 301; *Europa Yearbook*, 1985, p. 975).

In terms of educational structure, both China and Indonesia maintain centralized systems, with directives regarding guidelines for school organization and curricula originating from a central ministry of education. Nearly all schools in China are public, in that almost all are financed and controlled by the government. Most Indonesian schools are public, but a substantial proportion are conducted by private organizations, particularly by Islamic religious groups, that are obligated to follow government curriculum guidelines. In contrast, the British system, including both public and private schools, is administratively decentralized, with the power of decision over curricular matters largely in the hands of local authorities and individual schools' headmasters.

As we now consider the four propositions, we can recognize ways that the foregoing demographic, political, and economic conditions have influenced the three societies' educational provisions for learners defined as exceptional.

The propositions concern:

(1) how the terms *exceptional* and *equal rights* are defined,
(2) the level of a nation's commitment to educational rights,
(3) priorities in providing for educational rights, and
(4) economic influences on such rights.

Defining "Exceptional" and "Equal Rights"

Proposition 1: Societies can differ in the way they interpret "equal educational rights for exceptional people."

To clarify the significance of this proposition, we can inspect the way societies may vary in how they define *exceptional people* and *equal educational rights*.

Who Are the Exceptional?

Understanding how a society defines *exceptional people* is important for identifying who deserves the educational rights intended for *the exceptional*. But defining who is exceptional is far more difficult than defining who is

female when we speak of equal rights by gender or who is *black* when we talk
of equal rights by race. This is true because the problem of agreeing on what
exceptional means is complicated by: (1) a lack of consensus about which
personal characteristics are *exceptional* when educational provisions are
being proposed, (2) difficulties in measuring the extent of people's exceptionality, and (3) disagreements about where the cutting point should be for
separating the exceptional from the nonexceptional.

Disagreements about Personal Characteristics

The term *special education* is the phrase most frequently used to designate
provisions for aiding people who suffer personal handicaps that place them
at a learning disadvantage in a typical classroom. The kinds of handicaps
that concern us here are *personal* rather than *social*. By *personal*, I mean a
handicap that is an inherent characteristic of the individual—such as
blindness or deafness—which directly affects the person's ability to learn. In
contrast, a *social* handicap is an indirect barrier to learning caused by
prejudicial treatment of people because they exhibit some group characteristic, such as female gender, Oriental race, Jewish religion, or the like.

The most commonly recognized personal handicaps are disorders of
vision, hearing, body movement (bone, muscle, and nerve disorders), and
intelligence (mental retardation). In nearly all cultures, these are accepted
as barriers to learning, so they might be called "traditional" handicaps.
However, in certain societies in recent decades additional personal handicaps to learning have been identified. The most prominent are those listed
under such general, overarching labels as *perceptual-motor disorders* or
psycho-neurological learning defects. Beneath these umbrella labels, more
specific disorders are listed. For example, children who appear to have
normal vision, hearing, and "general intelligence" but still suffer great
difficulties in learning to read are called *dyslexic*. Those whose vision,
hearing, and "general intelligence" seem normal but who are unable to
grasp quantitative concepts are said to suffer *dyscalculia*. Ones with severe
handwriting problems are called *dysgraphic*. And as time passes, additional
subtypes of learning disabilities are described and labeled. In short, over the
years, the number of personal characteristics identified as handicaps to
learning has increased. And while all societies recognize the "traditional"
handicaps, they do not all recognize more recently designated types.

But the lack of consensus about who qualifies as exceptional does not stop
with the handicapped. At the other end of the scale of ability are people with
exceptionally fine skills. In certain cultures these unusually able people are
designated as deserving special educational provisions, but in other societies
they are not. Part of the reason that societies vary in the educational
opportunities they offer the highly skilled is that there is no general
agreement about how "superior abilities" should be defined. For purposes

of educational opportunity, some people identify *giftedness* as "general intellectual ability" or "exceptional superiority in a broad range of activities." And they use the term *talent* to refer to special ability in only one realm—mathematics, music, painting, dramatics, the dance, athletics, social relations, or the like. Then the question arises: Does either giftedness or special talent entitle a student to special educational treatment? Not all societies answer this question the same way.

In summary, to understand what is meant in a given culture by "educational rights for exceptional people," it is important to learn the sorts of personal characteristics that qualify individuals as exceptional in that culture. In way of illustration, consider the cases of Great Britain, China, and Indonesia.

The British Case

For Great Britain, Tomlinson (1982, p. 61) traced the officially recognized designations of persons with special educational needs over nearly a century, 1886–1981. She found that in 1886 there were only two statutory categories, both focussing on mental retardation, those of idiot and imbecile. By 1913 five more categories had been added—moral imbecile, mental defective (feeble-minded), blind, deaf, epileptic, and physically defective. In 1945 there were 12 categories, some incorporating more than one earlier designation (severely subnormal subsumed both idiot and imbecile), while other new varieties extended earlier categories (partially sighted was added to blind, and partially hearing was added to deaf). By 1981 the official types numbered 14, with several additional varieties suggested but not officially adopted. The 1981 list consisted of: child with learning difficulties (severe), child with learning difficulties (mild), blind, partially sighted, deaf, partially hearing, epileptic, maladjusted, disruptive, physically handicapped, speech defect, delicate, dyslexic, and autistic. Additional suggested categories included: neuropathic child, inconsequential child, psychiatrically crippled child, aphasic child, and others. The percentage of children in the school-age population who could be diagnosed as fitting into at least one of these categories could be as large as 20 percent (Tomlinson, 1982, pp. 55–56). These are the children judged to be sufficiently handicapped to deserve special education rights in Britain. When the gifted are added to this figure, the percentage qualifying for special-education opportunities under the present-day British conception of exceptionality might be as high as 25 or perhaps 30 percent.

The Chinese Case

At the beginning of the 1980s, the four types of personal handicap mentioned in China's *Encyclopedia of Education* as warranting special-education attention were those of blindness, deafness, marked mental retardation, and antisocial deviance (Special education, 1981–82, pp. 49–52). Li Hongtai, general secretary of China's National Research Foundation for Special Education, estimated in 1985 that the number of school-age children in the nation suffering such visual, auditory, and mental handicaps totaled half-a-million, which would represent perhaps two-tenths of one percent of the country's school-age population (Xu, 1985). Thus, compared to Great Britain, the proportion of children defined as handicapped and thus deserving special-education rights in China is very limited.

However, in contrast to the handicapped, the gifted in China have received a great deal of attention. It is true that the egalitarian movement during the Cultural Revolution (1966–1976) deemphasized people's intellectual differences and stressed, instead, disciplined communist political conviction. However, over the past decade the emphasis has shifted once more to a search for talent that can hasten the society's socioeconomic development. Much-publicized competitions are held to honor youths who display unusual ability in general academic attainment, in science, and in the arts. And *key schools* that offer scholarships and special opportunities for the gifted are accorded greater attention than in the past (Hawkins, 1983, pp. 154–155; Smerling, 1978–79, pp. 61–62).

The Indonesian Case

Present-day special education in Indonesia has derived from a legacy of provisions left by the Dutch when they relinquished colonial control over the island nation in the mid-20th century. Shortly after 1900, a newly awakened humanitarian spirit among the Dutch colonialists had motivated private groups in the Netherlands to establish in Indonesia a modest facility for each of four types of handicap—the blind, the deaf and mute, the mentally retarded, and the socially maladjusted (juvenile delinquents). These small centers continued until 1942, when Japanese armed forces ousted the Dutch and closed special-education facilities. After the close of World War II, the few special-education schools reopened, and an Indonesian orthopedic surgeon during the ensuing revolution against the Dutch (1945–1949) established a rehabilitation center for youths who lost limbs during the fighting.

After 1950, attention to the educational needs of the handicapped in Indonesia grew at a very slow rate until the mid-1970s, when efforts to aid the mentally and physically disadvantaged progressed at an accelerating pace. By the 1980s the emphasis in the Indonesian government's definition of *exceptional children* was still on the traditional categories of the blind, the deaf and mute, the mentally retarded, and the physically disabled. However, by now the official definition had expanded to include the cerebral palsied, the emotionally disturbed, the multipli-handicapped, the chronically ill, and the gifted (PPKSP, 1981, p. 1). Furthermore, the government's 1984 special-education curriculum distinguished between different degrees of handicap, such as between moderate and mild mental retardation. And beyond the officially recognized types of exceptionality, social workers and special-education personnel were also initiating activities to treat additional handicaps, including ones resulting from child abuse and neglect (*Final Report*, 1983).

However, estimates of the number of handicapped in the Indonesian population focussed only on disorders of vision, hearing/speech, and bodily movement, and on mental retardation. At the outset of the 1980s Indonesian officials used two methods to speculate about the number of children, ages 7–12, who suffered such disabilities. One method was to apply UNESCO's estimate that in most nations about 10 percent of the population will display such handicaps. So, if 15 percent of Indonesia's total population of 147 million in 1980 consisted of school-age children, there would be 2.25 million handicapped children in the nation. But the 1980 Indonesian national census identified slightly fewer than 255,000 handicapped school-age children, which is only 1.15 percent of the country's 7-to-12-year-olds, a figure less than 12 percent of the UNESCO estimate (DPD, 1981, p. 9). However, because the census takers could hardly be expected to diagnose handicaps with any precision, this census figure seems unrealistically low. Yet this census datum has served as the basis on which Indonesia's special education plans have been founded during the 1980s, representing a figure far below Britain's but still considerably above China's.

Measurement Problems

In most nations, methods for measuring acuity of sight and hearing are well established. Likewise, disorders of bodily movement, such as lameness or incoordination of the fingers and hand, are easy to recognize and describe. However, far more difficult and debatable are techniques for assessing intelligence and a variety of other characteristics, such as visual perception (as contrasted to acuity of eye function), auditory perception (as contrasted to acuity of ear function), coordination of simultaneous sight and sound perceptions, and others.

Consider, for instance, what is typically referred to as "general intelligence." Even in supposedly "advanced" and "enlightened" modern societies, most educators—and certainly the general public—fail to realize that a single score from a general intelligence test is an inaccurate, outmoded way to assess a person's mental abilities. Intelligent behavior is far more complex than what typical intelligence tests of the past have measured (Kail and Pellegrino, 1985). In recognition of this fact, psychologists and medical personnel continue to search for the most appropriate ways of determining who in a society qualifies as either exceptionally handicapped or exceptionally gifted in mental ability. And the ways currently used to arrive at this determination often differ from one society to another, as illustrated by present-day procedures in Great Britain, China, and Indonesia.

The British Case

In Great Britain, not only are there numerous evaluation methods used for diagnosing exceptional status, but numerous types of professional personnel are involved in the process. By the early 1980s, the officially recommended process for the diagnosis and placement of a school child who was suspected of needing special education included the following stages and personnel (adapted from Tomlinson, 1982, p. 93).

Stage 1. A classroom teacher or the school head (principal) judges that a child may need special education services.

Stage 2. The school head discusses the child's symptoms with a teacher who has had special education training.

Stage 3. The school head or the school doctor consults with other professionals (also at Stage 5, if necessary) and takes advice from the local education authority's special-education adviser.

Stage 4. The school head completes an SE-1 (Special-Education Form 1) to initiate the multi-professional assessment process. The process consists of (A) a medical officer examining the child and completing an SE-2, perhaps aided by advice from community health workers, (B) an educational psychologist completing SE-3 after administering intelligence tests and other assessment techniques, (C) a social worker perhaps completing another SE form after studying the child's family situation, (D) the classroom teacher, school head, special-education adviser, medical officer, educational psychologist, and social worker joining forces to evaluate the child's status.

Stage 5. If the diagnosis through Stage 4 is judged still to be inconclusive, more specialists can be called into the case, such as a neurologist or a clinical psychologist. Next, an officer of the local education authority (special-education adviser or educational psychologist) completes an SE-4. In addition, the child's parents have an opportunity to file an objection to the diagnosis and the recommended special-education placement of the child. Finally the child is assigned to the special-education program (out of 10 available types) deemed most suitable for the diagnosed condition.

In comparison to this complicated and relatively new procedure for identifying and placing the handicapped is Great Britain's simpler traditional way of finding intellectually gifted children. Intellectually superior youths who are to be accorded special learning opportunities have usually been identified by means of an achievement-test system operated by regional or university-attached examination boards. That is, students take tests in subject-matter fields to help determine the sorts of further education for which they may qualify. Traditionally such tests were administered at three stages of the child's schooling—the 11-plus examination at the close of primary education, "O-levels" (ordinary) at around age 16, and "A-levels" (advanced) at around age 18 or 19. By the 1980s the 11-plus examination had been eliminated, and a CSE (Certificate in Secondary Education) along with a more advanced test (General Certificate of Education as an equivalent of the "O-level" tests) had been introduced. These examinations, sometimes supplemented by measures of "general intelligence" or "academic aptitude," have been the chief means of selecting students who are to receive special educational opportunities for the intellectually gifted.

The Chinese Case

In contrast to the complex British system, the approach generally followed in China for identifying the handicapped has involved relatively simple observations of how a child's behavior compares with that of agemates. The task of diagnosing the gross sight and hearing disorders and the marked mental retardation which have been accorded special-education attention in China has required no use of sophisticated tests or of specially trained personnel. Nor has it been difficult to recognize those youths whose antisocial deviance warrants their assignment to reform schools. Thus, so long as the categories of handicap in China remain those of blindness, deaf-muteness, marked mental retardation (idiot, imbecile, slow-reacting), and delinquency, the job of identifying who deserves special education for the disabled is rather easy.

To locate students who deserve to enter key schools for the intellectually superior, the Chinese, like the British, use an achievement-examination system. Although the use of achievement tests for selecting students to enter key schools was suspended during the decade of the Cultural Revolution (1966–1976), in recent years examinations have again become the principal criteria for deciding who should attend key schools designed to promote intellectual excellence. Smerling (1978–79, p. 61) reported that in the latter 1970s the three requirements for enrollment in key schools were: (1) high marks on the national examinations in subject-matter areas, plus high-level marks in past schooling, (2) faithful political-moral awareness as defined by the Chinese Communist Party, and (3) good physical health.

The Indonesian Case

In several of Indonesia's larger metropolitical centers, special-education experts use standard vision and hearing tests as well as several foreign tests of intelligence that Indonesian psychologists have adapted for use in their country. However, such formal testing procedures are generally not used for identifying candidates for special education. Instead, the Ministry of Education has issued a brief manual for teachers and social workers to use in identifying exceptional children on the basis of easily observed symptoms and on the manner in which children perform simple tasks they are assigned. The manual includes a check list for each type of exceptionality, including giftedness (KKPLB, 1983). In 1981, the Ministry of Education announced its ambition to establish a network of assessment centers throughout the islands so that children suspected of suffering mental and physical handicaps might be properly identified. The centers would also be responsible for determining more accurately the incidence of handicaps in various parts of the nation (PPKSP, 1981, pp. 69–70). As a consequence, the procedures for diagnosing handicaps in Indonesia are more advanced than those used in China but less sophisticated and less complex than those routinely used in Britain. However, Indonesia appears less advanced than either Britain or China in efforts to identify giftedness.

Selecting the Cut-off Point

Determining a person's gender or religion or national origin involves deciding in which discrete category the individual belongs. But physical and mental abilities do not easily fit discrete categories. Instead, such abilities range along a scale. On a scale of eyesight there are gradual degrees between complete blindness and excellent visual acuity. The scale of hearing extends from complete deafness to highly sensitive auditory ability, and a scale of intelligence from extreme mental retardation to genius. So the task of determining who deserves the educational rights intended for the exceptional involves deciding where along the scale of ability to set the point that separates exceptional people from ordinary ones.

Not only do societies differ on where they set this cut-off point, but within a single society the cut-off point can change from time to time and from place to place (Tomlinson, 1982, p. 15). Our earlier example of changes in diagnostic categories over the past century in Great Britain illustrates this phenomenon. In Britain, as in other nations, the earliest categories of mental ability were ones that distinguished only the most severely disabled people (idiots and imbeciles) as deserving special attention. But by 1981 the cut-off point for special attention had moved much farther up the scale into the lower portions of the region that formerly had been considered "normal," so the exceptional now included children who experienced only mild learning difficulties. Likewise, people who were not entirely blind or deaf (the partially sighted and partially hearing) were, by the mid-1900s, identified as deserving special educational services.

The way this decision about the cut-off point influences who in the population is judged to deserve special education rights is illustrated in a comparison of Britain, China, and Indonesia. By the 1980s in Britain, the proportion of school-age children who could qualify for special attention because of mental disabilities—severe or mild, general or specific—might approximate 8 to 10 percent or more. In China in 1985, a random sample survey to identify mentally retarded or disabled learners placed the proportion of such children in the school-age population at one-third of one percent (Xu, 1985). As for Indonesia, we may recall that the 1980 census reported only 1.15 percent of school-age children as handicapped. Furthermore, only one-sixth of this number were reported as mentally retarded. Thus, on the basis of the census data, hardly two-tenths of one percent (40,000 children) of the nation's elementary-school-age population would be categorized as mentally retarded (DPD, 1981, pp. 9, 22).

One might assume that much, if not all, of the difference between the British, Chinese, and Indonesian percentages can be accounted for by differences in the way the three societies (1) define learning disabilities, (2) measure learning ability, and (3) set the cut-off point that separates the disabled from the normal. In other words, such a discrepancy in percentages would not likely result if all three societies used the same definitions, measuring techniques, and cut-off points.

What are Equal Educational Rights?

Even when people agree about which personal characteristics are exceptional and on how to measure them, they can still disagree about what is meant by *equal* educational rights. For some people, *equal* implies that everyone deserves a place in the regular educational system. This means that every child, of whatever ability, should have a chance to enter a typical classroom. Under such a philosophy, all learners are admitted to school and all are treated *equally*, meaning that everyone is treated the same. Those who fail to progress under regular instruction will usually drop out of school or be forced to repeat their present grade level.

But other educators have a different conception of *equal educational rights*. They subscribe to the motto: "Help each learner become all that he or she is capable of being." And because they recognize that all learners are not alike in personal characteristics, the education system must offer special provisions for the exceptional and not treat them all the same.

In the treatment of the handicapped, China has generally followed the first of these philosophies, whereas Britain has followed the second. Indonesia appears to be in transition from the first to the second viewpoints. As for the intellectually gifted, both China and Britain have provided them special learning opportunities, with Indonesia also intending to do likewise but at present still in the early stages of developing a systematic program to realize the intention (PPKSP, 1981, p. 10).

Levels of Commitment to Educational Rights

Proposition 2: Societies vary in their level of commitment to implementing a policy of educational rights for the exceptional.

In order to compare the commitment of different education systems to educational rights, we need indicators to use for judging a system's level of commitment. Below I propose two scales of indicators that are founded on the assumption that *equal educational rights* should not mean treating everyone alike. Instead, it should mean offering special provisions for the handicapped and gifted so they might make the most of their abilities. One scale focusses on stated policies and regulations, the other on implementation provisions. The reason for differentiating between policy and implementation is that there often is a discrepancy between educational regulations and actual practice. For example, virtually all modern-day governments have adopted a policy of providing compulsory, universal primary schooling. However, a large percentage of the world's primary-age children are still not in school. Policy statements can be viewed as the society's—or at least the government leaders'—stated intentions or ideals. Implementation provisions reflect the ability or willingness of the society to put policies into practice. I am suggesting that we are aided in understanding a society's philosophical and practical commitment to equal educational rights if we can locate where a particular education system belongs on the two scales. The steps on the policy-commitment scale range from the least serious commitment (Level 1) to the greatest (Level 4). Steps on the implementation-commitment scale also range from the least (Level 1) to the greatest (Level 5).

Levels of Policy Commitment

Policy statements or regulations can consist of:

Level 1. No mention of the exceptional.
Level 2. Concern for few varieties (4 or 5) of handicaps and/or giftedness.
Level 3. Concern for a moderate number (6 to 10) of handicaps and types of giftedness.
Level 4. Concern for a large number (more than 10) of handicaps and kinds of giftedness.

In our comparison of the three illustrative nations' policy commitments, it appears that Great Britain is on Level 4, Indonesia is on Level 2 and moving toward level 3, while China is between 1 and 2. These estimates are founded on the following considerations.

The British Case

Great Britain has a long history of legislation concerning the handicapped. The nature of typical policy provisions is illustrated by the following items excerpted from Tomlinson's (1982, pp. 32–35) lengthy recital of special education historical events in Britain. The 1899 Elementary Education Act urged, but did not require, local education authorities to provide special instruction for the handicapped. In the 1944 Education Act local authorities were obligated to ascertain children suffering from "a disability of body or mind" and to furnish proper education in special schools or elsewhere. The 1970 Education Act brought severely subnormal children into education. The 1981 Education Act specified that any child has special educational needs, or rights, if he has a learning difficulty which calls for special educational provision. In effect, over the years there has been a host of legislation focussing on the handicapped, with the proportion of the population encompassed by these provisions continually on the increase.

The Chinese Case

Until the mid-1980s, the basic education law in the People's Republic provided no special rights or facilities for the handicapped. However, according to Li (cited in Xu, 1985), authorities were considering adding special-education provisions in the revision of the national education law that was being contemplated in 1985.

The Indonesian Case

The original basic education law for Indonesia, formulated in 1950 and ratified in 1954, stated that:

> Special education is to be provided for those who need it. This means that individuals who suffer physical or psychological handicaps are to be educated in a manner that enables them to lead a decent life (PPKSP, 1981, pp. 5–6).

While this initial law thus established a general commitment to serving the handicapped, it has been only during the past decade that a serious emphasis on educating the handicapped has been reflected in legislation and policy statements. The commitment has been voiced mainly in relation to the government's attempts in the 1970s and 1980s to enroll all children, ages 7–12, in school (DPD, 1981, pp. 3–5). The typical official attitude toward the handicapped has also been reflected in political speeches, as in President Soeharto's remarks at the opening of a national center for special education in 1981:

The effort to educate handicapped children is not a task for only the government. It is the obligation of everyone, the government and all the citizens. Educating the handicapped is a humanitarian mission. Thus, I call upon everyone to help instruct our handicapped children so that in the future they can enjoy proper lives and not be dependent on others for their welfare (DPD, 1981, p. 21).

Not only has the government expressed serious concern for the educational rights of exceptional children, but a strong network of private organizations has evolved in support of such rights.

Levels of Implementation Commitment

Ways societies carry out special-education policies can include:

Level 1. No steps are specified for implementing policies, no special-education personnel are specified (nor are provisions made for training or acquiring personnel), and no funds are provided for programs.

Level 2. General aims and procedures for implementing policies are described, but no provision is made for preparing personnel, and no funds are provided for programs.

Level 3. Procedures for implementing policies are described, limited provisions for acquiring personnel are included, and a few funds are provided.

Level 4. Detailed procedures for implementing policies are furnished, standards to be met by personnel are specified, training and examination facilities for a moderate number of personnel are furnished, special facilities for educating the exceptional are established, research focussing on special-education issues is encouraged, and all of the foregoing activities are financed at a moderately strong level.

Level 5. The same as Level 4, except that there are more extensive provisions for facilities to èducate the exceptional, programs to train personnel, salaries for personnel, research activities, and funding special education.

In terms of implementation commitment, it appears that Great Britain is on Level 4, Indonesia is on Level 3 and aiming toward 4, while China is between 2 and 3.

The British Case

In 1983 Britain had over 145,000 physically and mentally handicapped students in special schools or special classrooms, (*Whitaker's almanack*, 1985, p. 1073). Thus, nearly 1.5 percent of the nation's 10 million primary- and secondary-school students were in special schools or classes, while a far larger number—perhaps as high as 4 to 7 percent—were provided some measure of special attention in regular classrooms. These services were available to both urban and rural residents.

The Chinese Case

In early 1985, Li (cited in Xu, 1985) reported that there were 319 schools for blind, deaf, and markedly mentally retarded children in China with a total enrollment of around 35,000, representing 7 percent of the estimated half-million blind, deaf, and mentally retarded children in the population. Xu also reported that there were fewer than 20 schools for children who were judged as suffering learning disabilities, but there were around 100 special classes attached to ordinary primary schools to serve these children. The number of learning-disabled pupils attending such schools and classes was between 2,000 and 3,000. In late 1985 the number of schools was reported to be 331 with an enrollment of 39,600 and approximately 10,000 faculty and staff members to the schools. Special classes for the mentally retarded in regular primary schools numbered 160 (Special education develops, 1985, p. 1). Therefore, less than 40,000 children and youths, out of a total school population of around 196 million, were in special schools or classes. This is two one-hundredths of a percent. Consequently, a pupil in Britain had a 70-times greater chance of being in a special school or class than did a pupil in China.

In the mid-1980s, most of China's special classes and schools were in large cities (Beijing, Shanghai, Tianjing). There were some facilities in coastal provinces (Shandong, Jiangsu), but Tibet had none, and Yunnan Province had only two schools for blind and deaf children.

The Indonesian Case

In 1952 there were ony four special schools for the handicapped in Indonesia. Since that time, however, the growth in facilities has been rapid. By 1981 there were 221 special schools and by 1985 around 300, with the increase due mainly to private organizations rather than the government. For example, official government attention to coordinating the nation's special-education efforts was not initiated until the mid-1970s, and by 1981 private groups were still operating 84 percent of the country's special-education schools (DNIKS, 1985, pp. 1–2). However, the government was providing additional teacher-education programs at advanced-secondary and university levels and was furnishing leadership in curriculum building.

By the mid-1980s, Indonesia had special schools for the mentally retarded, physically disabled, sight disordered, speech-and-hearing disordered, cerebral palsied, seriously maladjusted, and multipli-handicapped. Although plans were made to furnish special programs for the gifted and chronically ill, such programs were not yet in operation. The gifted continued to depend on their talent being recognized within the regular school program, with their superior academic performance and test scores providing them opportunities for advanced secondary and higher education.

In spite of such rapid recent growth in special education provisions, only a very small number of the nation's handicapped children were receiving special education in the 1980s. Even when the unrealistically low 1980 census estimate of the incidence of handicap among school-age children is used as a base, we find that only 3 percent of the handicapped (8,565 children) were in special education programs in 1981, and the percentage by 1985 could not have been much higher (DPD, 1981, p. 2). Hence, Indonesia still has a long way to go in fulfilling its policy commitment to educational rights for exceptional children.

The Majority Receive First Priority

Proposition 3: Societies give first attention to the educational needs of the more average majority and only later may attend to the needs of the exceptional minority.

For most areas of the world, the ambition of governments to furnish schooling for all their members has been a serious goal only since World War II. Prior to that time, extensive regions of Asia, Africa, and the Pacific Islands were under the colonial control of European powers, the United States, and Japan. And while the colonialists often said they favored widescale education for the native populations, in most instances this ostensible goal was not supported by actual provisions for schooling the masses. The bulk of Latin American nations, though politically independent of Spain and Portugal since the nineteenth century, continued to operate chiefly as feudal political-economic systems controlled by social elites that traced their ancestry to European origins. These feudal systems often provided no greater amount of schooling for the masses than had the colonial governments.

However, since World War II nearly all former colonies in Africa and Asia have gained political independence. In their new status, and stimulated by their membership in the United Nations, all have mounted socio-economic-development programs that include ambitious educational aims. Among the aims is that of furnishing universal compulsory schooling. Virtually all of them seek to provide at least 6 years of primary education, and a growing number are setting their goal even higher—to 8 or 10 years of education for everyone.

What bearing, then, does a society's progress toward universal schooling have on educational provisions for the handicapped? As Proposition 3 suggests, we can expect educational authorities to give first priority to furnishing education to the great mass of learners who have average or better ability. Only after facilities have been provided for the "average majority" (in whatever way a society defines such a term), will serious attention be given to special provisions for the handicapped and gifted. In societies which are still some distance from achieving universal schooling, "equal educational opportunity" typically means that everyone deserves the same chance to try the standard course of study offered in the schools.

There are several rather obvious reasons that special provisions for the exceptional are postponed until the nonexceptional have been served. First, the average majority of the population form a more powerful political body than do the exceptional. Not only are the nonexceptional far larger in number, but they have greater ability to voice their demands than do the mentally retarded, the blind, the deaf, and the lame. Therefore, the nonhandicapped majority can exert more effective political pressure to have its educational needs fulfilled than can the exceptional minority. Second, the nonhandicapped majority compose the labor force needed for the society's economic growth, so that an investment in educating the majority is expected to yield benefits in increased production and wiser consumption of goods throughout the society. The handicapped, in contrast, are seen as a financial liability and, from the viewpoint of economic development, less deserving of attention, so educational planners move more rapidly to train the productive majority than they do to aid the handicapped. Third, as a developing nation desperately tries to enroll all of its growing population of children in school, its educators are hardly able to train enough teachers and print enough textbooks to serve the average majority, much less to finance the more expensive services needed by the exceptional.

How, then, may these notions about the relationships between mass education and special education help explain provisions for exceptional people in our three exemplary societies?

The British Case

In Great Britain the movement towards mass education began in the nineteenth century, stimulated by the 1870 Education Act which established locally-elected school boards and authorized them to levy taxes to finance local schools. This act was followed in 1880 by the compulsory attendance law, with the result that soon the great majority of school-age children were enrolled in schools (Carrier in Barton and Tomlinson, 1984, p. 42). Consequently, Britain has a long history of universal basic schooling and thus would be expected to have begun giving serious attention to the needs of the handicapped a good many years ago. And, as noted above, that is actually what occurred.

The Chinese Case

Since at least the 1930s the Chinese Communist Party has been openly
dedicated to widespread schooling. But in the 1930s and early 1940s,
Japanese military forces occupied much of Eastern China, and at the same
time the Chinese Communists were in periodic conflict with the ruling
Nationalist Chinese Party (Kuomintang). As a result, the Communist Party
was not free to pursue its educational goals until it controlled the country's
mainland regions in 1949. However, the path toward universal schooling
would be a rocky one. The nation's large population, rapid population
growth, extensive land area (much of it mountainous), and the educational
setbacks occasioned by the disastrous Great Leap Forward (1958–1960) and
the Great Proletarian Cultural Revolution (1966–1976) combined to render
the pursuit of mass education most difficult. But a highly successful family-
planning program had, by 1982, reduced the nation's annual population
growth rate to 1.46 percent (Dong, 1985, p. 701), and the government
continued to invest large sums of money and great organizational effort in
schooling. As a consequence, major advances toward universal education
and universal literacy were recorded between 1949 and the mid-1980s.

It is difficult, if not impossible, to determine the true literacy and school-
attendance figures for the past three decades in China, because official
sources of statistics often vary dramatically. For example, one set of figures
places the proportion of school-age children (ages 7–11) enrolled in school at
49 percent in 1952, 85 percent in 1965, 93 percent in 1980, and 93.2 percent in
1982 (Dong, 1985, p. 702). However, another source states that the dropout
rate in 1980 was around 60 percent (Hawkins, 1983, p. 144). Under such
dropout conditions, the enrollment of school-age children in 1980 could not
have approached the 93 percent figure claimed in the first source. But
whatever the true figure may be, it is clear that while China was making
remarkable progress toward educating the masses, the nation had not yet
reached the goal of universal schooling by the mid-1980s. Furthermore, by
the 1980s there was still a great distance to go in achieving universal literacy.
Estimates of general literacy in the population placed the proportion of
people who could read and write at 35 percent in 1958, 50 percent in 1965,
and 65 percent in 1979 (Hawkins, 1983, p. 147).

In summary, then, by the mid-1980s, the People's Republic was still
endeavoring to make universal primary schooling and universal literacy a
reality. Therefore, we would expect—in keeping with Proposition 3—that in
the 1970s and 1980s serious attention to providing educational services for
the exceptional would still be at a relatively early stage of development. And
this is indeed the case, as can be illustrated with educational provisions for
the blind and deaf. Although the first education for deaf-mutes and the blind
dates back to the 1880s, by 1946 there were only 2,000 enrolled in the
nation's 40 existing schools. As further evidence that the need for special

education has not been viewed as critical, a delegation of American educators who visited China in 1977 discovered that the people they talked with felt that "mental retardation affects so few persons that it was not considered a problem in China." With 80 percent of the population in agricultural jobs, the major portion of Chinese society "makes limited demands for intellectual competence, and usually provides natural support within the family commune or the workers' residential district. . . . So long as Chinese society remains mostly rural and technologically unsophisticated, and so long as it remains committed to social cohesiveness and minimization of individual differences, mild mental retardation will surely continue to be of low priority" (Robinson, 1978 pp. 295–298).

Hence, while by 1985 more attention was being directed toward the schooling needs of exceptional children and youth, special education was still of little social import. As noted earlier, facilities for children judged to be mentally retarded or otherwise learning-disabled consisted of fewer than 20 special schools and around 100 special classes attached to ordinary primary schools, with the number of students enrolled in such programs estimated at between 2,000 and 3,000 (Xu, 1985).

The Indonesian Case

Indonesia's basic education law of 1950 committed the society to 6 years of compulsory, universal primary schooling for the entire populace. However, schools at that time were relatively few, the population was growing rapidly, and the economy was declining in strength. Consequently, efforts over the 1950s and 1960s to build more schools and to staff them with well-trained teachers always fell far behind the number needed. Then the early 1970s brought the nation a dramatic financial boost in the form of high prices for oil on the world market. A large portion of Indonesia's large oil profits was then invested in education, especially in the form of constructing more than 30,000 new primary schools over the 1974–1980 period (Postlethwaite and Thomas, 1980, p. 70). In 1973, an estimated 60 to 65 percent of children age 7–12 had attended primary school. By 1981 the government reported that close to 90 percent were enrolled in school, although a significant number of these still dropped out before completing the six-year program (DPD, 1981, p. 2). Such has been the progress in providing schools for the nonexceptional majority. But as noted earlier in this chapter, by 1981 only 3 percent (8,565 children) of the nation's estimated total of nearly 255,000 school-age handicapped were in special education programs. Hence, as in Britain and China, educational rights of the non-handicapped majority in Indonesia have been accorded serious attention before the needs of the exceptional minority are served.

Economic Influences on Educational Rights

Proposition 4: Provisions for educating the exceptional are influenced by the economic conditions of the society.

It may seem almost too obvious to mention that the more affluent a society, the more likely the society will furnish a greater array of special educational services for its exceptional members. And indeed, it is generally true that when funds to meet the demands of the average majority are more than sufficient, the handicapped and gifted can expect to receive greater attention, as illustrated in Indonesia when expanding oil revenues after 1973 stimulated the rapid increase of facilities for both normal and handicapped children. However, the relationship between a society's financial state and its provision of special services for the exceptional is not a simple one.

Consider, for example, financial conditions in China and in Great Britain in recent years. Over the first half of the twentieth century, much of the Chinese population lived near or below the poverty level, suffering from war, from such natural disasters as flood and drought, from an expanding population, from widespread illiteracy, and from low economic productivity. The great majority of the people have been peasants, engaged in low-technology agriculture while living in strongly supportive family clusters that protect and nourish their own members. In such societies, rarely is governmental recognition given to educational needs of the handicapped, nor is public money requested to meet such needs. Since there has been no historical tradition of public service to the handicapped in China, there is no serious outcry from the public when such services are not forthcoming.

In contrast, the British have lived in a heavily industrialized, increasingly urbanized society for nearly two centuries. During the nineteenth century, oppressive factory conditions affecting both child and adult laborers combined with the growing financial affluence of the British Empire to generate both a humanitarian spirit and funds to stimulate concern for the plight of the most severely handicapped. By the twentieth century these forces expanded the public's interest in the educational needs of a growing variety of people defined as exceptional. More and more special schools and classes were established throughout the twentieth century to furnish the educational services that the exceptional appeared to need. But in recent years, the British economy has fallen on hard times. Industrial production costs have risen, due both to labor strife and to the failure of the country's industries to keep up with the technological advances that have made other nations more effective competitors for industrial markets. In the 1970s and into the 1980s, both the government and private bodies have found it increasingly difficult to find the funds required for those special-education services to which the British have become accustomed. During this same period, the special-education practice known as integration or mainstreaming has become the vogue in Britain, in certain other European nations, and in the United States. The terms *integration* and *mainstreaming* refer to the policy of not segregating the handicapped or gifted into separate schools or into separate classes but, rather, placing them in regular classrooms with their non-exceptional agemates. It then becomes the task of the regular classroom teacher to provide whatever special aid such pupils require. Sometimes mainstreaming is complete. This means that the exceptional child is placed in the regular classroom full-time and is taught solely by the regular teacher. In other cases the mainstreaming is partial, with the handicapped child spending part of the day under the tutelage of the regular teacher, but receiving aid from a specialist the rest of the time, usually in a location outside of the regular classroom.

The strongest arguments adduced by advocates of mainstreaming are ones founded on a humanitarian rationale. The advocates' argument typically involves such convictions as:

(1) Handicapped pupils are usually different from their nonexceptional agemates in only one or two ways, so that in most other ways they are very similar to their agemates. Thus, the handicapped deserve to be in regular classrooms with their age peers so as to become accepted as "basically normal."

(2) In the broad society outside the school, the handicapped constantly interact with the non-handicapped so that it is desirable in the school setting for both the handicapped and their non-disabled agemates to practice living amicably and constructively together.

However, critical observers of the widespread popularity of mainstreaming in recent years have questioned the motives of at least some authorities who have enthusiastically endorsed integration as the major solution to the educational problems of the disabled. When mainstreaming becomes the principal mode of educating the handicapped, costly special schools and extra specialized personnel can be eliminated. In the case of Britain, Barton and Tomlinson (1984) observed that:

> There is certainly some indication . . . that some local authorities are interpreting the 1981 Education Act [which endorsed mainstreaming] as a license to close special schools and place children in normal schools without offering money or resources, an "integration on the cheap" feared by the teachers' unions. The whole mechanism for the assessment of children with special needs . . . invites a rhetoric that the "special needs" of large numbers of children are now being catered for in ordinary schools. The reality may be that no finance or resources are being offered to the schools either to "discover" or to cater for these needs (p. 71).

In summary, then, economic conditions within a society can affect the educational rights of the exceptional in ofttimes unobtrusive ways. Because

China lacks a history of liberal special education provisions, officials in China provoke essentially no public complaint if, for economic reasons, they fail to provide widespread special services. In contrast, Britain's history of ever-increasing special education provisions has built a public level of expectation that would prevent authorities from reducing such provisions for purely financial reasons. Thus, for officials who wish to save money during economically difficult times, the humanitarian argument for mainstreaming can serve as the publicly announced motive for eliminating expensive special schools and personnel.

In regard to societal expectations, Indonesian society would appear to fall somewhere between the Chinese and the British situations, yet somewhat closer to Chinese conditions. In Indonesia, as compared to China, there is greater official and public concern for educating the handicapped, but there has been no deepseated tradition of public responsibility for special-education services. The sense of social obligation is still developing. Indonesia's current experimentation with mainstreaming can be best interpreted against this background of a yet-evolving sense of public responsibility, which has been expressed chiefly in the provision of more special education schools and classrooms. So what is the principal motive behind the nation's mainstreaming sight-impaired children in small experimental programs since the late 1970s? Perhaps the move has been stimulated more by humanitarian, egalitarian motives than by financial considerations (Departemen Pendidikan dan Kebudayaan, 1983/84). In effect, I do not believe that, at least up to the present time, saving money has been the most prominent consideration in Indonesia's modest attempts at mainstreaming disadvantaged learners.

Conclusion

The dual aim of this chapter has been to offer four propositions that serve (1) to demonstrate several ways in which educational rights for exceptional people can differ from one society to another and (2) to suggest a number of causal factors that may help account for such differences. Implied in our comparison of Great Britain, China, and Indonesia is the conviction that the same propositions can profitably be employed for analyzing exceptional people's educational rights in other societies as well.

It should be apparent that the four propositions around which the chapter has been organized are not the only ones useful for this sort of analysis. Further propositions can be generated from such topics as (a) the influence of socioeconomic and ethnic status on who is furnished special education and (b) the effects of an egalitarian socio-political philosophy on educational rights for the exceptional.

As indicated early in the chapter, in all societies the educational rights of exceptional learners have received serious attention only after educational opportunities were already furnished to the more average majority of people. Yet, as the cases of Britain, China, and Indonesia have illustrated, the advances currently underway on behalf of the handicapped and gifted in these three representative nations bode well for the future. In the history of the world so far, the closing years of the twentieth century should be recognized as the period of the greatest understanding of, and greatest provision for, the educational needs of exceptional learners.

References

Barton, L. and Tomlinson, S. (Eds.) (1984) *Special education and social interests.* London: Croom Helm.

Britain 1985: An official handbook (1985) London: Her Majesty's Stationery Office.

Departemen Pendidikan dan Kebudayaan [Ministry of Education and Culture]. *Petunjuk teknis pendidikan terpadu di sekolah dasar* (Technical guide for mainstream education in primary schools) (1983/84) Jakarta: Author.

DNIKS (Dewan Nasional Indonesia untuk Kesejahteraan Sosial) [Indonesian National Council for Social Welfare] (1985) *Laporan perkembangan biro penyandan cacat DNIKS* [Report of the bureau for the care of the handicapped DNIKS]. Jakarta: Author.

Dong, C. (1985) China, People's Republic of: System of education. In. T. Husen and T. N. Postlethwaite (Eds.), *International encyclopedia of education, 2,* 701–705.

DPD (Direktorat Pendidikan Dasar) [Basic Education Directorate] (1981) *Pembangunan sekolah dasar INPRES untuk anak berkelainan usia 7–12 tahun dalam rangka persiapan pelaksanaan wajib belajar* [Developing the INPRES primary school for exceptional children, ages 7–12, within the preparation framework for implementing compulsory education]. Jakarta: Departemen Pendidikan dan Kebudayaan [Ministry of Education and Culture].

Europa yearbook (1985) London: Europa.

Final Report: South and Southeast Asian Regional Conference on Child Abuse and Neglect (1983) Jakarta: Ministry of Education and Culture.

Hawkins, J. N. (1983) The People's Republic of China (Mainland China). In R. M. Thomas and T. N. Postlethwaite (Eds.), *Schooling in East Asia,* (pp. 136–187). Oxford: Pergamon.

Human Rights: A compilation of international instruments (1983) New York: United Nations.

Kail, R. and Pellegrino, J. (1985) *Human intelligence: Perspectives and prospects.* New York: Freeman.

KKPLB (Kelompok Kerja Pendidikan Luar Biasa) [Special Education Work Group] (1983) *Alat identifikasi anak berkelainan* [Instrument for identifying the exceptional child]. Jakarta: Departemen Pendidikan dan Kebudayaan [Ministry of Education and Culture].

Postlethwaite, T. N. and Thomas, R. M. (1980) *Schooling in the ASEAN region.* Oxford: Pergamon.

PPKSP (Pusat Pengembangan Kurikulum dan Sarana Pendidikan) [Development Center for Curriculum and Educational Materials] (1981) *Pola dasar pengembangan pendidikan luar biasa* [Basic pattern for developing special education]. Jakarta: Departemen Pendidikan dan Kebudayaan [Ministry of Education and Culture].

Robinson, N. M. (1978) Mild mental retardation: Does it exist in the People's Republic of China? *Mental Retardation, 6,* August, 295–298.

Smerling, L. R. (1978–79) Admissions. *Chinese Education, 11* (4), 61–62.

Special education (1981–82) *Chinese Education, 14* (4), 49–52.

Special education develops rapidly in our country (1985) *People's Daily,* Oct. 4, p. 1.

Tomlinson, S. (1982) *A sociology of special education.* London: Routledge & Kegan Paul.

Whitaker's almanack (1985) London: Whitaker's Almanack.

Xu, J. L. (1985) Special education needs more attention. *Onlook Weekly,* March 11, p. 16.

A note of thanks is due Michael Gerber, Zhuang Jiaying, Titi Sayono, A. F. Tangyong, and Marsandi Wajawidodo for their aid in obtaining the sources of information upon which this chapter is based.

CHAPTER 5

The Right to Literacy[1]

Leslie J. Limage
UNESCO, Paris, France

This chapter examines and questions the complex contexts in which the right to literacy is evolving. The full implementation of this right has not been achieved in any nation. Hence, the first section reviews the international instruments concerning the right to literacy which are intended to inspire and influence decision-making in all nations. A second section of this chapter describes the extent and nature of illiteracy in the world. The chapter is devoted primarily, however, to the international debate concerning illiteracy.

This debate is presented in terms of three major approaches. The first approach is the pattern followed in most industrialized countries. A gradual growth of literacy over several centuries has been complemented by the introduction of compulsory primary schooling for all. This pattern will be illustrated by reference to the growth of literacy in England and Wales.

A second approach to implementing the right to literacy is the mass adult literacy and complementary education strategy which has been adopted by a number of socialist countries. The first such campaign undertaken on a national scale took place in the Soviet Union and it is the Soviet approach which has inspired many national liberation movements and socialist countries. This approach is illustrated with the experience of the Socialist Republic of Viet Nam.

The third major approach to literacy provision has been the policy of the majority of developing nations. Indeed, it may be argued that this third approach is something less than an overt strategy to provide access to literacy for all. Most developing nations have recognized their continued dependence on external economic and/or political constraints in an increasingly interdependent world. Frequently, national policy in these nations reflects externally imposed development models originating in international aid agencies' loan agreements or in other bilateral aid arrangements. In such contexts, developing nations, such as Brazil, have opted for limited target

[1] The views expressed in this paper are those of the author and in no way reflect those of the organization with which she is employed.

group efforts in adult literacy provision and have given priority to costly higher education.

The chapter concludes with a review of the prospects for universal literacy and common factors affecting all nations. All three groups of countries are confronted with a world recession. All nations are questioning the relevance and importance of the kinds of formal schooling and non-formal or lifelong learning provided to their citizens. The post-World War II emphasis on education to redress a whole range of social injustices and economic imbalances is being seriously questioned. Hence, the role of normative statements concerning the right to literacy and prospects for their implementation in the 1980s entails a new and realistic international commitment which, in many ways, remains to be identified.

The Right to Literacy: International Agreements and Programs[2]

The primary international instrument upon which all subsequent covenants, recommendations and declarations have been based is Article 26 of the *Universal Declaration of Human Rights*, adopted on December 10, 1948. The seriousness with which this Article was treated by the United Nations is further elaborated in the *International Covenant on Economic, Social and Cultural Rights*, Article 13, adopted on December 16, 1966. The Covenant received the requisite number of ratifications 10 years later. It thus entered into force on January 3, 1976. In terms of the country case studies in this chapter, The United Kingdom and Viet Nam have ratified the covenant, but Brazil has not yet done so.

A further series of standard-setting instruments has made reference to the importance of the eradication of illiteracy and the right to education without discrimination for all. The International Conference on Human Rights, meeting in Teheran on May 13, 1968, in its *Proclamation of Teheran* stated:

> The existence of over seven hundred million illiterates throughout the world is an enormous obstacle to all efforts at realizing the aims and purposes of the Charter of the United Nations and the provision of the Universal Declaration of Human Rights. International action aimed at eradicating illiteracy from the face of the earth and promoting education at all levels requires urgent attention (United Nations, 1981, p. 19).

Alongside the major UN human rights instruments emanating from the United Nations General Assemblies and Conferences, UNESCO has provided the forum in which the world community has met to set further educational and literacy goals and standards in a series of conferences and documents between 1960 and 1985. Although recommendations or declarations are not binding, each serves to prod and remind governments around the world of the goals for which they should be striving.

[2] See Appendices for summaries of relevant documents.

Illiteracy in the World

The significance of international instruments referring to the right to education or literacy only takes on meaning when the literacy situation in the world is examined. According to the most recent UNESCO study (UNESCO, Division of Statistics and Education, 1985) there are an estimated 889 million adult (15+ years) illiterates in the world in 1985 and 60 percent of them are women.[3]

This study corroborates the view that illiteracy is both a cause and a consequence of poverty and underdevelopment since 98 percent of the world's illiterates live in developing countries. Three-quarters of the total live in Asia, especially India and China. But the African continent has the highest rate of illiteracy, 54 percent or more. The illiteracy rate in Asia is 36.3 percent, and in Latin America and the Caribbean region, 17.3 percent. These percentages mask sub-regional differences and considerable disparities within nations. Table 5.1 indicates the extent of illiteracy by major region, and Table 5.2 gives some indication of sub-regional disparities by listing the countries with more than 10 million illiterates aged 15+ in 1985.

Alongside illiteracy figures and rates collected by UNESCO from official national sources, many industrialized nations are examining other indicators of illiteracy, such as school drop-out rates, numbers of young people leaving school without any certificate or diploma, military entrance examinations, census figures, and so forth. They are discovering a previously-hidden population of illiterates. Hunter and Harman (1979), and Kozol (1985) identify up to 60 million Americans lacking sufficient literacy and numeracy skills. At the beginning of the adult literacy awareness-raising campaign in

TABLE 5.1. *The Current Literacy Situation in the World and Major Regions*

Region	Population aged 15+, 1985 (millions)		
	Total	Literates	Illiterates
WORLD	3,203	2,314	889
Developed countries	931	911	20
Developing countries	2,272	1,403	869
Africa	300	138	162
Asia	1,833	1,168	666
Latin America and the Caribbean	253	209	44
LDCs	179	58	121

Source: Division of Statistics on Education, Office of Statistics. (1985). *The current literacy situation in the world*. Paris: UNESCO, p. 3. (All national statistics are provided by UNESCO Member States and are based on their own evaluation criteria. All figures are thus approximate.)

---

[3] Although UNESCO statistics are gathered regularly and officially, it is recognized that data gathering in many developing nations is frequently far from efficient and even literacy figures for industrialized nations are now being questioned.

TABLE 5.2. *Countries with more than 10 million illiterates aged +15 in 1985*

Country	Illiteracy rate (1985) (%)	Number of illiterates (millions)	Proportion of world total (%)	(cum. %)
India	56.5	264	29.7	29.7
China.	30.7	229	25.8	55.5
Pakistan	70.4	39	4.4	59.9
Bångladesh	66.9	37	4.2	64.1
Nigeria	57.6	27	3.0	67.1
Indonesia	25.9	26	2.9	70.0
Brazil	22.3	19	2.1	72.1
Egypt	55.5	16	1.8	73.9
Iran	49.2	12	1.3	75.2
Sub-Total (9 countries)		669	75.2	
Other countries		220	24.8	
World total		889	100.0	

Source: Division of Statistics on Education, Office of Statistics. (1985). *The current literacy situation in the world*. Paris: UNESCO, p. 8.

the United Kingdom in 1974–1975, the figure of two million adult illiterates was put forward as a realistic and cautious estimate of the extent of illiteracy in that country (Limage, 1975). Most recently, the French government has turned its attention to the potential existence of French nationals (not immigrants or immigrant workers) who may be illiterate and also estimates some two million adults in need (Espérandieu, Lion and Bénichou, 1984). Furthermore, some 100 thousand young people leave school in France each year without any school-leaving certificate and can be presumed to lack basic literacy skills. In a number of industrialized countries, including France and the Federal Republic of Germany, the extent of illiteracy among school leavers is being discovered as a direct result of youth unemployment schemes. As youth unemployment becomes increasingly grave throughout Western Europe and North America, government initiatives to provide initial employment or further training have frequently been reduced to basic education or pre-vocational programs.

The recognition that universal primary and secondary schooling are not guarantees of universal literacy is gaining credence. Hence, the international commitment to eradicate illiteracy in the world by the year 2000 involves concerted action in all nations of the world. The next sections look at the three major strategy approaches to achieve this goal.

Literacy in England and Wales

The Growth of Formal Schooling and the Spread of Literacy

Social historians and historians of education in several industrialized nations are increasingly dissociating the demand for literacy among working populations in the eighteenth and nineteenth centuries and the establishment of compulsory primary schooling. British historian of education, Brian Simon (1974), documents the context in which the working classes of nineteenth century England increasingly sought literacy skills in order to put forward their social and economic demands for better working and living conditions. Throughout the period, working people had set up their own reading circles and self-help groups. The working classes were highly mistrustful of any form of imposed instruction, assuming that it represented another type of social control. Indeed, the earliest charity schools and other educational initiatives intended for them forbade instruction in reading and writing. Rote memorization of biblical passages was considered an appropriate form of knowledge and would help the laboring poor to know their place in a certain social order.

This mistrust of instruction provided by authority has also been documented in France by Furet and Ozouf (1977), and in the United States by Bowles and Gintis (1976). On the other hand, these same historians describe the growth of formal schooling for many purposes other than literacy and numeracy transmission. French schools, for example, became the battleground between church and state and, in many ways, continue to convey such confrontation. In France, as in England and Wales or the United States, these historians have shown that the chronology and map of literacy is much less related to the establishment of a school system than to the history of social development. Thus the pattern for the growth of literacy in industrialized nations appears to be more or less similar (Limage, 1986). Hence, to portray the history of formal schooling as a continuum of progress from which schools in 1985 have somehow deviated prevents a serious analysis of just what schools have been called upon to transmit and, of course, obscures a study of the growth of demand for the right to literacy.

The 1944 Education Act and Secondary Education

The implementation of the right to literacy in England and Wales after World War II is closely related to the passage of the first major post-war educational legislation—the 1944 Education Act. Prior to World War II, in England and Wales as in many other industrialized nations, quality secondary education was accessible only to a few young people. The 1944 Education Act for England and Wales was the culmination of an ongoing debate concerning the amount and type of education which should be provided for all young people.

Prior to the War, secondary education for a very small percentage of young people was provided in private schools and in grant-aided "grammar schools" (Simon, 1974). The post-war compromise of the 1944 Education Act provided that local education authorities could set up several types of post-primary education: secondary modern, technical, comprehensive, grammar and private grant-aided schools. In fact, by 1961 more than 50 percent of secondary-age pupils were to be found in secondary modern schools. Educational reformers and Labour Party activists alike protested that the secondary modern school promoted the pre-war social selection. They argued that these schools were merely extended primary schools and their intakes were composed entirely of working class children. The elite continued to attend the grant-aided private and grammar schools, and the prestigious "public" schools. In the post-war period, many reformers inspired by equality of educational opportunity motives promoted the comprehensive school, a single secondary school for all.

Educational Reform: The Impact of School Organization and Finance on Achievement

As the finance and administration of education in the United Kingdom is the responsibility of local authorities, major national legislation and pressure for reform can only be applied indirectly. During the 1960s, a major movement against selection at age 11, prior to some form of secondary education and in favor of comprehensive schooling, gained momentum. In July, 1965, the Labour Government enacted "Circular 10/65," which invited local education authorities around the country to submit plans to reorganize their secondary schools along comprehensive lines. By 1970, approximately 29.2 percent of secondary age children were found in comprehensive secondary schools. Benn and Simon (1970) further document the democratization of education effort begun in the 1960s. For the most part, conservative local education authorities fought reorganization. Reluctantly, many authorities reorganized but continued to give preferential financial and staffing conditions to former prestigious secondary schools. And, of course, the conservative argument remained that quality would have to be sacrificed to quantity, that it was not and is not possible to cater to all children equally. Comprehensive schools were called upon to prove that they, too, could turn out as many young people as grammar and grant-aided schools able to pass "A" level and "O" level examinations. Given the examination orientation of secondary schooling, the equality of opportunity issue was slowly transformed into an effort to prepare an elite within comprehensive schools to pass these examinations allowing for university entrance. Thus, although these schools began with mixed-ability intakes, for the most part, by the third year of secondary schooling all the internal forms of selection (streaming, banding and so forth) well-known in American, French and German schools, were in place.

This internal selection and examination orientation also affects another important and much-debated factor in quality of educational provision: pupil/teacher ratio. As population growth declined across industrialized nations and economic constraint began to be felt in the 1970s, local education authorities were requested to reduce educational expenditure in England and Wales. Since the major educational expenditure is teachers' salaries, efforts were made beginning in 1974 to eliminate teaching posts, either by not filling vacancies as they arose or by making greater use of part-time and fixed-term teachers. Instead of taking advantage of decreasing pupil numbers to improve class sizes, the previous inequalities were accentuated. In primary schools, reception class size grew to 35 and higher in many cases as neighborhood schools were closed. At the secondary level, 11- and 12-year-olds were taught in classes of 30 or more while the very small number of young people staying on beyond the compulsory 16 years to prepare "A" and "O" level exams could very well be enjoying virtual tutorials of two to four students (Limage, 1975). By the return of the current Conservative Government, the comprehensive movement had been virtually halted and investment in education seriously curtailed.

The Adult Literacy Effort

Secondary educational reform in England still results in some 15,000 school-leavers each year who are virtually illiterate. In response to this situation, a movement to implement a national "Right to Read" campaign began in the early 1970s. In 1974, the British Association of Settlements, along with other voluntary bodies, set up a charter of demands—"A Right to Read! Action for a Literate Britain." They called for an all out national effort to eradicate illiteracy. At that time, it was estimated that approximately 5,000 adults were receiving literacy tuition and a figure of two million illiterate adults in need was advanced to draw attention to the size of the problem. In order to evaluate the success of the effort which was undertaken by the government in 1975, it is useful to review some of the charter's demands. First of all, the charter insisted that the government undertake a commitment to eradicate adult illiteracy by a reasonable date, 1985. Secondly, it was adamant that any serious attempt to deal with adult literacy should include an examination of what was going on in schools. In fact, the government had at its disposal the findings of the Bullock Committee and its report on reading, *A Language for Life* (Committee of Enquiry . . ., 1975). Then it was proposed that a special fund be created along with a national agency to assist local authorities and voluntary bodies in establishing literacy provision. An awareness-raising campaign should also be undertaken to enable both potential learners and the public at large to know that provision was available. All provision should be free of the usual budgetary conditions attached to adult education institutes. Tutors and organizers should be recruited, trained and paid according to the usual pay scale for teachers in public schools (the Burnham Scale) in order to insure quality and continuity of service. Although an important role was still to be played by voluntary bodies and volunteer tutors, there would no longer be excessive dependence on their services. Finally, a call went out to other sectors of public service and the media to assist in this effort.

The British Broadcasting Corporation responded immediately with a commitment to prepare a three-year series of programs and publications to be produced jointly with the British Assocation of Settlements and other bodies. The government met this commitment with a grant of one million pounds and the creation of an Adult Literacy Resource Agency to disburse these funds in a pump-priming initiative.

Campaign Results and Current Provision

As an awareness-raising effort, the adult literacy campaign was highly successful in terms of response from potential learners and voluntary tutors. Approximately 20,000 adults responded in the first phase of the campaign and, in the 10 years since that time, some 250,000 adults have received tuition either on a one-to-one basis or in small groups.

The accomplishments of this effort are better appreciated by a closer look at the context in which literacy tuition takes place. For the most part, local education authorities provide tuition within the framework of their adult education institutes. As in most other industrialized countries, adult education tends to provide leisure and non-vocational activities for an already affluent and educated public. Although local authorities have also tradition-ally provided some in-service training for tutors, they had no previous experience with training large numbers of volunteer literacy tutors who came forward as a result of the BBC programs and the publicity campaign.

In spite of the adverse economic climate, the Adult Literacy Resource Agency (ALRA) set about assisting in crash programs for the training of tutors, preparation of teaching material and advising on types and means for future provision. ALRA had its one-year mandate renewed for a two-year period (1976–1978) with quite different terms of reference. ALRA funding could not be used to pay teachers' salaries for local authorities, but it devised methods to employ some staff directly and assign them to local areas. By the end of its third year of operation, ALRA had helped to ensure that some provision was available in every local education authority. The central unit has had its mandate renewed and slightly altered on a virtually yearly basis since its initial creation. It has been constantly aware that the adults who come forward for tuition are those who are already highly motivated in their desire for a second chance at reading and writing skills. They have success-fully encouraged the adaptation of teaching practice to learner needs. In an attempt to reach the vast majority of adults who remain untouched by literacy provision, they have encouraged innovative approaches outside the adult education institute framework. They have provided funding for a number of special projects using shop fronts, buses, youth centers and so forth. Gradually they have taken on a responsibility to assist in literacy work for learners of English as a second language and basic education and numeracy.

The achievements of what is now known as the Adult Literacy and Basic Skills Unit (ALBSU) and the local education authorities and voluntary bodies in the implementation of the right to literacy are summed-up most effectively in an ALBSU publication:

> That a *framework of provision* has been created in each LEA area and maintained despite a difficult economic climate is a measure of the commitment of LEAs to this area of work. . . . ALBSU has long recognised the disparity of provision from area to area and the paucity of resources available but in an area of educational provision without clear legislative support it is reassuring to note that a framework continues to exist almost a decade after it first began to be established (ALBSU, 1983, p. 9).

Ideally, the Unit recognizes that its work should be included in an amendment of the 1944 Education Act "so that provision for adult and further education, including basic skills, is made an unequivocal duty of each local education authority in England and Wales" (ALBSU, 1983, p. 13). Nonetheless, the British literacy experience has provided a wealth of knowledge upon which many other industrialized nations are drawing. It has shown the commitment of organizers and tutors in a highly unfavorable economic climate. It is also continuing its action in a more general debate concerning the role and relevance of the entire examination system in British education. It may well be that the piecemeal reform which has characterized industrialized nations' response to increased demand for literacy as a basic human right is making some progress in the right direction. Although it would be unrealistic to affirm that universal literacy is presently achieved in any industrialized nation, the British experience illustrates progress made and problems to be solved.

Literacy in the Socialist Republic of Viet Nam

Literacy in the Revolutionary Context

A study of the literacy efforts undertaken in the Socialist Republic of Viet Nam provides an illustration of the second major approach to the implementation of this human right. Adult literacy campaigns and efforts towards universal primary education have been an integral part of Viet Nam's combat for national liberation and socialist construction since its declaration of independence from France on September 2, 1945. The complex context in which these efforts have been undertaken recall the Soviet and Chinese experiences. But the Vietnamese have also developed a highly national approach to eradicating illiteracy consistent with their own cultural traditions and national development goals.

Prior to 1945, militants seeking to mobilize their compatriots to overthrow French colonial rule, created the Association for the Propagation of Quoc Ngu (a Latinized alphabet much easier to learn than the traditional script). This Association began its literacy work in the North in 1938, in the center of the country in 1939, and in the south in 1943. At that time, as a result of underdevelopment and colonial rule, the illiteracy rate throughout Viet Nam was estimated to be 95 percent. Between 1938 and 1945, some 70,000 adults were taught reading and writing in semi-clandestine fashion.

The Declaration of Independence itself showed the importance attached to universal literacy:

> This new education is now in its organizational stage. It is certain that primary education should be compulsory. In the very near future, an order would be promulgated on the compulsion of the learning of the national script aimed at total literacy. To fulfill this extremely important task, we should not wait until things become normal, but, right in this difficult circumstance, we are resolved to carry it out (UNESCO, Regional Office for Education in Asia and the Pacific, 1984, p. 2).

This affirmation was quickly followed by a demand for commitment at the highest level. President Ho Chi Minh appealed in October, 1945, for a vast literacy campaign:

> In order to preserve national independence, in order to achieve national prosperity and power, all the Vietnamese people should be well conscious of their rights and obligations . . .; and first of all, they should know how to read and write the national script. . . . The illiterates should make every effort to learn. The literate husbands should teach their illiterate wives, the literate brothers should teach their illiterate sisters, the literate children should teach their illiterate parents, the literate masters should teach their illiterate servants, the rich should form classes at their private homes to teach the illiterates (UNESCO, Regional Office for Education in Asia and the Pacific, 1984, p. 3).

To understand the special role of literacy as a human right in the Vietnamese context, it is worth reexamining President Ho Chi Minh's exhortation. An abundant literature exists to explain and analyze the role of the individual in traditional Confucian society (Limage, 1975; Lê Thành Khôi, 1978). Briefly, the individual in the harmonious Confucianist tradition situates herself or himself in a complex network of social relations. Indeed, one's very identity is derived from one's place within society (Phan Thi Bac,

1966). So, when Vietnamese intellectuals returned from study in France with a knowledge of socialism, it was a reasonable step to envisage social change and national liberation in terms of reciprocal commitments such as those formulated for literacy mentioned above. Literacy acquisition was thus presented both as a human right for individual emancipation and as a social obligation to help in the effort to liberate the nation and build an independent society. It is this dual role ascribed to literacy acquisition which distinguishes the Vietnamese experience from the literacy efforts of industrialized or developing countries discussed earlier.

The Literacy Campaigns

In fact, several literacy campaigns were carried out as Viet Nam was progressively liberated. Also, alongside these campaigns, a complex system of complementary education for newly-literate adults engaged in combat and/or production was progressively established in spite of the war against the French and, later, American occupation. At the same time, a general education reform was implemented to provide universal primary schooling along the basic principles of national construction: "national, scientific and popular." These principles were applied to all aspects of education: adult literacy, complementary education, primary, secondary and university instruction. The reform involved the introduction of instruction in Vietnamese, rather than French, at all levels. It included retraining of teaching personnel and constant revision of the curricula and textbooks according to the changing needs of the war of liberation and national construction (Belloncle, 1984).

The key elements in each of the early campaigns in the North (1956–1958), and later in the South (1976–1977), were flexibility and adaptability to changing conditions. The pragmatism necessary to undertake literacy provision during wartime has also been coupled with a certain realism concerning limitations and difficulties.

The initial campaign was undertaken after the victory over the French at Dien Bien Phu in July, 1954, with make shift means. According to official estimates, some 1,929,642 Vietnamese between the ages of 12 and 50 learned basic literacy skills. The skills acquired were admittedly insufficient for active participation as militants or cadre in the liberation effort or in national construction. Hence, a system of complementary education was rapidly set up with a program and reading material constantly redefined or modified in the light of social, economic or political conditions. A survey of the earliest post-literacy reading material provided for the neo-literate shows the thoroughly social orientation of the effort. The Vietnamese sought inspiration in their own cultural traditions and rich oral heritage to inspire the population to greater effort.

Currently, a major effort continues to seek innovative ways to extend adult literacy and to provide universal primary schooling. The authorities are fully aware of the potential for relapse into illiteracy in areas in which the literacy campaigns were not followed by participation in complementary education or what is more generally called post-literacy provision.

Universalization of Primary Education

The effort to extend primary schooling along national, popular and scientific lines began with the first reform of education in 1950–1951. It was intended to prepare "good citizens, good cadres, and good workers." As in other socialist nations, emphasis was placed on study combined with productive work. The former French structure of a six-year primary and seven-year secondary system of schooling was changed into a unified system of 9 years of general education (4 + 3 + 2).

The second phase of educational reform corresponded to the restoration of peace and partition of the nation in 1954. The then Democratic Republic of Viet Nam (the North) undertook greater efforts to work towards socialist construction. The corresponding reform of education which took place in 1956 changed the structure of general education by adding one year at the third level (4 + 3 + 3). It also entailed revision of textbooks and curricula and began preschool provision.

After reunification of the country in 1975, national authorities were able to extend reforms to the South. In the former Republic of Viet Nam (the South), the heavily French-influenced educational system had shown some growth between 1954 and 1975, but wastage was extremely high. According to official statistics, out of 1,000 children entering school, only 407 would reach the fifth year. And of that number, some 223 would go on to secondary schooling. Only 54 would complete that level of schooling.

Thus, national authorities of the reunified Socialist Republic of Viet Nam began a reeducation effort in the southern regions in 1975 to pave the way for the socialist values already being taught in the North. The literacy campaign which was undertaken immediately after reunification was said to have reached its goal in 1978.

The next educational reform sought to provide a single school system for the entire nation. This reform's stated goals are (a) to educate the young from infancy to adolescence; (b) to extend education to the entire population including the ethnic minorities; and (c) to train and improve skills of all working people and to instill them with a higher level of political consciousness (Lê Thành Khôi, 1985). This reform continues to link education to productive work encouraging adaptation to local conditions.

Vietnamese authorities recognize, however, the unevenness with which universal primary education has progressed throughout the country. At present, provision is most extensive in the large cities and in the northern delta. Other regions have only limited provision, especially in the Mekong

Delta, the central coastal provinces and the northern midlands. The mountainous regions with their ethnic minorities remain the most disadvantaged in terms of educational provision. Authorities are also quite ready to revise aspects of the educational reform which are not adapted to local needs. A recent example of this flexibility is the change from a single school calendar suited to conditions in the North to several calendars corresponding to the agricultural seasons and the necessary upkeep of dikes for flood control in other areas.

Viet Nam faces another difficulty which it shares with other developing nations. Although the literacy rates improve, the absolute number of illiterates is steadily increasing. Hence, while government policy aims to reduce illiteracy to 7.3 percent for the age group 15–50 in the late 1980s, the absolute figure for illiteracy is projected to grow from 1,850 million in 1980 to some 2,181 million at the end of the decade. They further estimate that 90 percent of the illiterates at the end of this period will be children who have not attended school or drop-outs; and 50 percent will be from ethnic minorities.

This concern for providing universal primary schooling and literacy as overt policy goals also distinguishes Viet Nam's socialist construction effort from that of most developing and industrialized nations. The realism with which progress is evaluated indicates an unprecedented level of commitment. It is in terms of this measure of commitment, and not only in relative success, that implementation of the right to literacy is most fully understood.

Literacy in Brazil

Pre-1964 Reform, Cultural Diversity, and Economic Disparity

Brazil ranks among the nine nations with more than 10 million illiterates in their population. It is also the largest and most culturally and economically diverse nation in Latin America. Cultural diversity in the various regions of this country interacting with severe poverty and malnutrition has produced a wealth of traditional responses to need for social change.

In fact, just prior to the 1964 military takeover of Brazil, the country was in a state of social ferment due to the election of a populist president and major social and economic reform. The atmosphere of the period was summed up by a Brazilian writer and journalist:

> At this moment Pernambuco is the greatest laboratory of social experiment and the greatest idea factory in Brazil. . . . Two main factors have combined to favor the appearance of this Pernambucan climate of freedom: a movement of mass agitation which in a few years has provided the masses involved with an education they never had before, and the election, as governor of the state of a man of the people. . . .

Everything is new and everything is empirical. . . . Its poverty continues to be enormous, but its revolutionary activity, a search for solutions in all fields, gives it a vitality greater than any other state's (Callado, 1963).

At the same time, in the area of educational reform, Paulo Freire was working to extend his literacy for "conscientization" method whereby adults gained initial literacy skills in a period of 45 days. Between June, 1963, and March, 1964, all the capitals of the various states initiated training programs for monitors. The 1964 National Plan proposed the creation of 20,000 "culture circles," as the unit for literacy action was called. On April 1, 1964, a military takeover of the government of Brazil put an end to this literacy effort as well as to all other social reform. In exile, Paulo Freire has become known worldwide for his thought and action in the field of adult literacy in a context of mobilization for major social change.

Education and Development Since 1964

From 1964 onwards, investment in education took a quite different pattern. The "Brazilian Miracle," Brazil's development model followed since the mid-sixties has been characterized by a former president of the adult literacy effort, MOBRAL:

> . . . this model is founded on the orthodox view that all development processes must be supported by three pillars: economy, confidence, trade. The first requirement for rapid and sustained growth is the maintenance of a high rate of savings, making it possible to finance the investments needed to secure such growth. The second is the maintenance of a climate of rational thrift, stimulating confidence among producers and investors. The third is the existence of an expanding trade, capable of continuing to attract new investments and to increase output (Simonsen, as quoted in UNESCO, Regional Office for Education in Latin America and the Caribbean, 1975, p. 7).

In other words, Brazilian authorities opted quite openly for an economic policy in which priority is given to increasing the real national product rather than to improving the distribution of national income. The concentration of national income in certain sectors became increasingly accentuated between 1960 and 1970. UNESCO's 1975 study draws a definite linkage between economic policy and the nature and quality of educational expansion which should accompany it (UNESCO, Regional Office for Education in Latin America, 1975).

Despite Brazil's vast numbers of illiterates, investment in education and increase in enrollment levels has followed the pattern most prevalent among

developing nations, the government showing most concern with the higher
levels of education.

This policy choice to invest most heavily in higher education as opposed to
extending and improving retention in primary schooling has gone unchal-
lenged as the Brazilian economy has moved from the boom years of the late
sixties and early seventies to a severe recession which began in 1981. In
analyzing the impact of the recession on Brazilian children, Roberto
Macedo notes that for the entire period, 1960–1980:

> . . . growth rates of school enrollment in primary education lagged
> behind those of higher grades and that expansion was concentrated in
> college education. It is well known in Brazil that most of this expansion
> occurred in private colleges where to a larger extent education is
> considered a profitmaking activity like any other business (Macedo,
> 1984, p. 35).

It would appear that all educational reform which has been taking place
since the late 1960s is clearly linked to the government's willingness to adopt
development policies in line with standards set by the country's creditors.

The involvement of international aid agencies in defining national educational policy is also illustrated by World Bank support for the educational
reform of 1971 and the revision of that reform in 1982. Briefly, the World
Bank supported a project to encourage the reform of secondary education to
provide a larger place in the curriculum for vocational and technical
education. Previously, technical education as such was offered in special
technical secondary schools while general secondary schools prepared for
university entrance. Although this reform was considered necessary in the
light of economic policy and forecasts for manpower requirements, it
neglected a whole host of practical problems of implementation. An
evaluation by an expert from UNESCO on behalf of the World Bank
concluded that opposition to the reform was such that the quality of existing
provision was threatened and that "the school system cannot adapt its staff
and resources as quickly and radically as required by the changes taking
place in the production process" (UNESCO, Educational Financing
division, 1983, p. 13). Clearly the lesson to be learned is that educational
systems in both developing and industrialized countries cannot be directly
harnessed to manpower needs in a market economy.

Another factor affecting Brazil's efforts to expand educational opportunity goes beyond the impact of external agencies and creditors. In terms of
sheer numbers of children enrolled in schools, the task is enormous.
Retention rates are, however, of even greater concern. Philip Coombs
(1985) analyzes the quantitative growth of schooling in developing countries
and notes many cases of educational expansion similar to that of the
Brazilian pattern, i.e., a topdown expansion of higher education to the

neglect of quality and quantity in primary schooling. According to his examination of UNESCO statistics, Brazil reported a total enrollment, in 1975, of nearly 20 million pupils out of a total estimated population for the age group of 22 million. That figure represents a gross enrollment ratio of 89 percent. But Coombs' analysis concludes that only one out of four Brazilian children of age seven is likely to complete primary education. Thus wastage, drop-out and repetition within the educational system produces further illiterates to join the ranks of the adult illiterate population.

Adult Literacy in Brazil

The linkage between formal educational provision and a particular economic development policy also holds true for adult literacy efforts. This discussion began with reference to the state of social ferment in the country prior to 1964. The adult literacy campaigns which were springing up in several states lost their momentum and, in many cases, were forced to discontinue their efforts. In 1967, the government of Brazil, inspired by the UNESCO-sponsored functional literacy approach, undertook its own efforts to combat illiteracy. With the establishment of MOBRAL in December 1967, the government entered into a long term commitment to address the problem of adult illiteracy. In order to give the effort sufficient flexibility, MOBRAL was set up as an independent foundation, financed primarily through receipts from the Federal Sports Lottery. A 1969 decree stipulated that 30 percent of income from this lottery be used to finance literacy programs. A 1970 law allows voluntary tax contributions to be made to MOBRAL.

By 1970, MOBRAL was reaching 500,000 adult illiterates. In subsequent years, numbers have increased. It set targets for 1980 in which the adult illiteracy rate would be reduced to under 10 percent. Within target areas (urban centers to the exclusion of rural areas) and a target age group (adults between 15 and 35). The "functionality" of instructional content might also be defined in terms of goals to be achieved: a learner is considered literate who can "read and write his own name and address and those of his entire family; write short notes, send telegrams; solve simple minor problems concerning day-to-day occurrences; . . . and read and carry out written instructions" (UNESCO, Regional Office for Latin America and the Caribbean, 1975, p. 40).

In practice, MOBRAL has proven even more flexible than its originators had intended. In particularly poor regions of the country, such as the Northeast, MOBRAL accepts pupils under 14 years of age as primary schooling is either lacking or the children are already in the labor force.

MOBRAL is particularly well known in international discussion of finance for adult literacy schemes. The use of receipts from the national lottery means, in effect, that adult learners are actually financing their own instruction. As this amount is far from sufficient to increase and improve provision, local municipalities are encouraged to allocate additional funds for literacy work from their own budgets.

By and large, MOBRAL ranks among literacy efforts in developing countries charged with undertaking tasks far beyond the possibilities of their finance or actual mandate. It would be unrealistic in the face of such extensive illiteracy among all age groups to expect that field workers exclude young people of school age when they are located in areas where no schools exist. Nor is it realistic in terms of the close linkage between overall economic development policy of the country and external dependency to expect that the government finance the basic education of non-priority sector workers or, increasingly, the underemployed and unemployed. It is possible that, as a result of the recent political changes and elections, Brazil will be engaged in a transition to more democratic participation in decision making, which in turn will create, once again, greater possibilities for demanding the respect of basic human rights, in general, and the right to literacy in particular.

Literacy as a Human Right: Policy Choices and Future Prospects

The preceding discussion has looked successively at the major international standard-setting instruments and early programs extending the right to education in general and the right to literacy in particular. It then examined three major strategies adopted by industrialized, developing and socialist nations to respond to goals established by international agreements that have virtually no coercive power. Regional recommendations and declarations, international organization surveys and studies, and proclamations in scholarly and professional meetings of educators can only suggest and measure progress. In a period of economic austerity around the world, many countries are falling far behind the standards they have set for themselves in these international instruments. As the case studies have shown, however, no group of nations can be said to be most successful in providing the right to universal literacy. Each of the countries discussed has followed a different development model and the role ascribed to literacy is closely linked to that choice.

In conclusion, it would be useful to review some of the factors which appear to affect the implementation of the right to literacy in all three developmental models:

1. The scale and effect of any literacy effort depends on the level of political commitment at the national level.
2. The most disadvantaged populations, ethnic minorities and rural dwellers, are the most difficult to reach in both literacy campaigns and provision of formal schooling.

3. Mobilization of human and material resources for a long term effort are the only guarantees of progress in the implementation of the right to literacy.

4. Basic literacy skills are only retained when post-literacy reading materials and opportunities to apply these skills are available.

5. The participation of learners in formulating literacy goals and applications ensures motivation to continue classes and improves retention.

6. Wastage, drop-out and repetition in schools contributes to adult illiteracy and remedial learning should be available throughout formal schooling.

7. Within schools, class size, pupil/teacher ratio, teacher qualifications and availability of in-service training affect a child's opportunity to learn to read and write.

8. Malnutrition and poverty are consistently associated with adult illiteracy and impede children's capacity to learn.

Finally, across countries, commitment to eradicating illiteracy can be measured in terms of a periodic response to a certain number of questions: For whom is literacy provided and why? What language is selected for instruction? What level of provision is considered basic? What are the most effective ways in each context to motivate people to acquire literacy and to ensure that their children receive an even higher level of instruction than they have received? What are the consequences of leaving large numbers of people illiterate and what price will a nation pay in the future for such neglect?

A periodic response to such questions can provide an indicator of the level of commitment to the right to universal literacy.

References

Adult Literacy and Basic Skills Unit (1983) *Adult literacy and basic skills: A continuing partnership*. London: Author.

Belloncle, G. (1984) *Alphabétisation et éducation des adultes en République Socialiste du Vietnam* [Literacy and adult education in the Socialist Republic of Vietnam]. Paris: Agence de Coopération Culturelle et Technique.

Benn, C. and Simon, B. (1970) *Half way there: Report on the British comprehensive-school reform*. New York: McGraw Hill.

Bowles, S. and Gintis, H. (1976) *Schooling in capitalist America*. London: Routledge and Kegan Paul.

Callado, A. (1963) *Jornal do Brazil*, December.

Committee of Inquiry into Reading and the Use of English under the Chairmanship of Sir Alan Bullock, F.B.A., Department of Education and Science (1975) *A language for life* [Bullock Report]. London: Her Majesty's Stationery Office.

Coombs, P. H. (1985) *The world crisis in education: The view from the eighties*. New York: Oxford University Press.

Espérandieu, V., Lion, A. and Bénichou, J. P. (1984) *Des illettrés en France: Rapport au Premier ministre* [Illiterates in France: Report to the prime minister]. Paris: La Documentation Française.

Furet, F. and Ozouf, J. (1977) *Lire et ecrire* [Reading and writing]. Paris: Editions de Minuit.

Hunter, C. and Harman, D. (1979) *Adult illiteracy in the United States.* New York: McGraw-Hill.

Kozol, J. (1985) *Illiterate America.* Garden City, NY: Anchor Press/Doubleday.

Lê Thánh Khôi (1978) *Socialisme et développement au Viêt Nam.* Paris: Presses Universitaries de France.

Lê Thánh Khôi (1985) Vietnam: System of education. *International encyclopedia of education,* **9,** 5549–5551.

Limage, L. (1975) *Alphabétisation et culture: Étude comparative. Cas d'études: L'Angleterre, le Brésil, la France, la République Démocratique du Viet Nam.* [Literacy and culture: A comparative study. Case studies: England, Brazil, France, the Democratic Republic of Viet Nam]. Unpublished doctoral dissertation, University of Paris V.

Limage, L. (1986) Adult literacy policy in industrialized countries. *Comparative Education Review,* **30**(1), 50–72.

Macedo, R. (1984) Brazilian children and the economic crisis: Evidence from the state of São Paulo. In R. Jolly and G. A. Cornia (Eds.), *The impact of world recession on children* (pp. 33–51). Oxford: Pergamon Press.

Phan Thi Bac (1966) *Situation de la personne au Viet-Nam* [Situation of the individual in Viet-Nam]. Paris: Editions du Centre National de la Recherche Scientifique.

Simon, B. (1974) *The two nations and the educational structure, 1780–1870; Education and the labour movement, 1870–1920; The politics of educational reform, 1920–1940.* London: Lawrence and Wishart.

UNESCO. Regional Office for Education in Latin America and the Caribbean (1975). *MOBRAL: The Brazilian adult literacy experiment* (Educational Studies and Documents No. 15). Paris: Author.

UNESCO. Educational Financing Division (1983) *Brazil: Education and work, a decade of educational reform* (1971–1982). Paris: Author.

UNESCO. Regional Office for Education in Asia and the Pacific (1984) *Literacy situation in Asia and the Pacific*—Country studies: Socialist Republic of Viet Nam. Bangkok: Author.

UNESCO. Division of Statistics and Education. Office of Statistics (1985) *The current literacy situation in the world.* Paris: Author. (Available from Division of Statistics on Education, UNESCO, 7, Place de Fontenoy, 75700, Paris, France).

CHAPTER 6

The Right to Education for Multicultural Development: Canada and Israel

Vandra L. Masemann
Masemann & Mock Consultants, Toronto, Canada
Yaacov Iram
Bar Ilan University, Israel

Introduction

The right to multicultural development is one that is accepted to a greater or lesser extent in many countries.[1] The history of worldwide migration in the last several millennia, and more notably in the last two centuries, has resulted in a mix of peoples of various cultural, linguistic, and religious backgrounds within the boundaries of many modern nation states. It is now impossible to define nation states exclusively in ways that presuppose cultural, linguistic, or religious homogeneity within a general population (see Mitter and Swift, 1985).

The oppression of minority populations within nation states has run the gamut in the modern era from the outright slaughter and persecution of large numbers in situations of declared or undeclared war, to the systematic denial of the rights of full citizenship to transient workers, to the more subtle forms of linguistic or religious discrimination experienced by children in classrooms. All of these forms of persecution are a denial of basic human rights, by the state or by various parts of the population.

The right to multicultural development can be distinguished from the right to freedom from discrimination in that it focusses on cultural and linguistic retention and development in a pluralistic framework rather than on some of the more negative consequences of interaction between cultural groups. Multicultural education as it exists today in many parts of the world also has a secondary focus on the elimination of prejudice and discrimination (Kirp, 1979; Bullivant, 1981; Samuda *et al.*, 1984). It is basically an attempt to influence public opinion by promoting awareness and acceptance of diversity.

[1] The research on which the Canadian section of this chapter is based was funded by the Multiculturalism Sector, Department of the Secretary of State, Ottawa. The report on the Canadian research was published in 1985 (see References). Vandra Masemann acknowledges with thanks their support, and accepts full responsibility for the material used in this chapter.

This chapter presents case studies of two countries, Canada and Israel, in which multicultural development has taken place. Canada and Israel are chosen for a comparison of their approaches to multicultural education since they have both received a large number of immigrants in the last 40 years and have developed approaches in their educational systems to accommodate both the cultural and linguistic diversity of their populations. It presents the legal context within which multicultural policy has developed, a brief summary of the ethnic and linguistic diversity within each country, an overview of the state of teaching of the official languages and minority languages, and an analysis of ways in which multicultural education is dealt with in each country in relation to language, culture, and inter-group relations. Finally, a discussion of achievements and future goals is presented.

International Agreements Supporting Multicultural Development

The right to multicultural development encompasses a variety of aspects which must be clearly distinguished at this point. The wording of various international and national documents also enables these distinctions to be clearly understood.

The right to multicultural development is fundamentally the right for members of any cultural group to live in accordance with the precepts of their culture within the limits of constitutional or statutory law, and not to be persecuted on the basis of their ethnocultural affiliation. However, the philosophy of multicultural development has grown to mean, in addition, a more positive promotion of the benefits of the multicultural way of life, with its tenets of sharing, intercultural understanding, and equal access to the opportunity structure of the society.

In an examination of the documents which support this right, one can see the various shades of meaning that it encompasses.[2] Articles 2 and 6 of the *Universal Declaration of Human Rights* (1948) express an ideal for the protection of cultural rights of migrants everywhere, whether recent or long-settled.

The Universal Declaration clearly proposes education that is multicultural, recognizing that parents have the right to choose their children's education. In Article 13.3 of the *International Covenant on Economic, Social and Cultural Rights*, parents have the right to choose for their children "schools other than those established by the public authorities . . . to ensure the religious and moral education of their children in conformity with their own convictions."

Another aspect of multicultural development is the right to the enjoyment

---

[2] See Appendices for summary of relevant documents.

of cultural rights, which are spelled out as the right to an equal education, the right to participate in the cultural life of the society, and the right of minorities to enjoy their own culture, to profess and practice their own religion, or to use their own language" (*International Covenant on Civil and Political Rights*, 1966, Art. 27).

The *Declaration on the Elimination of All Forms of Racial Discrimination* (1963) states that "Discrimination between human beings on ground of race, colour, or ethnic origin is an offense to human dignity" and that "particular efforts shall be made to prevent discrimination . . . especially in the fields of civil rights, access to citizenship, education, religion, employ- ment, occupation, or housing." Racial equality is a concept that has not always been linked with multicultural development; but historically, racist regimes have certainly suppressed cultural development. Thus, racial equality is conceptually not possible as a feature of unicultural philosophies.

One document that addresses culture specifically is the UNESCO *Declaration of the Principles of International Cultural Co-operation* (November 1966). Article 1 states that each culture has a dignity and value, and every people has a right to develop its culture. This document also proposes cultural cooperation in its various aspects, but its provisions can be interpreted as applying to minority cultures as well as to the dominant culture in any society.

Thus, in the provisions of the various documents, the right to multi- cultural development encompasses basic individual rights of equality without distinction, equality before the law, educational rights, cultural rights, group rights of cultural and language maintenance, and freedom from persecution. The extent to which all of these rights can be reconciled in any political arena is played out in the history of any society. We now turn our attention to the specific legal provisions in Canada and Israel for the right to multicultural development.

Policies of Multiculturalism

The major problems concerning multicultural education in Canada and Israel are both similar and different. Canada has a population of indigenous peoples, descendants of early settlers, and recent immigrants from all over the world who live in a pluralistic society with two official languages, two major Christian religious denominations, and a multitude of other cultural attributes. The major problem is language and equality: ensuring that all children, regardless of linguistic and cultural affiliation gain access to the opportunities that are offered in the wider Canadian (and in many cases, North American) society.

Similarly, Israel has received immigrants from all parts of the world, and has an educational system which must accommodate to the cultural and linguistic needs of its students within the context of wider Israeli society.

However, Israel is also involved in ongoing relationships with countries on its borders and in incorporating an Arab population within its borders. Thus an emphasis on the Hebrew language, the Jewish religion, and on national identity tend to emphasize inter-cultural differences. In both countries, the emphasis on cultural or national identity is in difficult balance with an emphasis on inter-group relations, both within the country itself and with its neighbours. Policy-making must address this difficult balance.

Canada

The official Canadian policy of multiculturalism was proclaimed on October 8, 1971, but the groundwork for its proclamation had been laid for many years before then and from the beginning, rights to education concerning cultural differences have been linked with rights concerning religious and linguistic differences (Driedger, 1971, pp. 28–30).

Historically, cultural differences have been expressed through language. The 1971 policy of multiculturalism took a broad view of the cultural diversity of Canada, and stated that while there were two official languages in Canada, there was no official culture. Prime Minister Trudeau noted that "A policy of multiculturalism within a bilingual framework commends itself to the government as the most suitable means of assuring the cultural freedom of Canadians." He went on to outline the four main precepts of the policy.

First, resources permitting, the government will seek to assist all Canadian cultural groups that have demonstrated a desire and effort to continue to develop a capacity to grow and contribute to Canada, and a clear need for assistance, the small and weak groups no less than the strong and highly organized.

Second, the government will assist members of all cultural groups to overcome cultural barriers to full participation in Canadian society.

Third, the government will promote creative encounters and inter-change among all Canadian cultural groups in the interest of national unity.

Fourth, the government will continue to assist immigrants to acquire at least one of Canada's official languages in order to become full participants in Canadian society (Canada. *House of Commons Debates*, 1971, pp. 8545–46).

However, this policy did not have the force of constitutional law until a decade later, when the *Canada Act* and the *Charter of Rights and Freedoms* were passed. Linguistic rights with respect to the status of English and French as official languages are found in Sections 16–22 of the Charter. In these sections it is stipulated that citizens have the right to communicate with and receive services from various government institutions in either French or English, and that statutes and court services and proceedings shall be provided in both languages at the level of the Federal Government and the provincial government of New Brunswick, which is the only officially bilingual province.

Minority language educational rights are also outlined in the Charter; Section 23 stipulates that members of the English or French linguistic minority in a province who were educated in the minority language in that province have the right to have all of their children receive their education in that minority language, where numbers warrant.

In regard to Native people, the Charter specifically states that the rights and freedoms in it are not to be construed so as to abrogate or derogate from any aboriginal, treaty, or other rights and freedoms that pertain to aboriginal peoples, including the Royal Proclamation of October 7, 1763, or rights and freedoms that may be acquired through land claims settlement.

An overall provision is stated that "This Charter shall be interpreted in a manner consistent with the preservation and enhancement of the multicultural heritage of all Canadians" (Canada, Charter of Rights and Freedoms, 1982, Section 27). This provision will leave the way open for challenges in the courts on the basis of multicultural rights.

Israel

Israel's official policy of multiculturalism was stated in its Proclamation of Independence of May 14, 1948. In it, the newly created state of Israel pledged to:

> promote the development of the country for the benefit of all its inhabitants; . . . uphold the full social and political equality of all its citizens without distinction of race, creed or sex, and guarantee full freedom of conscience, worship, education and culture.

These principles have been incorporated in various pieces of legislation. For example, Clause 2 of the State Education Law of 1953 states:

> The object of State Education is to base elementary education . . . on striving for a society built on freedom, equality, tolerance, mutual assistance and love of mankind (Stanner, 1963).

Under this law, Jewish parents have an option between "State Education" (secular) and "Religious State Education" with the latter distinguished as religious in way of life, curriculum, teachers and inspectors (Ibid.). Parents have also the right to educate their children at non-official "recognized" schools outside the state system. This law enabled Jewish ultra-orthodox parents to establish an "independent school system" within the framework of "recognized educational institutions", subsidized by the state.

The Arab (Moslem and Christian) and Druze minorities formally enjoy full rights and formal equality in regard to education. Both Hebrew and Arabic are official languages of Israel. All educational laws and regulations apply equally to both Jews and Arabs with appropriate adjustments to the needs of the minority communities. In respect of their cultural and religious identity, the state maintains for the non-Jewish population separate schools within the state education system, with Arabic as the medium of instruction and a curriculum that includes the Arabic cultural heritage. Politically, these principles of equality for its citizens have been endorsed and elaborated by a succession of Israeli Governments.

Repeated policy statements regarding the intent to integrate the Arab citizens into the fabric of the Israeli multicultural society have undoubtedly been sincere. Nevertheless, their implementation over the years has been hindered by security considerations, economic factors, and socio-cultural factors such as the traditional Arab rural society (Bentwich, 1965; Kleinberger, 1969; Mar'i, 1978). As one writer has summarized:

> During the first two decades of the State of Israel, no clear program for the education of Arab children emerged. . . . Attention to all these problems—including education—was not a major commitment of Israeli officials whose more direct interests lay with security and the pressing needs of disadvantages Jewish immigrants (Bernstein-Tarrow, 1980, p. 84).

As an examination of the enabling legislation of both Israel and Canada has shown, multiculturalism is a policy that can exist in policy pronouncements and yet its implementation can be affected by many factors. First, policy-makers may be generalizing excessively about the possibilities for cultural and linguistic unity in essentially pluralistic frameworks. Secondly, the rights of individuals may be seen as in conflict with the rights of groups in a liberal democracy. Thirdly, external factors such as wars can present governments with pressing choices for resource allocation (Masemann, 1981).

Language Rights: Policies and Practice

The teaching of official languages in practice can present a vastly different picture from the official policy. In the following comparison between Canada and Israel, we see the complexities of teaching official and minority languages, the major emphasis on language in Canada as compared to the relatively minor concern with this issue in Israel.

Canada

Canadian multicultural education policies focus largely on the teaching of both *official languages* (English and French) and third language instruction in what have been designated as *ancestral languages* (languages of different minority groups). This section examines policies and practices in both these areas.

Official Languages

The teaching of the official languages in Canada has been complicated by the definition in the different provinces of English or French as the majority or minority language. Generally speaking, English and French have been the languages of school instruction in all of the provinces and territories. Historically, French has been taught almost universally in Quebec, and English has been taught almost universally in the rest of Canada.

The complications arise in the use by minorities of French and English as languages of instruction within in each province and as second languages to speakers of other languages. There are therefore six different programs in Canadian schools for teaching the official languages:

1. English for native English speakers as a majority or a minority.
2. French for native French speakers as a majority or a minority.
3. English for French speakers.
4. French for English speakers.
5. English for speakers of other languages.
6. French for speakers of other languages.

The official languages are also taught as second languages as part of a general liberal education. There is an enormous variety in types of courses offered, at the elementary and secondary levels, from short half-hour lessons to full day immersion-type programs which have the aim of full bilingualism. Parental choice and social class play a large part in the child's participation in such programs.

The third aspect of official language education is that of teaching newcomers or speakers of other languages. Since people immigrate to Canada at various ages, instruction cannot be provided to the children only during the regular school day. The Federal Government also provides grants to provinces and local school boards to conduct evening language classes for adults. In addition, language training for up to 30 weeks is provided for family bread-winners through the federal ministry responsible for immigration and employment (Canada, Multiculturalism Canada, 1985, p. 39).

Not all of those who require language instruction are necessarily immigrants, however. Programs for native people are provided in English or French as a Second Language, sometimes in conjunction with job training programs. Various sectors of the long-settled immigrant population have not been reached by language programs, notably the elderly and the women. Programs have been run by private voluntary agencies such as the YWCA and Frontier College to reach this population.

In summary, the right to instruction in and about one or both of the official languages is seen as a basic right in Canada. The official language policy promotes the foundation of intercultural understanding that is one of the main tenets of multiculturalism. As a later discussion demonstrates, the Israeli government has not formulated a bilingualism policy as such, although Hebrew and Arabic are the two official languages.

Ancestral Languages

The other large component of language teaching that occurs in Canada is the teaching of third languages, that is, neither English nor French. The guarantees for such languages are not nearly as clearly delineated in law as they are for the official languages, but they are a thriving aspect of the Canadian educational experience. Enabling legislation for third language teaching is found in the Education Acts of various provinces.

A summary of the scope of programs in native-Indian and immigrant languages gives some idea of the popularity of heritage language instruction. In Alberta, Saskatchewan and Manitoba there are several schools which offer bilingual programs in English, Ukrainian, German, Hebrew, Chinese or Arabic. These bilingual programs are relatively few in number and serve a few hundred children (Canada, Multiculturalism Canada, 1985).

The after-hours heritage language classes in public schools serve a much larger clientele, which numbers in the thousands. In Ontario, which has the largest such program, there were 81,993 students representing 49 different language groups in the 1981–1982 school year (Ibid., pp. 48–49). Heritage language instruction is also given in Greek, Italian, Portuguese, Spanish, Laotian, Vietnamese, Cambodian and Chinese in the province of Quebec (Ibid., p. 49).

In summary, the question of multicultural development in relation to heritage languages is a complex one (Masemann, 1978). The extent to which any citizen has the right to learn or speak a third language is a point of debate. The extent to which language and culture are inextricably mixed is also a matter of discussion. The extent to which third languages and their use in school, the arts, and the ethnic media contribute to the formation of a unique Canadian identity may be debated but it is also a distinguishing feature of Canadian life.

Israel

Hebrew and Arabic are both official languages of the State, but Hebrew is taught in the Arab schools as a mandatory second language from the third and fourth grades while Arabic is taught in Jewish schools only as an optional second foreign language.

In the Jewish sector, the revival of the Hebrew language (which had previously been kept for generations only as the language of daily prayer and of religious law and literature) became one of the basic symbols of Jewish nationalism and a means of cultural assimililation.

Following a decline in the use of Hebrew during the first years of Israel's independence as a result of mass immigration, in 1954 the government launched a massive program of "language transmission". Thousands of teachers, female soldiers and volunteers went to new immigrants' settlements and homes to teach Hebrew. These efforts restored the use of Hebrew among the adult Jewish population. According to the 1972 census, 88 percent of the people aged 14 and over used Hebrew as a daily spoken language and about 95 percent could carry on their daily business in Hebrew (Israel, Central Bureau of Statistics, 1974, p. 731).

An integral part of the process of immigrant absorption by various government agencies within "absorption centers" includes formal Hebrew instruction for a period of three to six months. Every immigrant is entitled to this basic right along with housing and employment.

The emphasis on the use of Hebrew in Israel is similar historically to the emphasis on English as a majority language in Canada. Moreover, the place of the French language in Canada has some important parallels with the place of Arabic in Israel. Both groups have considered themselves to be unassimilated minorities, with official language rights, but with the social reality of domination by a more powerful group. The place of third languages in each society is that of an "enrichment" model in which immigrants continue to retain some of their linguistic facility in the language of their place of birth. However, the place of Hebrew as a cultural, religious and national focus for Israeli citizens finds no parallel in the Canadian situation. We turn now to the other aspects of multicultural education which foster inter-cultural awareness.

Education for Multicultural Understanding and Intergroup Relations

Multiculturalism is a process through which a person develops competence in several cultures (Johnson, 1977). In pluralistic societies such as Canada and Israel, multiculturalism is necessary for individuals in order to move among varying cultural environments. Hence, multicultural competence includes the ability to communicate with, understand and participate in a cultural context other than one's own, within the same sociopolitical framework. The school has, therefore, been the major focus of efforts to teach multiculturalism, both in Israel and Canada, in relation to language, culture, and inter-group relations.

Israel

The three major cultural divisions in Israeli society to which multicultural policy is addressed are as follows: Sephardi (Oriental) and Ashkenazi (Western) Jews; religious and non-religious Jews; and Israeli Arabs and Jews. The situation of each is discussed in turn here.

1. Sephardim-Ashkenazim

The large waves of immigration brought about an incisive change in the fabric of the Israeli society, namely its ethnic, or geocultural composition. Whereas almost 90 percent of immigrants to Israel before 1948 hailed from Europe (Ashkenazim), almost half of the immigrants after 1948 came from underdeveloped, semi-feudal, traditional societies in the Middle-East and in Africa, north of the Sahara (Sephardim). Thus, the Jewish population of Israel underwent a radical change from preponderantly European in origin to a numerical majority of Orientals by the early 1960s. This trend of "orientalization" became a crucial issue for Israel.

This "orientalization" of its population presented Israel's society and its education system with the challenge of the rapid modernization and "westernization" of the Asio-African immigrants. The Sephardi immigrants were of large families, poor, many of them without formal education and therefore unprepared for a modern industrially oriented economy. Consequently, many of them were socially, politically and economically disadvantaged within the modern Israeli society. The immediate result was the development of a growing socio-economical gap, mainly in material well-being, occupational distribution, political power and in education (Smooha, 1978, pp. 151–182; Peres, 1976, pp. 101–134).

The commitment of Israeli society to bridging the ethnic socio-economic gap is expressed in the platforms of all political parties and by the Government. From 1948, education was conceived as the main tool for socio-political integration. As a result of various measures taken by the Ministry of Education and Culture during the last three decades, the educational inequality among Jews has almost disappeared on the primary and secondary school levels, though not in higher education (Iram, 1985). Much progress was made as far as the distribution of political power and socio-economic status were concerned.

But in the mid 1970s, political and educational debates concluded that the ethno-cultural issue was not a problem of inequality alone (Israel, Ministry of Education and Culture, 1976). Since 1974, the Ministry of Education and Culture has launched various programs aiming at strengthening the feeling of Jewish unity, to improve the self-image of these communities and to impart their cultural heritage to all students. These programs tend to stress the multicultural concept rather than the uniformity attitude of Ashkenazi (Western) cultural hegemony which prevailed in the past, and which alienated some segments of Oriental origin in Israel.

The ideological assumption which guided the Ministry of Education policy was that the ethnic problem was one of inequality in level of education, standard of living and political power, while a broad consensus negated ethnicity. Thus, through a new curriculum, it was hoped to restore the pride of the Oriental children, to mitigate their feelings of inferiority to the culturally and economically dominant European group and to minimize feelings of alienation from the Israeli society. The basic ideology adopted in 1976 was that the historical encounter of various Jewish ethnocultural groups in Israel must lead to a cultural synthesis, ensuring each group the opportunity to conserve and develop its cultural heritage.

To coordinate the educational activities, the Ministry of Education and Culture established in 1977, "The Oriental Jewish Heritage Centre", which was charged with "the cultivation, preservation and advancement of the Oriental communities' heritage and their cultural assets" (Israel, Ministry of Education and Culture, 1979).

It is too early to assess the merits of these educational programs and their potential long-term outcomes. However, there is no doubt that this change from uniformity and Western (Ashkenazi) cultural hegemony in ethnic policy in Israel has raised social awareness of the multicultural structure of the Jewish majority in Israel.

2. *Religious and non-religious Jews*

Another distinct aspect of multiculturalism among Jews in Israel is the division according to religious observance, whether religious, ultra-religious or non-religious. The religious Jews account for approximately 30 percent of the population and are mainly orthodox. They are distinctive in dress and way of life, and maintain their own separate schools and political parties. Their lives are guided by religious laws, and they tend to reside and marry within their group.

To minimize the danger of a Kulturkampf, the State of Israel followed the long-standing commitment of Zionism which, although founded mainly by secular Jews, sought to accommodate both its religious and non-religious followers. This came about when Israel sanctioned the pre-state religious status quo in four areas: 1. the Sabbath and Jewish holidays were to be official holidays; 2. Kashrut (religious dietary laws) were to be kept in state kitchens (e.g., army, hospitals, etc.); 3. religious law continued to regulate personal status; 4. religious education was to be recognized and funded by the State (Marmorstein, 1969, pp. 86–88; Birnbaum, 1970).

3. Israeli Arabs and Jews

This is the most complicated aspect of multiculturalism in Israel. The Israeli Arabs are a religious and cultural minority within a Jewish State. Following the Six Day War (1967) and the reunion of the Israeli Arabs with their Palestinian brethren in areas seized by Israel, there is a growing tendency among Israeli Arabs to see themselves as a national (Palestinian) minority as well. This adds complications to the already sensitive ongoing political and military conflict between Israel and the Palestinians (Smooha, 1984; Mar'i, 1978).

Much of the current pattern of Arab-Jewish intergroup relations is a legacy of the pre-state period. Arab and Jewish communities under the British Mandate (1920–1948) led separate lives, maintained separate economies, went to school in separate systems of education and practiced social exclusiveness to the extent of occasional armed hostility (Stock, 1968). After the establishment of the State of Israel and the hostilities which followed, there was a mass exodus of Arabs from the country, who believed they would soon return following the victorious Arab armies. Thus the percentage of Arabs in Israel dropped from 68 percent in 1947 to 11 percent in 1951 (Israel, Central Bureau of Statistics, 1981).

The reversal of status from a majority to a minority was a painful shock to those Arabs who remained in the newly proclaimed state of Israel. These people consisted mainly of the educationally, culturally, and economically backward strata of the rural areas, who were deprived of their political and religious leaders and of the social and intellectual elites (Kleinberger, 1969, pp. 307–322; Smooha, 1978, pp. 61–69). This accounts at least in part for the inferiority of Israeli Arabs in education and in other socio-economic aspects in comparison with the Jews.

Official policy toward the Israeli Arabs was dominated by three considerations: national security, the Jewish Zionist identity of Israel, and its democratic aspirations. Because most Arabs were concentrated in two rural border areas (prior to the Six Day War of 1967) and are linked by ties of kinship, religion, culture, heritage and history with the Arabs in countries which are in a state of war with Israel, they were distrusted or feared. National security was essential to both official policy and public opinion. Any policy toward the Arab minority was affected by the need to assure the Jewish character and Jewish majority of the State, including the allocation of resources for Jewish immigration and settlement. On the other hand, Israel officially granted civic liberties to its citizens and respected the right to separate identity of pluralistic groups. All these considerations sometimes give rise to situations characterized by contradictions (Smooha, 1978, p. 83; Sarsour, 1983, p. 113).

As already mentioned, Jews and Arabs in Israel maintain two separate educational systems. This segregation is viewed by Arab educational leaders as reflecting:

> the State of Israel's liberal approach which, in consideration for the members of the minority, allows them to provide their children with an education in the spirit of their culture and heritage (Sarsour, 1983, p. 124).

Despite the legal and factual segregation in education, there were no clear and distinct goals for Arab education in Israel. In 1972, the Ministry of Education and Culture issued "basic orientations for Arab education in Israel" (Israel, Ministry of Education and Culture, 1972; Sarsour, 1983, pp. 114–115; Smooha, 1984, p. 65). In 1975 the Ministry approved a formulation of common goals for all schools and specific goals for Arabs, Druze and Jews (Israel, Ministry of Education, 1976, p. 38). The specific goals for Arab education propose:

> to base education on the foundations of the Arab culture . . . on the aspiration of peace between Israel and its neighbours, on love of the homeland . . . loyalty to the State . . . uniqueness of Israel's Arabs and the knowledge of Jewish culture (Ibid.).

Arab critics point out that the national component in the Arab identity was ignored (Mar'i, 1978, pp. 50–55; Sarsour, 1983, pp. 118–121). As for curricular implementations of these goals, comparative studies show that while biculturalism (Jewish-Arab) is common in Arab education, it is rare in Jewish education (Peres, Ehrlich and Yuval-Davis, 1970; Mar'i, 1978, pp. 71–89; Sarsour, 1983, pp. 117–121). The Arab school curriculum includes extensive study of Hebrew language and literature, Jewish history, the Bible and other elements of Jewish culture, while Jewish students are scarcely exposed to Arab cultural heritage. Indeed, Arab students are bilingual and better equipped to live in a bicultural society than their fellow Jews. This of course is a general trend among cultural minorities that have no choice but to be multicultural in order to cope with society at large.

Despite the growth of the Arab educational system, there remain some pressing problems of equality when it is compared to the Jewish educational system. These are mainly problems of low performance in Arab schools and relatively lower educational achievements; higher dropout rate and lower school retention (Bashi, Cahan and Davis, 1981); uneven distribution of pupils between general and vocational tracks in the secondary schools; lower quality of teachers; and unequal resource allocations for school facilities, laboratories and curricular innovations (Israel, Ministry of Education and Van Leer Jerusalem Foundation, 1984, pp. 80–83).

While problems with multicultural education in Israel separate into three relatively clear categories, the situation in Canada at this time is quite different. A great number of different ethnic groups are part of the population, and a variety of programs in diverse areas have been established. The following section gives an overview of these programs.

Canada

The educational implications of the right to multicultural development in Canada are manifold. The teaching of languages is a component of such a response. However, many other aspects of the curriculum and of school organization have been affected by the cultural diversity of the population. Several excellent collections of readings in this area now exist, and in this brief chapter one can point only to the main features of multicultural education (Mallea and Young, 1984; Samuda *et al.*, 1984).

One feature has been a review of the content and the graphics of printed and film teaching materials for the existence of bias and stereotyping on the basis of ethnicity and race (also gender). Task forces have been established in several provinces and school boards, and recommendations have been brought forward for publishers for the portrayal of cultural and racial diversity (for example, see Ontario, Ministry of Education, n.d.).

Another related development has been the proliferation of curriculum materials specifically relating to multiculturalism. Study guides on the various cultural groups within a school board's jurisdiction are a common component of teaching materials, and speakers from various groups address teachers at professional meetings.

Advances have also been made in the training of teachers in cross-cultural and multicultural education. An umbrella organization, the Canadian Council for Multicultural and Intercultural Education, formed in 1981, is linked with provincial organizations to foster multicultural education concerns. They have held two national conferences for teachers with large numbers attending from across Canada. The level of awareness of teachers is steadily increasing, and they attended sessions on curriculum, classroom innovations, partnership with the community, intercultural communication, race relations, language, counselling, the media, women's issues, Native education, health and libraries (Canadian Council for Multicultural and Intercultural Education, 1985, pp. 22–26).

The pre-service training of teachers is also carried out in the faculties of education of both English and French universities in Canada. However, training in multicultural education tends to be an adjunct to the core curriculum concerns of student teachers and is not usually compulsory. The dilemma in multicultural teacher education appears to be that while multiculturalism is considered to be an ethic which pervades the entire curriculum, it is not seen as a teaching subject or even an area of specialization.

Teacher training is also being dealt with in in-service programs of the few individual school boards which have taken a long-term view of the task and are linking their teacher training with school board policies and programs. However, it should be noted that most school boards do not have any form of multicultural training at all. Several teachers' organizations are more active than school boards in this respect.

Another face of multicultural education has been the development of specific courses of study. Most provinces have developed elementary level social studies courses which deal with the cultural diversity of Canada, and some provinces also have such courses at the secondary level in history.

School-community relations have been adapted to the multicultural nature of school populations. In large urban centres, school notices are sent home in several languages, school-community liaison officers have been added to the school board staff, and translators are provided at public meetings.

In summary, the rights to multicultural development in Canada have great and varied implications for educational practice. The protection of group and individual rights to cultural development has led to the enormous proliferation of heritage language and culture classes and programs. The need to educate the entire school population concerning the multicultural diversity of Canada and about the need to protect every student from persecution has led to multicultural content in many curriculum areas, and intercultural and values education courses as well. The implications of these developments for school officials, administrators, teachers and resource staff have been profound as they have struggled to grapple with the ideal of a multicultural school environment. However, one sees in all of these changes in education an increasing awareness of group and individual rights to cultural development.

Thus a comparison between Canada and Israel's responses in multicultural education show a similar need to deal with official languages, religious differences, and ethnocultural differences. However, the responses have not been similar. The extent to which each country has made progress that could be called "achievement" is discussed in the following section.

Achievements and Future Goals

Canada

The achievements in allowing for multicultural development in Canada have taken a number of forms. The new Constitution and the Charter of Rights and Freedoms enshrine group and individual rights to education in one or both of the official languages. The very existence of an official multiculturalism policy and a Multiculturalism Sector in the Department of the Secretary of State are tangible evidence of an official commitment to multiculturalism. The existence of multicultural advisory councils in some provinces, of multicultural staff officers in provincial Ministries of Education, and of school-community liaison personnel at the local level also testify to such a commitment. The sheer complexity and variation of classes and programs in language and culture show the effect on the schools' curriculum. All of these policy developments and constitutional protections have been the outgrowth of a multicultural reality that pre-dated them.

However, there are areas where cultural development and equality is still a chimera. The place of Native peoples in the national fabric is still a complicated one, in which Native peoples feel that their cultural identity should not have to be part of a super-imposed multicultural identity (D'Oyley, 1983).

Much still remains to be done in race relations and the protection of individual rights of access to the power structure of Canadian society. It is still necessary to convince many long-settled European immigrants that the new immigrants from the West Indies, Asia, Africa and South America are also part of the Canadian reality. Even the official bilingualism policy is by no means accepted by all Canadians.

Probably the greatest remaining challenge is to convince officials in provincial ministries of education and school boards that a long-term commitment to multiculturalism is involved and that full-time permanent staff positions are needed. Long-term programs could then be formulated and implemented, the successes of which would be felt in the next generation.

Israel

Much has been achieved in three areas of multicultural education in Israel. Quantitative as well as qualitative progress has been made in the education of Oriental Jews and of Arabs in Israel. Nevertheless, we may conclude that the Jewish educational system to a certain degree overlooks cultural variations within the Jewish society itself (Sephardim/Ashkenazim) and outside of it as well. We have seen that much progress has been made in recent years towards including in Jewish school curricula material concerning Oriental Sephardic Jewish culture. However, these curricula pay too little attention to language and culture of Arab students, although there are signs of promising developments in this area as well. A new curricular unit, "The Arab Citizens of Israel" and proper textbooks have been introduced since the 1983–1984 school year (Israel, Ministry of Education and the Van Leer Jerusalem Foundation, 1984). This program is a unit in civic studies, part of which includes lively meetings between Jewish and Arab students

("Classes in Coexistence", *Time*, June 10, 1985). Also the Ministry of Education and Culture has introduced "Education for Democracy, Tolerance and Coexistence" as an "Annual Topic" for the 1985–1986 school year. The success of these programs may be seen in the years to come.

In spite of continuous efforts on the part of the educational system of Israel to cope with problems of multiculturalism, none have been resolved satisfactorily thus far. Since these problems are of a political, social and cultural nature and have implications beyond those of education, they cannot be expected to be solved by the educational system alone, but with the active support and involvement of other social institutions as well.

Conclusion

This discussion of the right to multicultural development in Canada and Israel has summarized the main provisions, both legal and constitutional, in each country. An overview has been given of the ethnic and linguistic diversity of each nation, and this has been linked with specific problems that have been addressed in educational programs devoted to the teaching of languages and to multicultural education in the broader sense. Each author has discussed the achievements and future goals in these areas, themes that can be seen in each country, and prospects for future policy development.

First, it seems that constitutional provisions are not necessarily a guarantee of equality or equity, particularly when there is disparity in status among ethnocultural and linguistic groups, and even more so when groups occupy dominant and subordinate statuses within a national framework.

Second, it is difficult to measure or assess the success of multicultural development and human rights since the qualities of tolerance and intercultural understanding are so evanescent, and may actually be threatened if cultural retention rather than cultural sharing is the outcome of programs for cultural development, or if political events such as warfare consistently present a negative picture of inter-group relations.

Third, multicultural development may be difficult to foster by government decree, if its foundations are not already laid in the history and social structure of a country.

Fourth, official language policy is an important part of multicultural development, and the educational framework of such policies demonstrates the degree of commitment to linguistic and cultural equality.

Fifth, the political realities of overt hostility to or subordination of groups may far outweigh the harmonious wishes of policy-makers or educators.

Sixth, there have been significant steps made in multicultural programming and ideas in the educational systems of both countries, but in the vast scale of things these programs are only the beginning.

And finally, there is a clear policy need in both countries to assess demographic trends and to plan for a future in which rights to multicultural development are safeguarded.

References

Bashi, J., Cahan, S. and Davis, D. (1981) *Achievements of the Arab primary school in Israel*. Jerusalem: Hebrew University. (Hebrew).

Bentwich, J. S. (1965) *Education in Israel*. London: Routledge and Kegan Paul.

Bernstein Tarrow, N. (1980) The education of Arab children under Israeli administration. *Canadian and International Education*, **9**(1), 81–94.

Birnbaum, E. (1970) *The politics of compromise: State and religion in Israel*. Cranbury, NJ: Fairleigh Dickinson University Press.

Bullivant, B. M. (1981) *Race, ethnicity and curriculum: New approaches to multicultural education*. Melbourne: Macmillan.

Canada. Charter of Rights and Freedoms (1982). Ottawa: Minister of Supply and Services.

Canada. House of Commons (1971) *Debates*. Twenty-eighth Parliament, 3rd Session, **115**(187).

Canada (1985) *Statistics Canada*. Ottawa: Minister of Supply and Services.

Canada. Multiculturalism Canada (1985) *Education: Cultural and linguistic pluralism in Canada*. Ottawa: Minister of Supply and Services.

Canadian Council for Multicultural and Intercultural Education (1985) *Developing partnerships: Report on the Second National Conference on Multicultural and Intercultural Education*. Toronto: CCMIE/CCEMI.

D'Oyley, V. (1983) Contested or non-assured rights. In D. Ray and V. D'Oyley (Eds.), *Human rights in Canadian education* (pp. 198–212). Dubuque, IA: Kendall/Hunt.

Driedger, E. A. (1971) *A consolidation of the British North America Acts 1867 to 1965*. Ottawa: Information Canada.

Iram, Y. (1985) Education policy and cultural identity in Israel. In C. Brock and W. Tulasiewicz (Eds.), *Education policy and cultural identity* (pp. 202–219). London: Croom Helm.

Israel. Central Bureau of Statistics (1950–1984) *Statistical abstracts of Israel*, No. 1–35. Jerusalem: Government Printer.

Israel. Ministry of Education and Culture (1972) Basic orientations for Arab education in Israel. *Basic goals in Arab education*. Jerusalem: Author. (Mimeographed).

Israel. Ministry of Education and Culture (1976) *Education in Israel in the eighties*. Jerusalem: Government Printer.

Israel. Ministry of Education and Culture (1976) Integration of Oriental Jewish heritage in educational institutions. *Director General Circulars, 37/2*. Jerusalem: Government Printer.

Israel. Ministry of Education and Culture (1979) Integration of Oriental Jewish heritage in educational institutions. *Director General Circulars, 39/4, 39/5*. Jerusalem: Government Printer.

Israel. Ministry of Education and the Van Leer Jerusalem Foundation (1984) *The Arab citizens of Israel: Interaction between Jews and Arabs in Israel*. Jerusalem: Government Printer.

Johnson, N. B. (1977) On the relationship of anthropology to multicultural teaching and learning. *Journal of Teacher Education*, **28**(3), 10–15.

Kirp, D. L. (1979) *Doing good by doing little: Race and schooling in Britain*. Berkeley: University of California Press.

Kleinberger, A. F. (1969) *Society, schools, and progress in Israel*. Oxford: Pergamon Press.

Mallea, J. R. and Young, J. C. (1984) *Cultural diversity and Canadian education*. Ottawa: Carleton University Press.

Mar'i, S. K. (1978) *Arab education in Israel*. Syracuse, NY: University Press.

Marmorstein, E. (1969) *Heaven at bay: The Jewish kulturkampf in the Holy Land*. London: Oxford University Press.

Masemann, V. (1978) Multicultural programs in Toronto schools. *Interchange*, **9**(1), 29–44.

Masemann, V. (1981) Comparative perspectives on multicultural education. In D. Dorotich (Ed.), *Education and Canadian Multiculturalism* (pp. 38–48). Saskatoon: CSSE Yearbook.

Mitter, W. and Swift, J. (1985) *Education and the diversity of culture.* Koln: Bohlau Verlag.

Ontario. Ministry of Education (n.d.) *Race, religion, and culture in Ontario school materials: Suggestions for authors and publishers.* Toronto: Ministry of Education.

Peres, Y. (1976) *Ethnic relations in Israel.* Tel Aviv: Sifriat Poalim and Tel Aviv University.

Peres, Y., Ehrlich, A. and Yuval-Davis. N. (1970) National education for Arab youth in Israel: A comparative analysis of curricula. *The Jewish Journal of Sociology,* **12**(2), 14–163.

Samuda, R., Berry, J. W. and Laferriere, M. (1984) *Multiculturalism in Canada.* Toronto: Allyn and Bacon.

Sarsour, S. (1983) Arab education in a Jewish state—Major dilemmas. In A. Hareven (Ed.), *Every sixth Israeli: Relations between the Jewish majority and the Arab minority in Israel* (pp. 113–132). Jerusalem: Van Leer Jerusalem Foundation.

Smooha, S. (1978) *Israel: Pluralism and conflict.* London: Routledge and Kegan Paul.

Smooha, S. (1984) *The orientation and politicization of the Arab minority in Israel.* Haifa: University Press.

Stanner, R. (1963) *The legal basis of education in Israel.* Jerusalem: Ministry of Education and Culture.

Stock, E. (1968) *From conflict to understanding: Relations between Jews and Arabs in Israel since 1948.* New York: Institute of Human Relations Press.

CHAPTER 7

The Right to Education for Employment and Mobility: Norway and Yugoslavia

Val. D. Rust
University of California, Los Angeles

Introduction

Even though education has been recognized as a human right, there remain certain educational spheres which limit equity and access. One of these spheres is the traditional organization of education for employment. Our task in this chapter shall be to assess the degree of progress that has been made in terms of human rights provisions mainly at the secondary school. It is of little use to prepare someone to function productively in the world of work, if that person is unable to exercise his/her craft in a productive manner. Unfortunately, that issue exceeds our objective here, for we must concentrate on equality and access issues pertaining to vocational and technical education rather than the opportunities available to work.

International human rights documents make explicit statements related to vocational and technical education. The *Universal Declaration of Human Rights* (1948) states that technical and professional education shall be made generally available (Art. 26). The *International Covenant on Economic, Social and Cultural Rights* (1966) stipulates that secondary education in its different forms, including technical and vocational secondary education, shall be made generally available and accessible to all by every appropriate means, and in particular by the progressive introduction of free education (Art. 13-2-b). The *Declaration on Social Progress and Development* (1969) reiterates that education should be made free at all levels (Art. II, 10, e).

While these UN statements stipulate that primary education is to be free, universal, and compulsory, education above that level is usually qualified. It is to be progressively introduced, meaning that where free education was not being realized at the time of the documents, it was recognized as a norm toward which subscribers ought to work. No statement has yet appeared which suggests that vocational training in some form ought to be universal, only that it be made generally available.

Besides the UN declarations, in the past three decades the International Labor Organization has also made a number of recommendations, including

121

the *Vocational Guidance Recommendation*, the *Vocational Training (Adult) Recommendation*, the *Vocational Training (Agriculture) Recommendation*, the *Vocational Training Recommendation*, the *Vocational Training (Fisherman) Recommendation*, and the *Vocational Training (Seafarers) Recommendation*. These spell out administrative issues such as financing and training standards, program curricula, methods of training, and international cooperation matters.

Two UNESCO documents are particularly pertinent. In 1962, UNESCO passed a set of recommendations concerning technical and vocational education. UNESCO revised its recommendations in 1974, setting forth general principles, goals and guidelines to be applied to vocational and technical education according to the needs and resources of each country. This represents the fullest general statement available regarding vocational and technical education by an international agency, within the framework of human rights considerations.

We shall deal with these recommendations later in this chapter, but it might be helpful to put our discussion in some historical context to give some sense of how nation states have attempted to secure greater human rights with regard to vocational and technical education. The discussion shall concentrate on Europe because that area of the world has served as a model for so much of the rest.

Vocational Education in the Modern Age

The emergence of the modern age in Europe some 200 years ago, with its factory system, nation state, and bureaucracy, broke the long-standing guild system and the apprentice tradition. The factory needed a different type of training. The very nature of the factory was to divide tasks into components. The tasks workers performed were routine and simple, so training was neither long nor difficult. The skilled craft system was no longer appropriate to these task-specific needs, so, during the nineteenth century, the skilled crafts declined dramatically.

As primary education became universal and people gained enough education to become involved in social and political affairs, they began applying pressure to restore some form of education that would extend beyond the narrow task-oriented training that was then available. France and Belgium were the first countries to introduce schools intended to train young handworkers but the system soon spread to other countries.

In spite of its rapid acceptance as a legitimate part of the schooling process, vocational education retained the stigma which had been attached to out-of-school vocational training in traditional Europe. It remained separate from, and inferior to, academic oriented schools, at least in terms of status, in spite of certain historical movements to correct this status imbalance. One of the major impulses to restore this balance came from

Marxist–Leninist revolutionaries of the past century, who claimed that the variety of school types was a deliberate mechanism to retain a separation between the laboring and the privileged classes.

After the Bolsheviks seized power in Russia in 1917, a concerted effort was made to eliminate these divisions and realize a uniform industrial school, "where teaching is closely connected with socially useful labor," but also where "the intellectual development of workers and peasants" is insured (Harper, 1937, pp. 20–21).

Progressive educators in America attempted to lower the barrier between vocational and academic studies by shifting the meaning of liberal education so that practical and utilitarian studies were no longer to be identified as being illiberal. For people such as John Dewey, occupational training could be "truly liberalizing in quality," if learned within a scientific framework that included more than mere skills development (Dewey, 1916, p. 235).

Indeed, America has been more successful than most countries in reducing prejudice against practical and utilitarian learning. Even in America, however, practical learnings continue to face many obstacles and challenges. The recent report of the National Commission on Secondary Vocational Education concluded that recent national study reports on the state of education have not given vocational and technical education the consideration it deserves. Consequently, the Commission issued its own report to fill the gap left by other reports. Two of the major challenges the report highlights have to do with access and equity issues (National Commission, 1984).

These two issues are most important for our discussion so we shall concentrate on those European systems that best illustrate our points. We have chosen to highlight Norway and Yugoslavia, because these two countries allow us to touch on activities in both Eastern and Western Europe. The two countries also represent a better blend of Eastern and Western European political ideologies than most others. In spite of this ideological similarity, the two are vastly different.

Norway and Yugoslavia

Norway is a long narrow country which is sparsely populated, having just over 4.1 million people. Except for about 25,000 Lapps in the north, the country is very homogeneous. Almost all inhabitants are Evangelical Lutheran and speak one of two official dialects of the Norwegian language. In spite of living in a state of dependency on Denmark and Sweden for several hundred years, Norway has had a distinct national consciousness for over 1000 years. Its standard of living is one of the highest in the world.

The government of Norway is a constitutional monarchy, but the real political power resides with the *Storting* or parliament, which consists of members elected by a system of proportional representation. The country has a tradition of extensive central control in political and administrative affairs.

Yugoslavia is smaller than Norway in terms of land mass, but its population is almost six times that of Norway, having over 23 million inhabitants. It is one of the youngest nation states in Europe having been created after World War II. Yugoslavia is declared to be one nation, but a multitude of languages (Cyrllic and Latin alphabets), religions (mainly Roman Catholic, Orthodox, and Moslem), as well as nations and nationalities exist. The nations include Croations, Macedonians, Montenegrins, Moslems, Serbs, and Slovenians. Nationalities are constitutionally designated as those national groups whose parent nations border Yugoslavia (Italy, Austria, Hungary, Rumania, Bulgaria, Greece, and Albania). The economic levels of these various groups are very different. Slovenians pride themselves in being at a level comparable to many Western Europeans, while those regions in the southern part of the country are very poor.

The country began as a highly centralized structure run by the Communist Party of Yugoslavia, but over the past quarter century the pervasive centrism of Yugoslavia has tended to break down until the leaders of Yugoslavia have come to accept a policy of genuine federalism where the six republics and two autonomous political provinces (Vojvodina and Kosovo) hold almost all of the political power. The economy and polity are run on the Marxist principle of self-management, with its anti-bureacratic and anti-statist implications. The basic idea of self management is that "all those who work in an enterprise—a factory, a business, a school—share as equals in the authority and power of running it" (OECD, 1981, p. 37).

The educational heritages of Norway and Yugoslavia are different also. The Norwegians have a long and strong history of education in the dualistic Western European tradition. Any discussion of equity must center on a shift in policy away from this dualism, and we find that the Norwegians have been as successful as any European country in breaking down the dualistic educational tradition and adopting a basic school which all children now attend for 9 years before branching into different streams of study. In fact, all pupils take the same subjects, without differentiated teaching, through the first 7 years of school and have but a limited set of optional hours in the eighth and ninth years.

Norway prides itself in providing a basic educational program of uniform quality throughout the country, even in those remote areas along the coast and in the north country. Attendance ratios are essentially 100 percent through the first 9 years, and they remain relatively high through upper secondary school.

While the Norwegians have struggled with structural school reform in recent decades, the Yugoslavs have struggled with quite a different problem. Immediately after World War II, the leaders of the young country were faced with a population that was largely illiterate and unschooled. Their task was to build a school system in an environment that did not possess schools, and this they have done. Whereas primary school attendance rates prior to World War II were negligible among the Yugoslav people, they quickly rose to almost 90 percent in the early 1950s and are now nearing 100 percent. Secondary school attendance rates are respectable with over 60 percent of an age level finishing secondary school in a given year (Georgeoff, 1982).

Yugoslav leaders followed the example of the USSR in setting up a common school form immediately after the war. The primary school consists of two 4-year phases. In the first phase, children learn with a teacher who teaches all subjects, while, in the second phase, children study under subject specialists who teach a curriculum that is centrally determined and consists of a long list of required subjects which focus on basic skills, preparation for secondary school and vocational training. Secondary school represents a further 4 years training, the first 2 years consisting of a continuation of a common required curriculum, mainly general studies. The last 2 years are intended to be occupationally oriented.

We turn now to human rights issues surrounding vocational and technical education in the two countries. These issues deal with the relationship between vocational and academic studies, the degree of access students have to vocational studies, and particular issues of women, minority groups, and the handicapped.

Human Rights Issues

Because these issues are best addressed in the UNESCO recommendations of 1974, we shall concentrate our inquiry on certain of its provisions.

I. An initiation to technology and to the world of work should be an essential component of general education . . . It should be a required element in the curriculum beginning in primary education and continuing through the early years of secondary education (Art. IV, 19).

The contrast between Norway and Yugoslavia is nowhere stronger than in the manner in which these countries define general education. Norway reflects a more conventional liberal arts orientation. In fact, the basic guidelines of the so-called 1974 *Mønsterplan* (revised in 1985), which sets the framework for the basic school (grades 1–9) aims and program, are almost devoid of references to vocational and technical education (Grunnskolerådet, 1985). Pupils are required to enroll in a uniform curriculum consisting of a certain number of hours of religion, Norwegian, mathematics, English, orientation subjects, nature studies, social studies, natural science, music, arts and crafts, physical education, and domestic science. None of these courses deals centrally with the world of work or with the role of technology in modern cultures, although some topics might be included.

The national curriculum does stipulate that some topics, including first aid, nutrition, traffic studies, consumer studies, environmental and nature conservation, and career guidance shall be integrated into the compulsory subjects. Some reference to the positive and negative attributes of technological society would be inevitable in these units.

A few optional courses are available in grades eight and nine, but these courses are organized and taught by the conventional teachers, who tend to offer topics similar to the subjects they teach within the already existing common program. Some school districts encourage pupils to engage in community-based work-study and community-based activities as a part of the optional program. These are popular in some districts, but on a national basis, these programs presently touch a relatively small number of pupils.

At the upper secondary level (grades 10–12), which consists of nine general streams of study, all students are required to participate in a substantial program of core courses. Just as in the basic school, these core courses fall within the conventional liberal arts orientation including religion, Norwegian, foreign languages, social studies, mathematics, natural sciences and physical education. Except for social studies, which does give some attention to topics such as the consumer society and the world of work, no consideration is given to vocational and technical education as a part of general education.

In contrast to Norway, Yugoslavia has embarked on a polytechnically oriented educational program typical of most Eastern European countries, following the early lead of the Soviet Union, which declared as early as 1917 that "labor, pedagogical as well as productive labor, will be made the basis of teaching" (Leary, 1919, pp. 113–114). Yugoslav policy makers insist that all students learn about and gain practical experience in the world of work as a part of their general education. A further aim is that all students leave secondary school with some work qualifications.

Even at the primary school level (grades 1–8) in Yugoslavia a major objective is "to increase the relationship of education to work, partially through a more intensive program of labor education . . ." (Georgeoff, 1982, p. 46). Of course, most of the curriculum is devoted to conventional subjects such as the mother tongue, natural sciences, mathematics, social science, geography, history, languages, physical education, art, and music; however, primary school pupils throughout Yugoslavia are required to take a course each year, usually beginning in grade four, which is related to work education. That course emphasizes industrial education and includes topics such as basic mechanics, metal work, and general technology (Georgeoff, 1982). Included in this program is an attempt to expose all students to production activities of local enterprises, either in the school workshops or in the enterprises themselves.

At the secondary level (grades 9–12), the first 2 years are generally uniform, regardless of locality or region, and include exposure to some vocational content and the life of work. Because secondary education is declared to be vocational in nature, the study of labor, its problems, technology and industrial processes, has taken on great importance. During these first 2 years, students engage mainly in theoretical studies but also spend time (usually two to three weeks) in enterprises in an attempt to familiarize themselves with the world of work and to prepare themselves for the remaining years at school when they actually become competent to exercise a useful vocational or trade skill (OECD, 1981). It is important to note that the more general mathematics and natural science courses have also undergone a transformation to include topics and content that is more appropriate to the advanced industrialized world (Szaniawski, 1978).

One of the major problems both countries face is the lack of teacher experience about the world of work. In fact, this seems to be a general problem. According to the National Commission on Resources on Youth, "teachers, like most adults, are often nearly as experience-poor as their students when it comes to the workings of their own communities" (NCRY, 1975, p. 52). Personal observations of Yugoslav teachers accompanying their classes into community establishments confirm this impression. Norway is no better off, in spite of the fact that Bergen Teachers College recently began a program of industrial teacher education for some of its primary teacher candidates, which includes a practicum experience in the industrial world. It is a small start, but may expand if it proves successful (Braanaas, 1977).

II. Technical and vocational education should begin with a broad basic vocational education, thus facilitating horizontal and vertical articulation within the education system and between school and employment (Art. II, 7).

Both Norway and Yugoslavia have made great efforts to develop an upper secondary school structure that will provide extensive options for pupils. No course of studies is a dead-end, but begins with a broad, general content that leads to other options. In Norway, the upper secondary school generally lasts for 3 years. Students apply to be admitted to one of eight branches of study:

General Education
Manual and Industrial Studies
Arts and Crafts
Fishing and Maritime Studies
Sport
Clerical and Commercial Subjects
Domestic Science
Social and Health Studies

A fundamental purpose of the *Upper Secondary School Law*, which took effect in 1976, was that the practical and general branches have equal status.

In many instances they exist side by side with each other. In theory, students may freely choose the branch in which they wish to study. They may also shift branches and begin another course at an appropriate level. Each branch is set up so that the student takes a general program during the first year before branching into a specialization the second and third years. The courses are also set up so that the vocational students may leave school with some qualification in the work world at the end of each year of study. In spite of this generally positive structure, a number of practical problems prohibit it from functioning as well as it might. We will address these presently, but we must first provide some outline of the structure of the Yugoslav upper secondary school.

All pupils who successfully complete the 8 year Yugoslav elementary school are eligible to apply for secondary schooling. A number of different types of schools have conventionally constituted secondary education, including *gymnasia* (general education), art schools, technical schools, trade or vocational schools, teachers' schools, and military secondary schools. As a consequence of the 1977 reform of secondary schooling, the *gymnasia*, technical schools and trade or vocational schools are being collapsed into a single entity which will reduce the social and academic distinctions that have characterized these schools.

Within this new framework, a common curriculum is to be found during the first 2 years of upper secondary schooling (Bezdanov, Frankovic and Sefer, 1980), consisting of the following spheres of education:

General Cultural Subjects
Socio-Economic Subjects
Natural Sciences and Mathematics
Production-Related and Technical Subjects
Electives

Because the secondary school has been designated as an institution to provide vocationally directed education, special emphasis is given to the natural sciences and mathematics, work related education, and polytechnical education. Students also engage in a few optional courses and in various forms of leisure-time activities such as youth and pupil cooperatives (Juhas, 1978). Thus, the program allows students to continue in school until they are 17 years old before they begin to channel themselves into specialized tracks. Students who complete this first phase of secondary schooling have an added advantage in that they possess a formal vocational qualification equivalent to those who have been engaged in work experience or on-the-job training for a comparable period of time.

It is in the second phase of secondary schooling that specialized vocational training takes place, while the number of common courses diminishes appreciably. In 1980, Yugoslavia came to an *Agreement on Unified Bases for Occupational Classification*, in which all occupations are classified in one of eight different levels. The first level simply requires completion of primary school, but the secondary school is intended to provide skills to meet the next three levels of skill (Nedeljkovic, 1980). Even those students in general education receive some specialized vocational or paraprofessional training though most plan to go on to higher education.

Yugoslav authorities wish to avoid the movement toward early specialization and even the growth of common courses that are strictly vocational in nature. Consequently, they have determined that approximately 70 percent of student time be devoted to general studies and 30 percent to occupationally oriented studies (OECD, 1981).

III. Vocational and technical education is readily available to all and for all appropriate types of specialization (Art. II, 7, e).

Different types of policy exist in Norway and Yugoslavia affecting the availability of vocational and technical education specializations. In Yugoslavia, vocational education is directly coordinated with the needs of labor at the local level through associated labor organizations. That is, the local community defines what vocational training programs should be locally provided. The assumption is that those workers who participate in the machinery of educational governance are in the best position to determine what programs are most suitable, both in the short-term and in the long-term.

The consequence of such a policy is that radically different types of vocational education configurations exist in different communities and parts of the country. On a national level, a wide array of vocational training programs and orientations are found.

Two problems have resulted from this policy. First, local communities are often inclined to make decisions based on narrow and specific needs rather than on more general and long-range needs, so that training does not prepare the young for changed conditions (Kintzer, 1978). Second, many communities rely on a single industry for their means of economic survival. In these locations a young person will have few choices from which to choose. Communities have attempted to overcome these obstacles through exchange arrangements, but, as we shall see, ethnic and language problems prevent this from being a fully satisfactory solution.

In Norway, the government has adopted a policy that all upper secondary school candidates are, in principle, free to choose which of the eight branches of study they will enter. The kinds of vocational education places across the country are much more uniform than in Yugoslavia, although there is also regional focus. For example, almost all of the nine types of fishing programs in the schools are located in three counties along the west and north coast of the country and do not exist in the other 17 counties, although several other counties have some types of maritime studies.

More typical, however, would be the situation found in the clerical and commercial branch. Every county offers the major lines of specialization, although many specialties are peculiar to a limited number of counties. The total number of specialties available somewhere in the country within each of the eight branches is impressive. For example, no less than 225 different types of courses are available in manual and industrial studies alone (Rådet, 1984). Of course, the large urban centers have the greatest variety of specialties, but they do have a policy of limited access to these places for students from other districts.

In spite of the rich offerings available, there remains a critical shortage of vocational and technical education places. Great efforts are being made to satisfy student demand, but so far that has not been possible and it is becoming clear that it will not occur in the immediate future, in spite of the fact that the number of places available for vocational training at the secondary level expanded by 40 percent between 1977 and 1983 (Rust, 1985). For example, in the social and health branch of study, only one in four applicants was admitted in 1980. In the manual and industrial branch, only two out of three applicants were admitted, while six of every ten were given places in fishing and maritime studies (*Utdanningsstatistikk*, 1982). One consequence of these shortages has been an increase in competition and a raising of the standards of admission. This brings us to the next human rights criterion.

IV. Vocational and technical education may be freely and positively chosen as the means by which one develops talents, interests and skills leading to an occupation . . . or to further education (Art. II, 7, b).

The ability to choose a program of study freely and positively involves a number of elements. First, the program must be available for study. Second, a young person must be able to gain access to it. Third, the choice must be looked at as a positive or good one. We have already addressed issues related to the first two of the elements and turn now to the third element: Is the option a positive one? We have already noted that throughout Western history, vocational and technical education have been viewed as less valuable than academic and general education.

Through the influence of science and technology, as well as political impulses, this dualism has been eroded during the past century (Rust, 1977, Ch. 5). Eastern European countries have been especially active in attempting to break down the dualism and build a unified school appropriate for everyone. Scandinavia has been especially successful among Western European countries in instituting these reforms. In fact, Norway possessed the foundations for a 7-year national common elementary school as early as 1896.

In spite of the structural reforms that have taken place, elitist values persist in most countries. Yugoslavia exemplifies this persistence. Until recently, a strict distinction was made between training for production and education for white collar occupations. Blue collar workers were classified according to the complexity of their craft skills (unskilled, semi-skilled, skilled) and white collar workers were classified according to their school qualifications (primary, secondary, higher). One of the major objectives of the revised classification of occupations was to break down this dualism and redefine occupations on a basis quite different from that in the past (Nedeljkovic, 1980).

In spite of these changes, in practice, students whose grades are poor generally drop out of school after they complete primary education or they seek admission into the schooling tracks designed for skilled workers. Students with good grades enter the track designed for general education and higher education (Georgeoff, 1982). Because the curriculum is generally common in the first phase of secondary school, students still have the option to shift tracks, but admission to the second phase of secondary school is by public competition with priority given to pupils with higher general marks achieved in the first phase.

The value orientation mentioned above is quite obvious in application ratios, where insufficient applications are received for some occupational training programs, while excessive applications are received for those places that prepare for white collar occupations. White collar jobs remain more attractive because of their status and salary advantages, and young people gravitate toward these advantages (Bezdanov, Frankovic and Sefer, 1980). Even those students who may not qualify for the better secondary schooling places are often able to circumvent the rules and gain admission either through connections of parents or through falsification of records (Woodward, 1983).

In many respects, Norway has been more successful than Yugoslavia in breaking down the dualism between vocational and general education. One of the aims of the *Upper Secondary School Law*, taking effect in 1976, was to give equal status to practical and theoretical education, by insuring that students in all branches could proceed to all types of higher education, if their performance was of a sufficient standard. This means that a bright young student can prepare for a vocation at the secondary school but also look forward to a future place at the university if he/she wishes.

The general education branch of the Norwegian upper secondary school was also opened up so that any student who had successfully completed primary school was theoretically eligible to enter. In 1980, for example, all but 4 percent of general education applicants were eventually admitted to that branch (*Utdanningsstatistikk*, 1982). In contrast, the government is unable to provide all the places that are requested in the vocational sector, because these are so much more expensive than general education places; consequently, it has been necessary to establish a restricted enrollment policy. Within any utilitarian framework, where demand exceeds places, the value of these places rises, and some of the brightest students are now competing for those few vocational education places. For example, the average examination and course scores for students qualifying to enter the plumber, painter, barber, dietician or tailor streams must be at least one full grade point average above those entering general education. The scores must be more than two grade points higher for an upholsterer and they must be what Americans would call "straight A's" for those entering the photography and dental assistant streams (*Utdanningsstatistikk*, 1982).

Education policy is not entirely responsible for the unusual shift in standards to qualify for vocational training. Norway is a progressive social democracy where salaries, health benefits, retirement advantages, etc., are relatively uniform across all occupations. Tax laws are such that there is little advantage gained by great wealth. Consequently, when the young decide on a vocation they tend to turn their attention to more subtle considerations, such as length of training, opportunity to be in the mountains or near the sea, vacation periods, amount of stress, and conditions of work, which play a large role in these decisions. A young person would tend to think twice about becoming a medical doctor when he/she knows that this profession requires about a decade of training beyond secondary school but insures a salary that is not even twice that of an unskilled sheet metal worker (*Statistisk Årbok*, 1984).

The tendency of bright students to opt for vocational education will be greeted with some applause by those who have worked to equalize the general and the practical branches of learning. However, we must face a difficult reality; this condition has begun to create severe difficulties for those who have a history of low achievement in school. In the past, vocational education was a means of personal advancement and development for those who did not do well in school. Today, these students are systematically being excluded from this opportunity because their places are now being taken by students who have excelled in school. The Norwegians are taking some steps to help these low achieving students, as we shall see in section VII below, but the situation remains unsatisfactory.

V. Vocational and technical education is available to all language and ethnic minorities in a community as well as to all social classes.

Although the 1974 UNESCO recommendations fail to address this issue directly, they do stipulate that vocational and technical education should contribute to the elimination of all forms of discrimination. Because it is central to both the Norwegian and the Yugoslavian cases, we focus directly on this recommendation.

Norway does not have the ethnic diversity found in Yugoslavia; however, it does have its minority populations, particularly in Finnmark, which is the county in the far north. More than half the Lapps of Europe occupy this region. Their language is an Ugro-Finnic variant, and they were highly discriminated against for several decades. Since 1969, however, the Parliament has allowed them to use their own dialect (there are three major dialects in Norway) as the language of instruction, while Norwegian is taught as a second language. Great efforts have been undertaken also to provide some cultural learning in their schools.

In terms of most indices of growth, that part of the country is one of the most disadvantaged in Norway, but just as in Yugoslavia, it is making more progress than most other areas, mainly because there is greater room for improvement. In 1977, only 62 percent of the young people leaving the basic school were going on to secondary school. The national average at the time was 79.5 percent. In the next 4 years, the percentage of young people entering secondary school in Finnmark had risen to 72.8 percent. This represented a dramatic increase, but it remained far behind the national average, which had risen to 83 percent, and was approximately five percentage points behind the next lowest county, which was sending 76.8 percent on to secondary school (*Utdanningsstatistikk*, 1982).

The expansion of educational opportunities has taken place both in general and in vocational education. Finnmark can boast of having some specializations in each of the nine branches of secondary school (Rådet, 1984), and an expanding number of opportunities are available for school leavers to work and to do service in the community as a part of the middle school program (Grunnskolerådet, 1985).

In Yugoslavia, with its multiple language and cultural groups, special attention is given to preserving even the smallest of these groups. Article 247 of the federal *Constitution* guarantees each nationality "the right freely to use its language and alphabet, to develop its culture," while Article 170 stipulates that "propagating or practicing national inequality and the incitement of national, racial, or religious hatred and intolerance shall be unconstitutional and punishable." (Yugoslav Federal Executive Council, 1974).

The language of instruction in the schools is carried out not only in the major Yugoslav languages but in the nine languages of nationalities living in the country (Albanian, Bulgarian, Czech, Italian, Hungarian, Rumanian, Ruthenian, Slovak, and Turkish). In the four Ruthenian schools, for example, children enjoy instruction and a full set of textbooks in that language. The textbooks cost no more than texts in all other languages, in spite of the great differences in their costs of production.

At the national level, inequality is a fact of life, simply because there is great economic disparity between sections of the country and some sections are not able to provide education at a comparable standard as other parts. Those socio-economically underdeveloped republics of Bosnia-Herzegovina, Macedonia and Montenegro as well as Kosovo are recipients of a national policy of accelerated economic development but they remain far behind the wealthier areas of northern Yugoslavia (Mladenovic, 1982).

In the educational sphere, the federal government has maintained a grant-in-aid program which has offset the funding disparities to some degree. For example, while the per capita social income of Kosovo is only one third that of Yugoslavia, its educational budget is over one-half that of the country as a whole (OECD, 1981), and while the number of secondary students in Croatia grew by 235 percent between 1952 and 1970, it grew by a startling 751 percent in Kosovo during the same period. This means that the rate of school attendance of the 15–18 age group rose from 13.6 percent to 29.8 percent; however, it remained far behind the northern areas of the country (Steinman, 1972).

At the republic level, other equity problems become apparent. We have seen that occupational training options are closely aligned to community interests, and although no overt discrimination is allowed to take place, the fact is that available training places are usually in enterprises with a particular language or ethnic tradition. A young person who wants that training, but who belongs to a different ethnic group, is extremely hampered. For example, Slovenia is the dominant culture of the Slovenian Republic, but there is an Italian population along the western border. In spite of extensive republic and communal statutes to insure equity, it is impossible to provide vocational training in the case of most Italians in their mother tongue.

The problems faced by minority groups have often been dealt with through the "politics of circumvention," where some level of denial of the problems has been practiced (Neal, 1984). Here it must be stated that Yugoslavia is moving slowly toward a sense of unity. Discrimination will slowly diminish in such a climate.

VI. Vocational and technical education is available . . . on a basis of equality to women as well as men. (Art. II, 7, f).

We recall that women were historically excluded from access to most of formal education. Many girls were educated, but that education took place in the confines of the home and household. It was not until the Age of Enlightenment in the eighteenth century that formal education for females gained attention in Europe; however, even during the nineteenth century, when schools were opened to women, they were largely under private sponsorship and those which provided vocational training focussed on the few vocations for which females were deemed to be uniquely suited.

Conditions for women have changed over time and in our day two major considerations come into play. First: Are women attaining a level of education comparable to that of men? Second: Are women being excluded from certain types of occupational preparation?

With regard to the first consideration, Norwegian females finish school at rates comparable to males through the primary and secondary levels. They far outstrip the males at the first two levels of university study (level I does not lead to a degree and level II leads to the first degree). However, the rate drops dramatically when we consider graduate level studies. Only 6.9 percent of all doctorates awarded in 1982 were to females.

What progress has been made in recent years in terms of female enrollments? In 1971–1972 only 43.1 percent of those graduating from secondary school were females. During the next 10 years equity was achieved in terms of secondary school leavers. While only 42.7 percent of young females were leaving the first level of university study in 1971–1972, the balance had shifted to 55.3 percent by 1981–1982. The shift in percentage differences at the second level was even more dramatic, because only 37.3 percent of university II leavers were female in 1971–1972, and the figure had shifted to 54.6 percent 10 years later. While some progress was made at level III, it remained highly disproportionate and the number of females gaining doctorates barely shifted at all during that time.

Even though female completion rates at secondary school are now higher than male rates, substantial discrepancies continue to exist in the types of branches. Norway remains a country where sharp distinctions are drawn in the occupations women choose and the occupations men choose. In terms of rights issues, there is no discrimination, but in terms of personal choices, the cultural values that dictate these choices remain quite traditional.

Data on Yugoslavia are not very current, but certain conclusions can be drawn from those that are accessible. Females essentially gained parity with males at the primary level by the beginning of the 1960s. They remained far behind the males at that time in terms of secondary school attendance, but were quickly closing the gap during the 1960s. Higher education remains out of reach for a good portion of the population through the entire period, with only slight progress being made. However, the proportion of females in the highest levels of study is greater than in Norway.

Turning to the various types of schools at the secondary level, a great discrepancy continues to exist in terms of some of the types of schools females are attending. The discrepancy is most apparent in terms of schools for skilled workers, where only 29.6 percent of the students are female. Because two out of every five secondary students are in these schools, it becomes obvious that equity has not been attained in terms of people who select more conventional skilled occupations. We must keep in mind, however, that our equal rights criteria stipulate only that places be available, not that they actually be selected by an equivalent percentage of females.

It might also be helpful to note the ability of women actually to enter the work force in Norway and Yugoslavia. In 1981 in Yugoslavia, 36 percent of the total work force were women. That figure had doubled since the time that Yugoslavia had been taken over by the partisans during World War II (Rådet, 1984). In Norway 41.9 percent of the work force were women in 1983, which also represents a sharp increase in the last decades (*Statistisk-*

Årbok, 1984). We must conclude that women appear to move toward emancipation in both the countries we are observing.

Conclusions

Pertinent process objectives of the 1974 UNESCO recommendations on vocational and technical education have been reviewed. It has not been possible to go beyond the objectives themselves and assess the degree to which these have contributed to broader social objectives such as greater democratization, improved quality of life, or critical intervention on the scientific and technological aspects of contemporary civilization, but it has been possible to make some judgments about the degree to which two countries have satisfied certain schooling objectives. We had chosen the two countries not only because they allowed us to touch on differences and similarities in the activities of both Eastern and Western Europe, but because we initially felt that they had made exemplary progress in achieving a measure of success.

We found that, in spite of obvious strengths, both countries have decided weaknesses in their programs. For example, Norway adheres to the liberal education tradition to the exclusion of a broad focus on technological society in its general education program. Yugoslavia maintains a rigorous policy of local decision-making which results in policy decisions that are often narrow and short-sighted. These are two examples of conditions which could and should be defended; however, they possess a shadow side that is almost inherent in the condition. No thinking person would recommend eliminating these two traditions in order to correct that shadow side.

Any progress toward ultimate resolution of these problems ought to be made within the context of the larger culture, but progress from this point must be incremental and cautious.

References

Bezdanov, S., Frankovic, D. and Sefer, B. (1980) The policy and system of education. *Yugoslav Survey*, **21**(3), 115–146.

Braanaas, T. (1977) *Norsk industri og grunnskole/pedagogisk høyskole* [Norwegian industry and basic school/pedagogical college]. Bergen: Bergen Teachers College.

Dewey, J. (1916) *Democracy and education*. New York: Macmillan.

Georgeoff, P. J. (1982) *The educational system of Yugoslavia*. Washington: United States Department of Education International Education Program.

Grunnskolerådet (1985) *Høringsutkast til mønsterplan for grunnskolen* [Draft of the model plan for the basic school]. Oslo: Universitetsforlaget.

Harper, S. N. (1937) *Source book on European governments*. Princeton: D. Van Nostrand Co.

Juhas, M. (1978) Educational reform in Yugoslavia. *Yugoslav Survey*, **19**, 75–95.

Kintzer, F. C. (1978) Educational reforms in Yugoslavia. *Educational Record*, **59**(1), 87–104.

Leary, D. (1919) *Education and autocracy in Russia from the origins to the Bolsheviki*. Buffalo: University of Buffalo Press.

Mladenovic, M. (1982) Development of economically underdeveloped republics and the autonomous province of Kosovo. *Yugoslav Survey*, **23**(1), 3–22.

NCRY (National Commission on Resources for Youth) (1975) *Resources for Youth Newsletter.* New York: National Commission on Resources for Youth.

National Commission on Secondary Vocational Education (1984) *The unfinished agenda: The role of vocational education in the high school.* A report sponsored by the National Center for Research in Vocational Education at Ohio State, funded by the U.S. Department of Education. Columbus, OH: Ohio State University.

Neal, F. W. (1984) Yugoslav approaches to the nationalities problem: The politics of circumvention. *East European Quarterly,* **18**(3), 327–334.

Nedeljkovic, C. (1980) Social compact on uniform criteria for the classification of occupations and vocational qualifications. *Yugoslav Survey,* **21**(4), 147–154.

OECD (Organisation for Economic Cooperation and Development) (1981) *Reviews of national policies for education: Yugoslavia.* Paris: Organisation for Economic Cooperation and Development.

Rådet, P. (1984) Women, work and self-management in Yugoslavia. *East European Quarterly,* **17**(4), 459–468.

Rådet for videregaende opplaering (1984) Ekstra elevplasser [Extra Pupil places]. Oslo: Rådet for videregaende opplaering.

Rust, V. D. (1977) *Alternatives in education: Theoretical and historical perspectives.* London: Sage.

Rust, V. D. (1985) Norwegian secondary school reform: Reflections on a revolution. *Comparative Education,* **21**(2), 209–217.

Statistisk Årbok (1984) Norges offisielle statistikk, Oslo: Sentral byrå.

Steineman, Z. (1972) Development of the schooling system and changes in the educational composition of the population. *Yugoslav Survey,* **13**(4), 105–120.

Szaniawski, I. (1978) Trends and problems in the integrated curriculum of vocational and general education in socialist countries. *International Review of Education,* **24**, 131–141.

Utdazmningsstatistikk (1982) *Utdanningsstatistikk: Viederegaende skoler* [Educational statistics: Secondary schools]. Oslo: Statistisk sentralbyrå, Oct. 1.

Yugoslav Federal Executive Council (1974) *The constitution of the Socialist Federal Republic of Yugoslavia.* Belgrade: Yugoslav Federal Executive Council.

Woodward, S. L. (1983) Inequalities and Yugoslav political stability. In D. N. Nelson (Ed.), *Communism and the politics of inequalities.* Lexington, MA: Lexington Books. pp. 165–188.

CHAPTER 8

The Right to Lifelong Education in Kenya and the United States with Special Reference to Adult Education

Jean Davison and Kal Gezi

Introduction

Education in its broadest sense is lived—it is an integral part of every person's life whether planned or unplanned, formal or non-formal. As Kenyan scholar Jomo Kenyatta once observed, "education begins at the time of birth and ends with death" (1968, p. 23). Several nations have demonstrated the possibility of lifelong learning practices, including the Soviet Union, India and China. At the same time, an increasing number of scholars recognize that schooling within a lifelong context accounts for only a small percentage of most people's education (Cropley, 1980; Coombs, 1985). Much of what is learned on a day-to-day basis occurs in non-formal and informal contexts. Because improved medical practices have caused an extension of the human life-span in many parts of the world, much of an individual's education now occurs in adulthood.

Though several individual countries set earlier precedents in adult education (e.g. folk high schools in Denmark, adult literacy in the USSR, China and Vietnam), the first international attempt to address the needs of adult learners was at the World Conference on Adult Education held by UNESCO in 1960. This and the Teheran conference 8 years later brought to world attention the existence of millions of adult illiterates. The need for placing adult education within a lifelong context was intensively discussed at the third UNESCO conference on adult education held in Tokyo in 1972 and was further articulated in the UNESCO document *Learning To Be* (1972). The role of adult education as a significant and integral part of lifelong learning was reinforced by UNESCO member states at the General International Conference held in Nairobi, Kenya, in 1976. The resulting document entitled *Recommendation On The Development Of Adult Education* (UNESCO, 1976) warns that adult education must not be considered an "entity in itself", but should be viewed as an "integral part" of a global scheme for lifelong education and learning. Such a scheme is aimed at "restructuring the existing education system" and developing

139

"educational potential outside the education system" (UNESCO, 1976, p. 5). UNESCO's most recent declaration on the rights of adult learners (The Right To Learn, 1985) makes adult education a continuing priority even in a period of increasing international austerity (Limage, this volume, Chapter 5).

A working definition of adult lifelong learning is a change in an individual's knowledge, attitudes, and/or skills over time as a result of *direct* experience (observation, discovery, inspiration) or *indirect* instruction and demonstration. Learning is either self-directed or it constitutes participation in organized instruction. It has both cognitive and affective aspects.

For purposes of examining national efforts to expand human rights in such a vast field as lifelong education, our discussion is necessarily limited to policies affecting adult education that often translate into formal programs. We shall use the *Recommendation On The Development Of Adult Education* (UNESCO, 1976) as the yardstick for evaluating the extent to which the right to lifelong education has been implemented and expanded in two contrasting countries—Kenya, a developing African nation, and the United States, a western industrialized nation. The 1976 UNESCO document makes it the responsibility of each member state to "recognize adult education as a necessary and specific component of its education system and as a permanent element in its social, cultural and economic development policy" (1976, p. 7).

That adult education has a role to play in the expansion of human rights and opportunities over the lifespan is illustrated by the recent interest in lifelong learning as an educational process (e.g. Skager and Dave, 1977; Cropley, 1980; Lowe, 1982; Darkenwald and Merriam, 1982; Gichuru, 1984). During the 1982 Harare Conference held by UNESCO for African educators, priorities were outlined that include the need to re-integrate lifelong educational strategies with formal measures in order to expand opportunities to those adults who previously have had little or no contact with formal education, including nonliterates, women, and the handicapped as specifically recognized groups. Thus, the recognition that the rights of particular adult groups need to be addressed in national decisions related to the expansion of adult education opportunities is mandated by UNESCO's policies.

The discussion in this chapter begins with an examination of Kenya, where adult education since independence from Great Britain in 1963, has until recently played second fiddle to an overwhelming demand for formal schooling by a still largely nonliterate rural population. By contrast, the United States case demonstrates a long history of compulsory formal education in which continuing education at the adult level is but one phase. We begin with Kenya's experience to illustrate ways in which UNESCO recommendations are translated into national programs that contribute to the expansion of human rights in a developing African country.

The Kenyan Experience[1]

Background

Like many developing African nations, Kenya has a population that is characterized by a rapid growth rate (4 percent per year) and unequal distribution by age group with nearly half of its population of 16,500,000 under the age of 15. Additionally, over half (52 percent) of Kenya's total population is nonliterate (Kenya, Department of Adult Education, 1985, p. 15). In 1979, the Central Bureau of Statistics estimated that 5 million persons above the age of 15 years lacked sufficient literacy skills for reading. Of the total nonliterate, 62 percent are female and 38 percent are male, indicating a discrepancy in equality of opportunity to gain literacy.

Characteristic of most African countries, Kenya has a population predominantly located in rural areas (85 percent) whose members depend upon agriculture and to a lesser extent on herding for their subsistence. At the same time, only 17 percent of Kenya's land is arable (Best and DeBlij, 1977). Such figures indicate that without increased agricultural inputs in the form of water projects, land conservation methods and improved techno-logical innovations such as the use of fertilizer, much of Kenya's growing population will continue to live on the small portion of its existing arable land. The alternative is migration to an urban center. As young Kenyans become formally educated, they tend to leave the rural areas in search of wage employment in the few urban centers where existing job opportunities do not meet the demand for increased jobs. It is within the context of a largely nonliterate or only semi-literate agricultural society with a rapidly growing population and high unemployment rate that adult education programs addressed to expanding human opportunities must be viewed.

In the post independence years since 1963, much of the nation's develop-ment efforts have been directed toward achieving formal education for children at the primary and secondary levels. Kenya's educational system, based on the British model, is hierarchically arranged with achievement examinations eliminating all but the most academically capable at three levels; the end of primary (Standard Seven—which is equivalent to 7th grade), the third year of secondary ("O" Level) and the end of high school ("A" Level) which acts as a final screening for university. By 1980, the percentage of Kenya's Gross Domestic Product (GDP) in educational expenditure was 7 percent as compared with 4.8 percent for the whole of Africa and 5.6 percent for the world (Kenya, Department of Adult Edu-cation, 1985, p. 11).

Of the total primary school-age population in 1982, 92 percent were

[1] The author of this section gratefully acknowledges the assistance received from Dr F. A. Karani, Principal of the College of Adult and Distance Education, University of Nairobi, and Mr David Macharia, Director of the Department of Adult Education.

enrolled in the lower grades through Standard 5, the equivalent of fifth grade in the US (Kenya, Ministry of Economic Planning and Development, 1983, p. 37). At the same time, high drop-out rates occurred in the last two grades (6 and 7) particularly among girls (74 percent) who are often forced to leave because of pregnancy or to contribute to female family labor (Kagia, 1983). Education at the primary level is not compulsory and children who achieve minimal literacy sometimes drop out to work at home herding cattle, farming or caring for younger children, or they may seek wage employment if they are boys.

Older adults began to receive training through agricultural and health extension courses in the 1960s, and for literate adults the Institute of Adult Studies, University of Nairobi, was set up to provide residence courses, extra-mural courses, and distance education including correspondence and radio-transmitted courses. While residence and extra-mural courses cater largely to the urban educated elite who constitute a small percentage of the population, distance education and regional adult education training centres partially serve the needs of rural skills among rural adults who are the vast majority. At the same time, lack of literacy skills among rural adults, especially women, is a major problem. The first national literacy campaign was undertaken by former President Jomo Kenyatta in 1966 with limited success. Part-time teachers were hired to teach adult nonliterates but they were poorly compensated and few adults in rural areas were motivated to attend. The major thrust in literacy education, as we shall see, began with Kenya's second president, Daniel arap Moi, in 1979.

Currently, Kenya is blessed with a multifarious array of programs directed toward meeting the needs of adult learners. Government ministries and departments, non-governmental organizations, voluntary groups and the Institute of Adult Studies at the University of Nairobi, to mention a few, are in the business of providing literacy programs, nutrition and family life classes, self-help and extension courses, and in-service training for professionals. Rather than attempt to explain all the programs designed to meet adult learners' needs in Kenya, the discussion will be limited to programs designed to expand the educational rights of the following three disadvantaged adult groups identified by the UNESCO conference held in Harare—the nonliterate, women and the disabled.

Education for Adult Literacy

By far the greatest effort in Kenyan adult education has been devoted to literacy programs. By 1979, the Kenya government recognized that the number of adults unable to read or write had not decreased appreciably for several reasons—the previous literacy efforts were partially ineffective because the funds and personnel allocated by the Government were insufficient; in addition, adults were more committed to educating their children than themselves; and finally, the high drop-out rate at the end of the fourth or fifth year of school meant that many children left formal education only marginally literate and soon lapsed back into illiteracy (Odhiambo and Macharia, 1985). Consequently, the failure to achieve full adult literacy was partly a result of the Government's lack of commitment and partly a consequence of educational priorities of Kenyan citizens.

Following the death of President Kenyatta in 1978, with the inauguration of President Daniel arap Moi, a new National Development Plan (the Fourth) was launched for 1979–1983. The main thrust of the plan was the eradication of poverty with the elimination of adult illiteracy becoming a major focus. Early in 1979, members of the Board of Adult Education, the Division and the Ministry of Economic Planning and Development met to formulate a plan of action. The result was a mass enrollment plan which would increase the number of students in the first year (1979) from 200,000 to 750,000 in the final year, with the hopes of enrolling a total of 4,150,000 adults by the end of the nationwide campaign in 1984 (Odhiambo and Macharia, 1985, p. 145). To assume responsibility for the campaign, the Department of Adult Education was created within the Ministry of Culture and Social Services and 4,000 full-time staff members were recruited, of which 3,000 were literacy teachers. In addition, 5,500 part-time teachers were hired. The Government demonstrated its intent to eradicate adult illiteracy by increasing its financial commitment to literacy education from 400,000 Kenya pounds in 1978–1979, prior to the campaign, to 900,000 Kenya pounds by the end of 1979, with the figure reaching 4 million Kenya pounds by 1983–1984 (Odhiambo and Macharia, 1985, p. 145).

The new literacy campaign was given wide coverage by the Kenyan media and through the efforts of politicians, voluntary organizations and local leaders, the enrollment (415,007) in adult literacy programs in the first year (1979) was twice that expected. However, the following year the numbers dropped slightly to 398,877, and by 1982 had dropped still further to 343,888 (Kenya, Department of Adult Education, 1985, p. 29). Though no study has been made to investigate why the enrollment figures dropped, the Department of Adult Education suggests that inadequate allocation for adult education classes, including the payment of teachers, and the drought in 1982 may have been contributing factors (Kenya, Department of Education, 1985). The drought forced women farmers in many parts of Kenya to search for alternative sources of food or to stand in food lines. Because the majority of participants in adult literacy programs are women (nearly 80 percent), the search for food may have taken precedence over literacy in drought stricken areas. As Limage (Chapter 5, this volume) and Davison (1985) argue, primary basic needs such as food and health outweigh the need to literacy among people in developing countries.

Though two out of the five million nonliterate Kenyans identified in 1979 have attended literacy classes over the past 5 years, no figures are available for drop-out rates or rates of completion. Therefore, it is difficult to know how many of the total number of participants actually achieved full literacy. Further, regional discrepancies in the availability of programs and in enrollment exist. While programs in areas close to Nairobi and other urban centers are well staffed and attended, programs in pastoral areas in the north far from Nairobi are almost non-existent.

The major thrust of the current national development plan (1984–1988) in adult education is literacy retention. While the number of adult literates has increased, the demand for post-literacy materials has not kept pace. With the recognition that literacy materials for neo-literates must be relevant to the needs of a largely rural population has been a shift to themes of health, nutrition and agriculture that directly impact the qualify of life in rural areas. Consequently, the Department of Adult Education is currently seeking funding for the wide-spread dissemination of post-literacy materials produced by UNICEF's GOBI project. GOBI is the acronym that stands for Growth charts monitoring a child's nutrition rate; Oral rehydration therapy; Breastfeeding; and Immunization. UNICEF has produced simple reading materials for the purpose of educating mothers to each one of the four foundations of child health with the long-range goal of reducing infant mortality. Additional materials will be produced by other organizations around the themes of family planning and family life education.

Finally, in order to make literacy more relevant to the needs of women in rural areas, the Department of Education in cooperation with the Women's Bureau (Ministry of Culture and Social Services) and Maendeleo Ya Wanawake (Progress of Women) Organization, which serves as an umbrella organization for local self-help groups, is exploring ways of integrating literacy with existing women's group activities.

Addressing the Educational Needs of Women

In the wake of the UN Decade of Women Conference held in Nairobi, 1985, renewed attention is focussed upon the educational needs of women in developing countries. While the 1967 UN *Declaration on the Elimination of Discrimination Against Women* and the *Convention on the Elimination of All Forms of Discrimination Against Women* (1981) make significant recommendations (see Chapter 3, this volume), the *Forward-Looking Strategies of Implementation For The Advancement of Women* (1985) outlines specific obstacles to equality, development and peace, and recommends concrete measures for overcoming such obstacles. The document addresses obstacles to equality in both formal and nonformal education, including equity in educational facilities and school equipment, prevention of female educational wastage and a vigorous commitment to eradicating female adult illiteracy.

While the ratio of female-to-male participation is nearly equal at the first level of education in Kenya, at the secondary level female participation lags (39 percent) and at the tertiary level it is significantly small, with female students registered at the University of Nairobi accounting for less than 20 percent of the total student population (Eshiwani, 1983). At the adult level, no break-down by sex is available except in literacy classes where women account for 80 percent of the participants nationwide.

Though women predominate in literacy classes, the number who actually attend is far less than those who have never attended. In an educational survey of 176 adult rural women in Bungoma and Kirinyaga Districts (1983–1984), one of the authors found that only 37, or 21 percent, had ever attended an adult education class and many of those had dropped out after a short period of time. The most often cited reasons for non-attendance are too much work, poor health or eyesight, and lack of relevancy to the immediate socioeconomic needs of the respondent. Consequently, adult educators in Kenya are exploring ways in which literacy can be integrated with existing development programs for women rather than offered as a separate class at the end of the day.

The Tototo-Kilemba approach to education for rural development offers a model. Tototo-Kilemba refers to a women's self-help group established in eastern Kenya which has four goals: income-generation, nutrition education, literacy, and community problem-solving. The philosophy of the group is that "learning should be organized within the context of community development as perceived by the participants" (Gakuru and Clark, 1980, p. 4). By integrating literacy and numeracy skills with the other three areas, the women's group members see the usefulness of literacy.

The women's self-help movement which has cultural antecedents in mutual aid and cooperative labor groups in Kenya, accelerated in the late 1970s as a result of the UN Decade of Women so that by 1983–1984, 16,346 women's groups had registered with the Women's Bureau (Mbeo, 1985, personal communication). Because such groups already have an organizational structure and self-articulated goals often involving income-generating activities, they provide a receptive environment for non-formal education. Rural women see their groups as educative agents where learning and teaching are reciprocal—"We put up lessons for those not in school" was the way one Kirinyaga woman phrased it (Davison, 1984, p. 15).

The needs of women's groups are often similar—to improve their homesteads and agricultural production, collective farming, livestock rearing, leadership training and literacy. In order to implement specific projects, women organize themselves to learn particular skills and knowledge associated with each project, often inviting government extension workers to assist them. The mode of learning is through observation and demonstration—seeing and doing. Women are taught how to set up a bakery, a tree nursery, or a bee-keeping project through visits to similar women's projects. Capital is raised through member contributions, loans, and/or donations

from private and public organizations and in the process women learn
record-keeping and banking skills. In addition to raising the socio-economic
status of the group's women, the non-formal education provided by the
groups build self-reliance and confidence among semi-literate and nonliterate women who may never have had the opportunity to be self-
supporting. Such education is relevant because it is both practical and
participatory and thus meets the objectives of the 1976 Recommendation on
the Development of Adult Education adopted by UNESCO. For this
reason, literacy education will be most useful if it is integrated with women's
groups' programs.

Adult Education for the Disabled

Two UN documents protect the rights of disabled persons—the 1971
Declaration on the Rights of Mentally Retarded Persons and the 1975
Declaration on the Rights of Disabled Persons. During 1981–1982,
UNESCO organized a series of seminars for the East African region in
Nairobi on special education to meet the needs of the disabled. While
recognizing that the education and training of disabled persons is necessary,
the 1975 declaration acknowledged that developing nations are able to apply
only "limited efforts" to achieve such ends in view of other educational
priorities. The UN International Year of the Disabled Person further
highlighted the need to design educational programs that would allow for
full participation and equality.

In Kenya, special education programs are addressed to the needs of four
categories of disabled: the blind, hearing impaired, physically disabled and
mentally disabled. Thus, the classification more nearly resembles the
Indonesian case described by Thomas (see Chapter 4, this volume) than that
of an industrialized nation like the United States. While most of the
attention in Kenya has been directed toward special programs for children,
there is increasing awareness on the Government's part of the need to
provide special adult education for the disabled and those teaching disabled
persons. To this end, the Ministry of Education now provides training for
teachers working with mentally and visually handicapped children at
Highridge Teachers College while Kamwenja Teachers Training College
trains adults working with the hearing impaired (Kilonzo, 1984). Thika High
School for the Blind outside Nairobi caters to young adults, while several
vocational training centers have been set up to meet the special needs of
blind adults including Machakos Vocational Centre, Kapenguria Sheltered
Workshop and Sikri Agricultural Training Centre for the Blind and Deaf
(Kilonzo, 1984, p. 10). Additionally, a number of organizations such as the
Kenya Society for the Mentally Handicapped, Kenya Society for the Blind
and the Association for the Physically Disabled of Kenya, which often
include disabled members, provide educational facilities for adults.

Traditionally, African societies had few persons recognized as disabled and those few were integrated into and taken care of by the extended family. Consequently, there was little awareness of the specific problems of the disabled. Given such widespread lack of awareness, the Kenya government has undertaken a campaign to educate a wider audience to an acceptance of disabled persons and their special needs through radio and television programs. Thus, through the encouragement of UNESCO in the early 1980s, Kenya's thrust in special education for adults has been twofold; to provide training for the disabled and to educate the Kenyan society to an acceptance of disabled persons and a recognition of their special needs. Throughout its efforts to meet the needs of disabled learners, the Government has sought advice of the disabled and has incorporated disabled participants in designing programs to meet their needs. Therefore, Kenya's effort with respect to expanding the rights of disabled learners more nearly meets the objectives of the 1976 UNESCO document on adult education, that advocate including the needs of participants and use of their different experiences in planning and implementing programs, than has occurred in the cases of nonliterates and women. While women's participation in designing programs at the national level is solicited, few women at the sub-locational level have been included in the decision-making process until very recently. Nor has there been much attempt to include rural nonliterates in designing and evaluating literacy programs. At the same time, literacy has stimulated an interest in social and economic development and in reading. Thus, Kenya's efforts to expand adult educational opportunities contrast markedly with those of the United States which has a much longer history of formal education based in local communities.

The US Experience

Background

The United States provides an example of a nation which has a long tradition of providing free, open and compulsory public schooling for its youth and vast educational opportunities for its adult population. In the past, adult education in the United States depended on voluntary efforts. In 1730, Benjamin Franklin established the "Junto," which was a continuing inquiry group to discuss important ideas, and organized the Philadelphia Library to house books which could be read and discussed by the Junto. The establishment of the Lyceum in 1826 was aimed at enabling members to study and share knowledge, and within less than a decade, several thousand lyceums were in operation. The Mechanics Institute, which began in 1831, provided a variety of agricultural, science and history programs for workers. In 1874, the Chautauqua Institute was created to train Sunday school teachers, but the Chautauqua movement soon became a national movement providing liberal arts education at different sites and by correspondence.

Public resources, such as libraries and school and university outreach programs, became a focus of adult education. Land grant institutions such as the universities of Wisconsin, California, and Minnesota were the forerunners in providing extension and continuing education programs. Agricultural extension, which was based on the Morrill Act of 1862 and the Hatch Act of 1887, set out to interpret scientific data to farmers by offering demonstrations and relevant programs. And subsequent legislation and expenditures over the decades through the 1970s have expanded human rights to lifelong education opportunities.

Sources of Adult Education

According to the National Center for Education Statistics (US Bureau of the Census, 1984), the first major source of adult education in the United States is public schools and postsecondary institutions. Public schools offer a variety of options such as the adult school, adult classes in the afternoon and evening, trade and vocational schools and programs. Community colleges usually offer three kinds of classes: credit, non-credit and community service. Colleges and universities provide extension education including off-campus courses, tele-communication programs, internships and correspondence programs in addition to non-traditional study. The second major source of lifelong learning opportunities is the non-school sector which includes community organizations, professional and labor associations, business and industry, government agencies, tutorials and others. In most cities, programs are offered to adults and children by museums, libraries, recreational agencies and religious institutions. Employers represent the third largest providers of adult education. Most large corporations in the United States have their in-house training programs for their employees. Some have contracts with universities for specialized programs. Some, such as Xerox, have established their own campuses and their own cadre of instructors. Courses offered by such corporations are often approved for transfer by colleges and universities. The courses cover a range from the job-related skills to academic skills and graduate level technical subjects.

With the proliferation of providers of lifelong education, a large array of programs and courses has become evident from the highly specialized topics to the more general areas of study. Among the major offerings in adult education are the basic skills, vocational, technical, liberal arts, sciences, recreational, personal development, parenting and family support, community and civic development and general and cultural enrichment.

Participation in Adult Education

According to National Center for Education Statistics (NCES, 1983), adult participation in adult education has increased by 30.8 percent between 1969 and 1975, and by 20.6 percent between 1975 and 1981. Several factors expanded the participation of adults in lifelong learning activities. First, the "baby boom" generation of the 1950s was now into the ranks of adults. Improvements in health care have also contributed to longer life spans among Americans, so there were more adults in 1981, totaling over 272 million (NCES, 1983). Second, the changing economic conditions are forcing many people to update skills, learn to perform in new job settings and acquire new skills not required before such as tele-communications and computers. Third, the continuous push for ending job discrimination and for enhancing equal work opportunities for all Americans, as reflected by various laws and regulations, such as Title IX and affirmative action programs, spurred on the training of new entrants to the world of work and to the new avenues for upward economic mobility. Fourth, we have been undergoing a revolution in the expansion of knowledge making it imperative for people to seek new information in order to cope, adjust, and progress in an age of rapid change.

The definition of adult education and the differing questions used by surveys in this field influence the reported rate of participation. If the survey defines adult learning as self-directed learning, it could find, as Tough (1971) did, that 98 percent of the adults are engaged in lifelong education. But if the survey defines adult learning as participation in organized instruction as NCES (1983) did, it could come up with as low a rate of participation as 12.8 percent. Still, if the survey restricts its definition of adult education to learning for academic credit or certificates, the rate of participation becomes even lower. But a 27–33 percent range would seem to be a reasonable estimate of adult participation.

Previous education, age and area of domicile seem to be associated with participation in adult education. The rate of participation in adult education increases with the increasing educational level of participants. Those who had 5 or more years in college had 31.1 percent participation rate in adult education as compared to the 2.2 percent rate for those who had 8 years of schooling or less. There is a general agreement among researchers that educational background has a positive impact on participation in adult learning.

Older adults, 55 years and over, tend to have the lowest participation rate as compared with younger adults; in 1981 more women were participants than men. Several factors could have contributed to the increased participation of women in adult education. Clearly, there has been a change in women's roles and options from traditional homemakers, who had limited career options, to emancipated persons who now have the opportunity to choose from expanding career options. The American women's movement brought about greater awareness of women's rights and needs which in turn led to various laws protecting equal opportunity and equal worth, and making sex discrimination illegal in the halls of academe and in the marketplace. In addition, technological advances resulted in time-saving devices at home providing women with more time to pursue other interests. Furthermore, high divorce rates and changing economic needs of families, coupled with expanding career opportunities, have stimulated many women to return to school to improve their skills and enhance their employment alternatives.

Even though the rates of participation are lower for Black and Hispanic adults than for White adults, ethnicity, according to some writers, may not have a direct effect on the rate of participation. What affects participation are such related factors as previous level of education and motivation. White high school dropouts are less likely to participate in adult education than Black college graduates (Cross, 1981). However, this writer argues that the participation of high income adults regardless of ethnicity, is greater than that of lower income adults because poverty tends to hinder the degree of schooling and the motivation to pursue further studies. Hence, White and ethnic persons with lower economic backgrounds are less likely to participate in adult learning than economically-privileged Whites and ethnic individuals.

Focussing on the specific economic and civic rewards of adult education, data from the US Office of Vocational and Adult Education indicate that as a consequence of being enrolled in an adult education program, 117,000 adults acquired a job in 1981, approximately 74,000 advanced to better positions and 141,000 pursued further training. In the same year, 38,000 adults were removed from public assistance and over 40,000 voted for the first time (Federal focus, 1985).

Current Issues

It is commonly agreed that a great deal of money is expended on adult education in the United States, if one adds public funds spent by federal, state and local authorities, to all private expenditures. But it is also evident that the federal government and most states lack a clear policy regarding adult education. Furthermore, in the current era of large budget deficits, budget cuts have begun to reduce expenditures on adult education on national, state and local levels. These cuts underscore our lack of total commitment as a people to the continuous investment in our adult citizens' education.

Even though strides have been made in extending educational opportunities to more adults in the United States, the task by no means is complete. Concerted efforts should be made to provide adult education opportunities to more segments of the population such as the economically-disadvantaged, minorities, the non-English speaking, migrant workers, women, the elderly, the handicapped and the functionally and marginally illiterate, to enable them to fully exercise their rights to lifelong education. There are about 27 million Americans who are illiterates today, and 44 percent of Blacks and 56 percent of Hispanics are considered to be functionally or marginally illiterate (Kozol, 1985). Programs addressed to their literacy needs would expand their opportunities for further adult education.

Therefore, in order to guarantee the adult's right to lifelong education, there is a need to establish a national comprehensive policy on lifelong learning, in partnership with the states which spells out clearly the responsibilities of each partner and places adult development as a priority on the national agenda. This policy should be supported by continuous funding and coordination among federal, state and local agencies. Further, data sources need to be established on the quality of adult programs, their staff and clientele, and the effects of these programs on personal, community and national development. There is a need to publicize relevant, multi-lingual, inexpensive, and accessible classes and activities to attract more under-educated adults and expand opportunities to adult education and constructive citizenship. The changing national and state manpower and human needs in the United States must continually be examined in order to adequately plan and implement economic and human development programs in this country and enhance the opportunities for employment and mobility to all citizens.

In summary, adult education in the United States is pluralistic and decentralized and it has greatly been expanded over the years to more adults despite occasional budget belt-tightening and cyclical economic downturns. Access to lifelong education and the quality of what is being offered will be enhanced by strong national and state commitments and a clear vision of how to provide greater learning opportunities for all citizens now and in the future.

Conclusion

The needs of adult learners in a developed country such as the United States are very different from adult learners in a developing African country such as Kenya. Whereas the emphasis in many American adult education programs is upon retraining, advanced training or enrichment in specialized fields due to the rapid change in business and industry, adult education in Kenya focusses on development education by stressing basic skills in literacy and numeracy, health education and nutrition, as well as inservice training and distance education. Though the United States has a much longer history in the field of nationally recognized formal education, Kenya has made great strides toward achieving equality of opportunity in education in a few short years since independence in 1963. In fact, Kenya's total educational expenditures on education in 1981 constituted the same percentage (6.8 percent) of the national product as the United States for the same year (UNESCO, 1984).

Judged by the UNESCO recommendations from the Nairobi conference, how well are Kenya and the United States implementing the recommendations on adult education? It is evident that Kenya has followed the UNESCO precepts and that the United States had many of these precepts incorporated in their programs even before the UNESCO declarations.

While both countries have attempted to emphasize personal development, the participation of individual adults and groups in decision making at all levels of the learning process has been peripheral and often an after-the-fact process. Furthermore, while adult education is aimed at personal and community development, there are no longitudinal studies of how such learning contributes to an individual's or a community's lifelong development.

Kenya, a relatively small country with a predominantly rural population, addresses the needs of adult learners at the national level. Because the country has high unemployment and school-leaver rates, the central government initiates short-term planning goals that are incrementally defined. Kenya's national policy focusses on literacy and vocational training which are implemented by various government ministries, university, and private agencies. In the United States, on the other hand, adult education is decentralized, with most policy decisions occurring at the state and local levels. For this reason, there are few federal manpower studies related to adult learning needs and there is no comprehensive national policy on adult education comparable to that of Kenya.

The Kenyan use of educational media, such as radio and television, in adult education is increasing but it has a long way to go to catch up with the technological advances which allow the United States to deliver courses via satellites, sound and video tapes, television, movies, computers and an enormous variety of educational materials. As the use of telecommunications media in adult education increases, it is evident that both countries need to train more qualified teachers to work with a broad spectrum of media and with different adults in various fields of study. Teachers need to learn the needs of special groups of adults, the strategies best suited for them and the methods of involving them as active learners.

In both countries, adult education policies clearly indicate the desire to produce self-reliant, confident adults capable of making decisions that enhance their own self-development as well as that of their social communities. Though faced with very different economic and sociocultural circumstances, there is no doubt that progress has been made in both Kenya and the United States to expand educational opportunities to include more adults. Through continued efforts, the future in both nations bodes greater progress toward the goal of achieving the right of every individual to participate in lifelong education.

References

Best, A. C. and DeBlij, H. J. (1977) *African Survey.* New York: John Wiley and Sons.

Coombs, P. H. (1985) *The world crisis in education: A view from the eighties.* New York: Oxford University Press.

Cropley, A. (Ed.) (1980) *Towards a system of lifelong education.* Hamburg: Pergamon Press and the UNESCO Institute for Higher Education.

Cross, K. P. (1981) *Adults as learners.* San Francisco: Jossey-Bass.

Darkenwald, G. G. and Merriam, S. B. (1982) *Adult education: Foundation of Practice.* San Francisco: Jossey-Bass.

Davison, J. (1984) Adult basic education: The needs of rural women. *Berc Bulletin* **9,** 14–18. Nairobi: Kenyatta University College, Basic Education Resource Center.

Davison, J. (1985) Achievements and constraints among rural Kenyan women: A case study. In G. S. Were (Ed.), *Women and development in Africa* (pp. 268–279). Nairobi: Gideon S. Were Press.

Dewey, J. (1938) *Experience and education.* New York: Macmillan.

Eshiwani, G. S. (Ed.) (1983) *A study of women's access to higher education in Kenya with a special reference to mathematics and science education.* Nairobi: Kenyatta University College, Bureau of Education Research.

Federal focus (1985) *Thrust for educational leadership,* **15,** 26.

Gakuru, N. and Clark, N. (1980) Preliminary finding of Tototo-Kilemba approach to education for rural develoment. *Kenya Journal of Adult Education,* **8**(2), 4–8.

Gichuru, F. X. (1984) Education for all: Thrusts of UNESCO before the year 2000. *Berc Bulletin,* **9,** 3–7.

Kagia, R. (1983) Sex differences in educational opportunities. In G. S. Eshiwani (Ed.), *Report of the National Seminar on Women's Access to Higher Education* (pp. 79–83). Nairobi: Kenyatta University Bureau of Educational Research.

Kenya. Department of Adult Education (1985) *Towards elimination of illiteracy: Kenyan perspective and suggestions for a regional programme.* Nairobi: Author (Mimeograph).

Kenya. Ministry of Economic Planning and Development (1983) *Kenya: Development plan: 1984–1988. Nairobi: Government Printer.*

Kenyatta, J. (1968) *Facing Mt. Kenya.* London: Secker & Warburg (originally published 1938).

Kilonzo, F. M. (1984) Current services for special education in Eastern Africa—A report. *Berc. Bulletin,* **9,** 6–11. Nairobi: Kenyatta University College, Basic Education Resource Centre.

Kozol, J. (1985) *Illiterate America.* Garden City, NY: Anchor Press.

Lowe, J. (1982) *Education for adults: A world perspective.* Paris: UNESCO, Oise Press.

M'Beo, A. (1983) Education for All. *UNESCO Courier,* (5), 3.

National Center for Education Statistics (1983) *Digest of education statistics.* Washington, DC: US. GPO.

Odhiambo, D. and Macharia, D. (1985) The Kenyan experience. In P. Fordham, (Ed.), *One billion illiterates: One billion reasons for action* (pp. 144–158). Toronto, Ontario: International Council for Adult Education and Bonn, Germany: Deutsche Stiftung fur internationale Entwicklung (DSE).

Skager, R. and Dave, R. H. (1977) *Curriculum evaluation for lifelong education.* Oxford: Pergamon Press and the UNESCO Institute for Higher Education.

Tough, A. (1971) *The adult's learning projects: A fresh approach to theory and practice in adult learning.* Toronto: Ontario Institute for Studies in Education.

UNESCO (1972) *Learning to be.* Paris: UNESCO.

UNESCO (1976) *Recommendation on the development of adult education.* Nairobi General conference. Paris: UNESCO.

UNESCO (1984) *Statistical yearbook.* Paris: UNESCO.

US Bureau of the Census (1984) *Statistical abstract of the United States: 1985.* Washington, DC: US, GPO.

CHAPTER 9

The Rights of Parents, Students and Teachers in Canada and the Philippines

Romulo Magsino
Educational Foundations,
Memorial University of Newfoundland,
St. John's, Newfoundland,
Canada

Introduction

Formulation of international documents which define individual and group rights is premised on the assumption that such rights will be officially recognized and provided for by various national governments. Not unexpectedly, governments of different countries appear to respond to international documents in varied ways. Thus, apparently, the Philippines and Canada are perceived differently by the world community with respect to their commitments to human rights documents produced by the United Nations or any of its many agencies. Having issued several reports detailing national efforts to implement these rights, Canada has frequently appeared as a commendable example of a democratic society which guarantees rights to its citizens. On the other hand, subjected to martial law for a number of years and freed from an autocratic rule only recently, the Philippines has been criticized for gross violations of human rights (Amnesty International Mission, 1976).

Ascertaining the fidelity of various countries to the rights identified in international documents requires extensive study. This paper contributes towards that study by exploring comparatively the rights of parents, students and teachers in the Philippines and Canada. In pursuing this objective, the author will refer to specific statements on rights of parents, students and teachers in these two countries and then proceed to indicate the provisions that have been made to meet such statements. Outstanding problems in both countries will also be explored.

International Instruments[1] on Parents, Students and Teachers

In contrast with other identifiable groups (e.g., women, prisoners, disabled persons, etc.),[2] parents, students, and teachers have not yet been singled out for special attention in international documents by the United Nations or its agencies. However, references to rights that relate to such specific groups are scattered, even if sparsely, in these documents. Thus, parental rights may be inferred from Article 12 of the *Universal Declaration of Human Rights* which prohibits arbitrary interference with one's family or home. Article 16, which is echoed as Article 10, 1 in the *International Covenant on Economic, Social and Cultural Rights*, establishes entitlement of the family to protection by society and the state. Article 26, 3 declares that parents have a prior right to choose the kind of education that shall be given to their children. Parental choice of education for their children receives further elaboration in the *International Covenant on Economic, Social and Cultural Rights* whose Article 13 binds the states to respect parental right to establish and direct educational institutions and to send their children to non-governmental schools in order to ensure the young's religious and moral education in conformity with parental convictions. This right is reiterated in the *International Covenant on Civil and Political Rights* (Art. 18, 4) as well as in the *Convention against Discrimination in Education* (Art. 5, 1, b).

The student right to education is asserted in the *Universal Declaration of Human Rights* which mandates (in Art. 26) free education at elementary and fundamental stages, enjoins states to make technical and professional education generally available, and requires equal accessibility to higher education on the basis of merit. It also states what it perceives to be the aims of education, namely, the "full development of the human personality"; "the strengthening of respect for human rights and fundamental freedoms"; "promotion of understanding, tolerance and friendship among all nations and social or religious groups"; and "furthering the activities of the United Nations for the maintenance of peace". Similar provisions are found in the *International Covenant on Economic, Social and Cultural Rights* (Art. 13, 1), in the *International Convention on the Elimination of All Forms of Racial Discrimination* (Art. 5, d, v), and in the *Convention against Discrimination in Education* (Arts. 4 and 5). While not addressing students directly, other international documents such as the *Declaration of the Rights of the Child,* the *Declaration on the Promotion among Youth of the Ideals of Peace, Mutual Respect and Understanding between Peoples,* the *Declaration on the*

---

[1] Unless otherwise indicated, the international documents referred to are found in the United Nation's *Human Rights: A Compilation of International Instruments* (1978).

[2] UN documents singling out specific groups are, for example, *Declaration on the Elimination of Discrimination against Women, Declaration of the Rights of Disabled Persons,* and *Declaration of the Rights of the Child.* These and others are summarized in the appendix of the book.

rights of Mentally Retarded Persons, and the *Declaration on the Rights of Disabled Persons*, carry ramifications for the rights of students.

International documents hardly ever mention teachers and their rights. Article 13, 2, e. of the *Universal Declaration* states, however, that "material conditions of teaching staff shall be continuously improved." Moreover, a special Intergovernmental Conference convened by UNESCO in 1966 adopted the *Recommendation Concerning the Status of Teachers*. This document separately itemizes specific professional freedoms and rights of teachers apart from many other teacher entitlements related to further professional education, advancement and promotion, tenure, disciplinary procedures, and medical examinations, among other things. Further, it enumerates teacher entitlements to conditions of effective teaching such as class size, hours of work, ancillary staff, teacher aides, annual holidays with pay, leaves of absence, and others.

Despite the paucity of specific statements on parent, student, and teacher rights, one might well insist that the rights of these groups are not limited to these statements. Insofar as they are human beings just like every other, they are entitled to human rights set down in the international documents.

Formal Statements on Rights: The Philippines

Philippine justice within which rights of parents, students, and teachers could be located is based on diverse elements. It has been affected by a substratum of native customary law which shaped and reflected the attitudes and beliefs of the people towards the law and its administration. Its chief ingredients consist of a distinctive combination of civil (Roman) law and the common law. The civil law foundations of Philippine justice took roots through three centuries of Spanish rule; the principles and procedures of common law developed as a result of a half-century of American tutelage in the art of self-government. Thus, the body of Philippine law today largely includes several codes (e.g., Civil Code, Penal Code, etc.) and a large number of statutes, as well as "judge-made" laws and a (1973) constitution which incorporates many legal principles similar to those found in its American counterpart (Hayden, 1972).

Parental Rights

Catholicism, imbedded in the Filipino way of life by Spanish missionaries and through the nation's long colonial status, inevitably helped establish the primacy of the family as the basic institution in the country. Thus, it is not surprising to discover that international human rights statements on the protection of the family have their counterpart in the *Philippine Constitu-*

tion, 1973.[3] Its Art. II, Section 4, reads: "The State shall strengthen the family as a basic social institution." Pre-dating this constitution, the *Civil Code of the Philippines, 1949* contains several principles related to the family as an institution including a ban on any agreement or custom which destroys the family (Art. 218) and an assertion that "In case of doubt, all presumptions favour the solidarity of the family" (Art. 220).

Family solidarity in the Philippine setting clearly involves parental authority. The *Code* (Art. 220) goes on to say that "Every intendment of law or fact leans towards . . . the authority of parents over children. . . ." *Presidential Decree No. 603*, 1974 (known as the *Child and Youth Welfare Code*), enunciates the parents' primary right to their children's upbringing, particularly "in relation to all other persons or institutions dealing with children's development" (Art. 43), and affirms their right to discipline their offspring (Art. 45).

The primary right of the parents to provide for the upbringing of their children has given rise to certain corollary rights explicitly recognized by law. The *Constitution* declares that "The natural right and duty of parents in the rearing of the youth . . . shall receive the aid and support of the government" (Art. II, 4). A more concrete expression of this principle is found in the *Education Act, 1982* (Sec. 5, 1) and in the *Civil Code* which requires the government to establish schools in every locality in the country (Art. 359, 1). Parents who have children enrolled in such schools have the right to organize themselves to discuss matters related to the total school program, and to gain access to their children's school records (*Education Act, 1982*, Sec. 8).

The right of parents or private individuals to establish private schools has had a long tradition in the Philippines. Indeed, as in many other countries, educational endeavor in the country was begun by missionaries and private individuals seeking to provide basic attainments for the people. They retain the right formally to establish schools provided they conform to procedures and requirements for incorporation of private schools as specified by law.[4] Even in public schools, the right of parents to have their religious convictions transmitted to their young is also assured. Thus, Article XV, Sec. 8 of the *Constitution* guarantees the teaching of religion in public elementary and secondary schools without cost to parents (or the government) upon their request in writing.

---

[3] President Corazon Aquino has recently announced the dissolution of the Philippine Parliament and the formation of a body which will formulate a new constitution (*Citizen, Ottawa*, March 26, 1986, p. A7). It is very likely, however, that present constitutional provisions affecting education will remain largely untouched.

[4] A change in requirements occurred in 1982 when the *Education Act* stipulated that new private schools to be established must incorporate as non-stock educational corporations. However, existing stock schools are not affected by this requirement. Through private schools, whether religious or secular, parents are provided the choice in the education of their children (Dizon, 1983, pp. 47–48).

Student Rights

The Philippine Constitution declares that the State shall promote the physical, intellectual and social well-being of the youth (Art. II, 5). In pursuit of this policy, the *Child and Youth Welfare Code* specifies in Article 8 that "In all questions regarding the care, custody, education and property of the child, his welfare shall be the paramount consideration."

With such explicit concern for the young, it is not surprising that the Philippine government should come up with bold statements concerning their rights in education. The *Constitution* (Art. XV, 4) requires the government to maintain a system of free public elementary education and to establish and maintain a system of free public education at least up to the secondary level in areas where finances permit. Presupposing the existence of systems of education, the *Education Act* stipulates, as a matter of policy, that the state shall safeguard the welfare and interests of students (Sec. 5, 2), and then enumerates nine rights for students. In addition to all these, the *Child and Youth Welfare Code* specifies that no child shall be refused admission to public schools (Art. 71); that assistance to parents to ensure children's attendance may take various forms such as school supplies and lunches, etc. (Art. 72); that public nursery and kindergarten schools shall be maintained whenever possible (Art. 73); that there shall be at least classes for special children in every province and, if possible, special schools for the physically handicapped, the mentally retarded, the emotionally disturbed, and the specially gifted (Art. 74); and that officials shall ensure provisions for adequate classrooms, facilities, and hazard-free environment for the young as well as free access to dental and medical services (Art. 75).

Teacher Rights

Compared with statements on parental or student rights, those on rights of teachers are just as extensive. The *Civil Code* states that teachers and professors shall exercise substitute parental authority (Art. 349) and exercise reasonable supervision over the conduct of the child (Art. 350). Expressly, however, they are prohibited from using corporal punishment. Not unexpectedly, the *Education Act* incorporates a list of rights for all school personnel (Sec. 10) which applies to teachers and another list of special rights (Sec. 11) for teaching or academic staff. However, the 1966 *Magna Carta for Public School Teachers (Republic Act No. 4670)*, together with its implementing *Rules and Regulations*, could prove to be the most extensive listing of rights for teachers anywhere. Pre-dating the UNESCO *Recommendation Concerning the Status of Teachers* with which it shares similar provisions, the Filipino teachers' *Magna Carta* includes items related to their entitlements with respect to probationary period, tenure, transfer, safeguards in disciplinary or administrative proceedings, conditions of work, salaries, allowances, other benefits, leaves of absences, and organizational rights and freedoms. Such rights are slightly modified, and supplemented, by *Presidential Decree No. 1006* (1976) which aims at the professionalization of teachers and at regulating their practice in the country.

Formal Statement on Rights: Canada

A sharp contrast immediately arises as we move from Philippine law to Canadian law. Evident in the preceding discussion is the assumption that the rights enumerated apply to all parents, students and teachers across the Philippine archipelago. Confronting a nation made up of 1,007 islands and of 87 language groups, national authorities—whether colonial or Filipino— have been compelled to adopt centralized mechanisms to counteract disper- sive forces in the country. A central government implementing uniform laws throughout the country has thus been a necessity. In sharp contrast, as a confederation of provinces zealously guarding provincial rights, Canada came into existence through compromises in the allocation of federal and provincial powers.

The *Canadian Constitution* grants the federal government jurisdiction over marriage and divorce, and the provincial governments jurisdiction over solemnization of marriage as well as property and civil laws. Further, criminal law is left with the former, while authority to make laws dealing with children and their welfare is vested in the latter. This division of powers has resulted in some awkward arrangements and has required special efforts to avoid duplication of activities. The allocation of governance over children and over educational matters to provincial governments has also meant that some degree of variation can be found in the legislation concerning these two areas. Similarities are pervasive, however, and this section of the chapter shall concentrate on them.

Parental Rights

A former British colony and still attached to her mother country, all of Canada (with the exception of Quebec) has inherited the system of common law. In common law countries, the interrelationships between the parent and the child remained for a long time a subject of ethical and moral standards rather than of enforceable laws. Still, common law recognizes some degree of parents rights to custody or possession of their children, to visit the child (when separated from the parent), to determine his or her education and comportment, to determine religious upbringing, to disci- pline the child, to choose medical treatment, to consent to marriage, to consent to the child's adoption, and to appoint guardians (Eekelaar, 1973).

In Canada, the family has enjoyed the right to function with minimum interference, particularly from the state, and intervention is seen as justified only in cases of significant parental fault (Canadian Council on Children and Youth, 1979: 60 ff.). It remains true, however, that rapid social change and appalling family conditions during the last century have resulted in the enactment of legislation to provide children with needed care and protection (Sutherland, 1976). The result is an uneasy tension between the tradition of parental control and the principle of the best interests of the child. The ambivalence is apparent in various provincial legislations on child welfare and the family in the country (Schlosser, 1984).[5] In any case nowhere in these legislations can be found an explicit enumeration of parental rights so prominently etched in relevant codes in the Philippines.

Erosion of parental rights in Canada is most apparent in education. Development of extensive systems of schools in each province has been accompanied by the accumulation of administrative institutional policy and decision-making which has curtailed parental control of the education of their children. Nevertheless, educational statutes and case law have formally recognized and provided for parental right with respect to religious education. Also, in most provinces, parental choice in education is formally and effectively recognized through a system of separate religious school systems and secular private schools (Bargen, 1961; Wilson, 1981).

Student Rights

The Canadian concern for the well-being of the young is reflected in numerous provincial statutes that justify state intervention in several areas involving the child and his family. While traditionally, children have received protection only where marked parental abuse or neglect is present, more recent developments have broadened the nature of parental fault.

Court decisions on educational cases also reflect some recognition of an identifiable right for the young. Thus, in the *McLeod* case (1952), the court said that, in coming to its decision, it was compelled to regard the interests of children as paramount, that these interests were inherent in the province's schools act, and that all its provisions . . . must be read in that light. Indeed, as Parry (1975) shows, case law has firmly established the right of the pupil to receive from teachers and educational officials the care and protection that a judicious parent would give to the child.

In Canada, provincial schools acts grant schools the power to control the conduct of pupils. This power, based not only on the doctrine of *in loco parentis* but also on the need to maintain order for educational purposes, has been generally respected by the courts (Bargen, 1961). With a long tradition of autonomy, school boards have so enjoyed discretionary powers that recognizing and providing for student rights have remained slow processes,

[5] The Canadian Council on Children and Youth (1979) has compiled a comprehensive list of statutes related to children in various provinces.

particularly in relation to their exercise of civil and political rights (Sweezy, 1969). However, the picture looks much brighter in relation to welfare-oriented rights (Magsino, 1977–1978), such as access to education and to educational provisions appropriate to one's needs, for which relevant statutes have been legislated in various provinces. As will be noted later, however, some vexing shorcomings are still encountered.

Teacher Rights

Common law tradition, which defines the school board-teacher relationship as one between master and servant or between employer and employee, has served as the framework for teacher rights in Canada. The details of this relationship have become very complicated over the years and now many different legal sources of teacher rights are involved (MacKay, 1984). For educational purposes, each province has statute laws, regulations which implement them, and quasi-judicial bodies (e.g., board of reference) partly responsible for carrying out specific provisions of the laws. Moreover, the courts have developed a body of case law which has clarified statutory provisions affecting teachers (McCurdy, 1968, Chapter 3). All these have contributed towards teacher security and well-being *vis-à-vis* occasional capricious and malicious actions by school boards, particularly in relation to dismissals and promotion.

Clearly, however, the formation of professional organizations in the provinces must be regarded as one of the most salient factors in the growth and protection of teacher rights in Canada. As Nediger (1981) has pointed out, teacher organizations using collective bargaining as a powerful weapon have brought about significant changes not only to school board-teacher relationships but also the process of decision-making on educational policies. Presently, salary, condition of employment and, in general, all economic concerns of teachers are legitimate areas for negotiation between teacher organizations and school boards under collective bargaining statutes.

What is notable in all this is that, with respect to the entitlements of Canadian teachers, students, or parents, we do not generally find them enumerated explicitly as rights in any specific document(s). However, this fact has not prevented these groups from enjoying a substantial number of rights within educational systems.

The Reality of Rights in Education

Official recognition of rights in public documents paves the way for their exercise. Unfortunately, there is very often no guarantee that enjoyment of rights will be attained even with the best of intentions in such documents. It is apparent that, in varying ways, both the Philippines and Canada have made valiant attempts to provide for the rights they have officially recognized. It also appears that more can be done. This section will highlight a number of current achievements and possible areas for future efforts.

The Philippine Situation[6]

Philippine efforts in education throughout the 1900s have been remarkable. Whether intended to promote social welfare, to aid parents in the education of their young, or to ensure children's well-being, expenditures in education and the associated growth of the educational enterprise reveal a national commitment that belies economic difficulties. The educational enterprise has always demanded a substantial share of expenditures, devouring between 11 to 16 percent of the annual national budget in the 1980s. The 1984 allocation, for example, was P8,082,376,000 (about 15.12 percent of the entire governmental appropriation). This is clearly a huge jump from the allocation for education in the amount of P194,154,899 in 1957.[7] The proposed budget for 1986 in the amount of P11.6 billion represents a P2.4 billion increase from the 1985 budget of P9.2 billion. This increased allocation, proposed despite economic dislocations following the turbulence arising from the Aquino assassination in 1983, is simply another step in the constant escalation of expenditures on education.

In 1957, the average per child allocation was P57.89. By 1983, the figure has gone up to P412 per elementary pupil and P1,102 per secondary student. In 1984, the allocation went up to P479 for the elementary pupil. Included in the education budget was the allocation for special education programs for 45,335 and 58,925 mentally gifted, retarded, behavior-problematic, hearing-impaired and physically handicapped pupils in 1983 and 1984, respectively.

Health and nutrition programs have also received attention. In 1984, a total of 650,000 public elementary pupils were examined and treated by 51

---

[6] Unless indicated otherwise, the data and information on Philippine education in this section have been drawn from

    Bulletin today. Education tops budget allotments. August 9, 1985a, 10.
    Bureau of Elementary Education, Special Education Division. Special Education: A New Deal for the Handicapped and Gifted (1983), Leaflet.
    Department of Education (Philippines). *Annual Report*, 1956–1957.
    Isidro, A., et al. *Compulsory Education in the Philippines*, 1952.
    Ministry of Education, Culture and Sports. *Annual Report*, 1983; 1984.
    Ministry of Education, Culture and Sports. *Statistical Bulletin*, 1982.
I am pleased to acknowledge the generous assistance of Dr Abraham Felipe, Deputy Minister, MECS, and of Ms Flordeliza J. Penalosa and Filipina Villapando (Information and Publication Service, MECS); Ms Susan Regalario (Planning Service, MECS); and Ms Ofelia Sinay (Special Education Project, Special Education Division, MECS).

[7] Comparative figures must be treated with caution, considering the fact that the government devalued the peso and relaxed exchange controls not only in 1960–1962 but also in 1970 (Hawkins, 1976), and that severe inflation hit the country in the first half of both the 1970s and the 1980s. In any case, the current exchange rate is around 18 pesos for every American dollar.

medical officers in different school divisions. Public health nurses participated in the control of communicable diseases through health inspection of 1,679,682 pupils. Dental services were extended to 54.4 percent of the targeted clientele. Further, under the nutrition project, supplementary snacks were distributed to 3,705,335 school children. Financial and food supplies in various forms (wheat flour, dried skim milk, rice, etc.) continued to be given to feed 880,518 underweight school children in 1985.

Finally, attention was also given to the improvement of the quality of education through textbook projects and school building programs. At the elementary level, 12,000,711 copies of textbooks and teacher materials were printed and distributed, while 1,282,352 copies were delivered to public secondary schools. At the same time, demand for new and replacement classrooms at the elementary level was met through the construction of 69,410 new classrooms from 1980 to 1984.

Meanwhile, teacher welfare was not forgotten. To help teachers meet their financial needs, flexible school work schedules have been adopted to allow them to engage in income-generating activities after work hours. Loans from the national bank have been facilitated to enable generation of backyard projects for extra income. Earlier, the former minister of education, Jaime Laya, had also directed agencies concerned to pay teachers appropriate wages for extra services such as taking the census, registering voters, counting votes during elections, and other community-helping, officially-sanctioned activities. More importantly, he had adopted measures including salary adjustments based on additional academic credits earned and years of experience gained, merit increases, over 10 percent across-the-board pay increases, P100-increase in cost-of-living allowance, and creation of 15,000 additional positions for Master Teacher I. Future measures are contained in a comprehensive financial plan already prepared and intended to make teaching positions competitive with those of other professions requiring commensurate skills and training.

Unfortunately, herculean efforts throughout the decades have not solved several serious problems and issues in Philippine education. As the National Manpower and Youth Council put it, the general problem has to do with a constantly growing school population outpacing the availability of inputs and resources in education. At all levels, but particularly at the elementary and the secondary levels, inadequacy of classrooms, teachers, textbooks, equipment, and others, prevails. Where they are available, the question of their quality remains. At the level of management of schools, it is felt that there are certain inadequacies, resulting in the failure to ensure efficiency in the administration and supervision of schools. Further, it appears that regional disposition of educational resources and opportunities is marked by unequal distribution, particularly at the disadvantage of the central and southern regions of the country (National Manpower and Youth Council, 1985, pp. 35–37). These problems have clear implications for the rights of parents, students and teachers insofar as these problems result in the failure of government to meet their entitlements.

Inadequate schooling provisions account partly for the fact that, despite the high Philippine literacy rate in comparison with other developing nations, 5.8 million (10 and older) Filipinos are unable to read and write. Their illiteracy certainly hampers their pursuit of equal opportunities in life. Equally disturbing is the fact that rural Filipinos still lag behind their urban counterparts in obtaining literacy due to concentration of better facilities and teachers in urban areas (Magno, 1984, pp. 12–13). In fact, for the majority of Filipinos, access to formal education is limited to elementary schooling, a reality not helped by failure to enforce compulsory attendance and by a high drop-out rate (*Guro*, 1984, p. 21). For those who have had access to the school system, much learning is of dubious quality. A recent survey (Torres, 1984a, p. 1) found that 30 percent of 13,600 public schools studied were substandard. This problem is not confined to public schools. Without financial support from the government, many private schools have been pushed towards not only commercialization but also towards frustrating teacher-learning conditions like large classes, inadequate equipment, and unqualified teachers (Torres, p. 3). Teacher quality, whether in public or private schools, remains a real problem. A recently publicized survey by the National Science and Technology Authority and the Ministry of Education revealed that over one-half of the country's science teachers in secondary schools are not qualified educationally and thus are in need of massive in-service training (*Bulletin Today*, 1985, p. 10).

The Canadian Situation

The willingness of the Canadian government to render reports to the United Nations with respect to the implementation of human rights in the country may well indicate its confidence that it is meeting the mandates of the international documents it has officially adopted. Of greatest relevance in this study are four reports, three of which relate to the provisions of the *International Covenant on Economic, Social and Cultural Rights*. These are the *Report of Canada* on Articles 6 to 9 (1980), on Articles 10 to 12 (1982), and on Articles 13 to 15 (1985). The fourth *Report of Canada* pertains to the implementation of the provisions of the *International Covenant on Civil and Political Rights* (1979).[8]

Canada's commitment to the principles enumerated in these documents is reflected in the mechanisms it has established to promote the implementation of such principles. Before acceding to the two international documents in 1976, the Government of Canada obtained the agreement of all the provinces to adopt the measures needed to implement the covenants in their

[8] I am pleased to acknowledge the assistance of Ms Maureen O'Brien and Mr Steve Jackman (St. John's Regional Office, Secretary of State) who kindly gave me copies of the *Reports*.

jurisdictions. In 1975, a federal-provincial conference on human rights agreed on procedures and mechanisms for implementing the two instruments. It also set up a continuing federal-provincial committee of officials responsible for human rights. This committee, which meets twice a year, has been an effective liaison between federal and provincial governments in the implementation of the Covenants. Further, the federal government has an interdepartmental committee on human rights which regularly examines questions related to the Covenants' implementation. Some of the provinces have counterpart committees.

Report of Canada (1982) in Articles 10 to 12 presents a detailed account of what both levels of government have accomplished to satisfy the requirements of these articles. From the report, it is obvious that the Canadian governments have traveled a long way in providing for the protection of the family, mothers and children (Art. 10); for the right to an adequate standard of living (Art. 11), and for the right to physical and mental health (Art. 12).

In Canada, parental right to assistance from government in the education of their young has been provided for extensively through the development of public school systems. It is worth mentioning that, despite the public school movement, parental right to educational choice has remained to a large degree.

Report of Canada (1985) in Articles 13 to 15 focusses on educational matters. While education is a provincial concern, there are pockets of federal responsibility, particularly involving children of indigenous people and of military personnel. As the *Report* notes, the federal government has succeeded in ensuring free primary and secondary education of virtually 100 percent of all these children through attendance at federal, provincial and private schools. Also, it has met its obligation related to fundamental education of adults who did not obtain schooling earlier through national training programs and through the efforts of the Department of Indian Affairs and Northern Development and of the Correctional Services of Canada. Aside from contributing financial assistance for the construction, expansion and renovation of schools, the federal government has passed legislation to ensure the material conditions of the teaching staff in federal schools and has set down guidelines on the basic remuneration and benefits of their teachers.

Clearly, however, provincial governments shoulder the bulk of the responsibility for meeting the rights of parents, students and teachers in education. There is good reason to believe that much of this responsibility is being discharged by these governments. While there are some differences in the range of educational opportunities they make available, by and large the governments are, as the *Report* shows amply, generally successful in satisfying the requirements of the relevant article in the covenant.

Such rights as are found in education and school acts and in collective bargaining agreements have seen not only implementation by relevant parties but also enforcement by the judiciary in the country. Courts have consistently upheld sections of laws which protect teachers. For example, in an early case (*Metcalfe v. Board of Trustees of Moose Jaw District No. 1*, 1938), a Saskatchewan court insisted that the right to a proper notice prior to termination is obligatory and that a teacher's being eligible for superannuation is no reason to act otherwise. More recently, a British Columbia court ruled in favor of two teachers who were suspended without pay for not appearing before a school board's meeting to determine their involvement in staff problems in the school. The court held that the board did not follow the procedures laid down in the relevant legislation and ruled in favor of the teachers (*Johnstone v. Langley School District No. 35 Board of Trustees*, 1979). In Alberta, a court which ruled in support of a superintendent dismissed summarily declared that his school board was bound to act fairly and was under a duty to afford him a required hearing (*McCarthy v. Calgary R.C. Separate School District No. 1 Board of Trustees*, 1979). The Canadian court has also played an important role in upholding teacher rights under collective bargaining agreements. Thus, in *Syrette v. Transcona—Springfield S.D. No. 12* (1976), a Manitoba court decided in favor of a teacher dismissed in contravention of an agreement, then in force, which disallowed termination of any teacher's contract during the year.

Finally, the *Report of Canada on Implementation of the Provisions of the Covenant* (on civil and political rights) highlights the commitment of the federal and provincial governments to the many rights stated in the Covenant. However, how such legislation relates to parents, students, and teachers, specifically with respect to their civil and political rights within educational systems remains unclear. The wide-ranging authority vested in school boards, the lack of civil rights guarantees in the past, the absence of precedents in courts supporting civil or political rights and the consequent hesitation of lawyers to push cases before courts of law (Sweezy, 1969, pp. 298–299) have prevented the growth of civil libertarian tradition in the field of education in the country.

Thus, in spite of fairly heavy litigation pitting school boards against teachers, academic and civil rights cases have seldom reached Canadian courts. Seventeen years ago, McCurdy (1968) saw potential for litigation in relation to teachers' right to select and assign controversial or "objectionable" readings in literature classes. So far as can be ascertained (MacKay, 1984, p. 279), this potential has not been actualized although one related case has been recorded (*Re Busche and Nova Scotia Teachers' Union*, 1975). This involved the right of a teacher to speak out publicly against her union. Urged to engage in an illegal walkout by the teachers union, she wrote two letters to a local newspaper editor, both critical of the conduct of the meeting which decided on the walkout. When the union's professional committee found her guilty of unbecoming conduct and recommended a reprimand, she went to the court to quash the decision. The court ruled in her favor.

Student rights advocates may find even greater problems for young people. Despite recognition of and provisions for their well-being in schools, the traditional exercise of authority and discretion by educators has prevented full enjoyment of welfare rights by students. Frequently, in settling cases which involve educators' exercise of authority, courts have been mainly concerned with examining whether punishments imposed on students have been meted out for just and reasonable cause; whether the educators have acted out of malice; whether the power exercised has been abused; or whether the punishment has been rendered capriciously, excessively, or carelessly.

Nevertheless, increased recognition and protection of student and teacher rights may be expected. Still, the expected expansion of teachers' and pupils' civil, political and academic rights should not draw attention away from other problematic areas needing careful scrutiny. One such area concerns the right of private school parents to receive support from the government in educating their children. Clearly, as an aftermath of the public school movement, private schools are treated differentially and disadvantageously by governments, and private school parents are consequently twice burdened financially for pursuing their religious, or value convictions. However, if freedom of beliefs is a fundamental and protected freedom according to the *Canadian Charter*, it can be argued that its exercise cannot be used to treat private school parents differentially. Thus, based on the principle of human right to equal treatment, there appears a strong case for funding of private schools, unless stronger, over-riding considerations obtain (Shapiro, 1985).

Some Concluding Observations

The Philippines and Canada exhibit similarities with respect to the issue of rights in education. Both countries have exerted much effort to provide for the educational entitlements of their populations. Further, the correspondence between the stated rights entitlements in Philippine documents and whatever can be gleaned from scattered sources in Canada is striking. Clearly, both countries officially subscribe to the principles and rights promulgated by the United Nations and/or its agencies. Justifiably, we might infer that, at least in part, the two nations are motivated by the same aspirations which guide their educational endeavors. This may be explained by the fact that Filipinos have accommodated western cultural values and legal-moral principles during their long colonial relationship with Spain and the United States. It does not appear to matter that civil law serves as the framework of rights in the Philippines while common law serves the same role in Canada. True enough, with a centralized politico-legal system, the Philippines is able to formulate its policies uniformly all across the land. And, with its civil law foundation, it has shown tremendous boldness in incorporating statements on specific rights of particular groups like parents, students and teachers in its major general and educational documents. Such uniformity and specificity of formulation of rights are clearly missing in the Canadian scene. Still, their absence has not encumbered Canadian school systems in providing for such rights. In fact, Canadian systems seem to cater to these rights more effectively than the Philippine systems do.

It is only fair to observe that the Canadian record in recognizing and meeting educational clienteles' rights entitlements, as identified in various UN documents, is quite creditable. This is consistent with the conclusion reached by the Organization for Economic Cooperation and Development (OECD, 1976, p. 31) that "the development of education in Canada appears as an enormous *organisational, administrative and staffing achievement.* . . ." Unfortunately, the same cannot be said of Philippine education. Valiant efforts have not remedied the festering illnesses that plague the educational scene.

Perhaps, it may be said that Philippine efforts have not been consistent enough. Since 1972, when martial law was declared, budget allocations for military and infrastructure purposes have outstripped the educational budget whose average annual share of the governmental financial pie from 1973 to 1984 was 13.5 percent. This sharply contrasts with the average budget allocation of 31.4 percent from 1956 to 1972 and, even more glaringly, with the average allocation of between 35 and 40 percent from 1964 to 1968 (Association of Catholic Universities of the Philippines Secretariat, 1985, p. 260; MECS *Annual Report*, 1984, p. 63). Considering the debilitating effects of inflation, the continuing rise in enrollment, and the awesome shortcomings in the system, the present education minister himself had to conclude that "education has to recover at least a major part of its traditional share in the national budget" (Laya, 1984, p. 18). Such catching up does not appear urgent in Canadian education, although increased allocation will go a long way in meeting more fully the rights of its clientele. The Canadian education budget has remained fairly constant at around 7.5 to 9 percent of the gross national product from 1967 to 1980 after climbing consistently from a low of 2.4 percent in 1950 (*Statistics Canada*, 1983). On the other hand, the Philippine education budget, which has never been more than 3.3 percent of the annual gross national product since 1955, reached its low of 1.92 percent in 1980 (Association of Catholic Universities of the Philippines Secretariat, 1985, p. 260). Clearly, because providing for the rights of the educational clientele requires suitable and adequate resources, the Philippine government has to allocate to schools a vastly increased share of the nation's gross national product if it is to satisfy the requirements of the international human rights documents. Already heavily indebted, with a substantial portion of the national budget earmarked for interest payments, it is not clear that the financially-troubled country can afford increased educational allocation.

Nevertheless, the recent dramatic replacement of the Marcos regime by the Aquino government which is committed to national transformation could bring about significant change in governmental priorities. Already, the government has decreed general amnesty for communists and has released ideological leaders imprisoned by Mr Marcos. Also, plans are afoot to negotiate further autonomy for the Muslims in the South. Should these moves achieve positive results, military expenditures could be substantially reduced and other pressing areas like education could receive greater financial allocation. While bound to encounter legal and technical problems the new government's attempt to recover enormous wealth stashed away by Marcos and his cronies could shore up the depleted treasury. Moreover, the American government's promise to assist Mrs Aquino in the task of national rebuilding appears firm. All these could add up to greater resources for a nation struggling to meet various needs.[9] All these are, necessarily, speculative. However, the change of government provides at least a new beginning for a people whose courageous resolve, so crucial to the overthrow of a corrupt regime, can be harnessed in time of peace.

However, critical as increased financial allocation may be, the fact remains that comparative affluence alone does not translate into provisions to meet rights of educational clientele. For instance, in Canada, which reputedly is a "have" country, some provinces (e.g. British Columbia and New Brunswick) have yet to legislate mandatory provisions for appropriate and free education for handicapped or special children. It is not clear, either that the problems noted by the Organization for Economic Cooperation and Development in 1976 have been resolved satisfactorily. What is needed, whatever economic circumstances characterize a country, is the recognition not only that education is a major contributor to national development but also that it is an area where individual and group entitlements to human rights make urgent and compelling claim against government. It is such recognition that should provide justifiable grounds for policy decisions on national governmental priorities.

[9] See *Newsweek*, March 10, 1986, 18–37; *Time*, March 10, 1986, 18–40.

References

Amnesty International (1976) *Report of an Amnesty International Mission to the Philippines*. London: Amnesty International.

Association of Catholic Universities of the Philippines Secretariat (1985) *The Filipino Teacher in the '80s: An empirical study*. Manila: ACUP.

Bargen, P. (1961) *The legal status of the Canadian public school pupil*. Toronto: Macmillan.

Canadian Council on Children and Youth (1979) *Legislation related to the needs of children*. Toronto: Carswell.

Dizon, A. (1983) *Education Act of 1982 Annotated*. Manila: Rex Book Store.

Eekelaar, J. M. (1973) What are parental rights? *The Law Quarterly Review*, **6**, 210.

"Formal education for most Filipinos and at Grade School level." *Guro*, December, **21** (Supplement of *Education and Culture Journal*) 21.

Hawkins, E. K. (1976) *The Philippines: Priorities and prospects for development*. Washington, DC: World Bank.

Hayden, J. R. (1972) *The Philippines: A study in national development*. New York: Arno Press (reprint).

Isidro, A., Canaře, J. Manalang, P. and Valdes, M. (1982) *Compulsory education in the Philippines*. Paris: UNESCO.

Johnstone v. Langley School District No. 35 Board of School Trustees, 12 B.C.L.C. (1979)

Laya, J. (1984) Resource allocation for the public school system. *Education and Culture Journal*, October–December, **1**, 1–19.

Magno, F. (1984) The widening gap in RP urban, rural literacy rates. *Guro*, December, **21** (Supplement of *Education and Culture Journal*) 12–13.

Magsino, R. (1977–1978) Student rights in Canada: Nonsense upon stilts? *Interchange*, **8**, 52–70.

MacKay, W. (1984) *Education law in Canada*. Toronto: Emond-Montgomery Publications.

McCarthy v. Calgary R.C. Separate School District No. 1 Board of Trustees, 4 W.W.R. 725 (1979).

McCurdy, S. (1968) *The legal status of the Canadian teacher*. Toronto: Macmillan.

McLeod v. Board of School Trustees of School District No. 20 (Salmon Arm) 2 D.L.R. 562 (1952).

Metcalfe v. Board of Trustees of Moose Jaw District No. 1, 2 D.L.R. 641 (1938).

National Manpower and Youth Council (1985) Problems and strategies in formal education. In *Philippine HRD yearbook 1985* (pp. 35–37). Manila: Author.

Nediger, W. G. (1981) *The impact of collective bargaining on financial gains and management rights in Canadian education*. Paper presented at the 1981 Conference of the Canadian Society for the Study of Education, Halifax, Nova Scotia.

Organisation for Economic Cooperation and Development (1976) *Reviews of National Policies for Education—Canada*. Paris: OECD.

Parry, D. M. (1975) *Teacher liability and tenure*. Unpublished master's thesis, Memorial University of Newfoundland, St. John's.

Philippines (1949) *Civil code*.

Philippines (1973) *Constitution*.

Philippines (1980) *Civil code*. Republic Act No. 386.

Philippines Ministry of Education, Culture and Sports Information and Publication Service (1983) *Education Act, 1982*.

Philippines. Department of Education (1957) *Annual report, 1956–1957*.

Philippines. Ministry of Education, Culture and Sports (1983) *Annual Report*.

Philippines. Ministry of Education, Culture and Sports (1984) *Annual Report*.

Philippines. Ministry of Education, Culture and Sports. Planning Service (1982) *Statistical Bulletin*.

Philippines. Special Education Division. Bureau of Elementary Education (1983) *Special education: A new deal for the handicapped and the gifted*. Pamphlet.

Presidential Decree No. 1006 (Decree Professionalizing Teaching) (1976).

Re Busche and Nova Scotia Teachers' Union 62 D.L.R. (3d) 330 (1975).

Report of Canada. Articles 6 to 9, International Covenant on Economic, Social and Cultural Rights (1980) Ottawa: Ministry of Supply and Services.

Report of Canada. Articles 10 to 12, International Covenant on Economic, Social and Cultural Rights (1982) Ottawa: Ministry of Supply and Services.

Report of Canada. Articles 13 to 15, International Covenant on Economic, Social and Cultural Rights (1985) Ottawa: Ministry of Supply and Services.

Report of Canada. International Covenant on Civil and Political Rights (1979) Ottawa: Ministry of Supply and Services.

Schlosser, M. J. (1984) Third party child-centered disputes: Parental rights v. best interest of the child. *Alberta Law Review*, **22**, 394–416.

Shapiro, B. (1985) *The report of the Commission on Private Schools in Ontario*. Toronto: Government of Ontario.

Statistics Canada: Financial statistics of education (1983) Ottawa: Ministry of Supply and Services.

Sutherland, N. (1976) *Children in English Canadian society: Framing the twentieth century consensus*. Toronto: University of Toronto Press.

Sweezy, G. (1969) Free speech and the student's right to govern his personal appearance. *Osgoode Hall Law Journal*, **7**, 293–307.

Syrette v. Transcona-Springfield School District No. 12, 67 D.L.R. (3d) 568 (1976).

Torres, E. (1984) Why is there a need to prioritize education? *The ASI Option*, **4**, 1, 3.

United Nations (1978) *Human rights: A compilation of international instruments*. New York: United Nations.

Wilson, J. D. (1981) Religion and education: The other side of pluralism. In J. D. Wilson (Ed.), *Canadian education in the 1980s* (pp. 97–113). Calgary, Alberta: Detselig Enterprises.

CHAPTER 10

The Right to a Political Education

Carole L. Hahn
Division of Educational Studies
Emory University

Introduction

International documents assert that all human beings should possess basic civil and political rights such as the rights to vote and run for office, rights to freedom of expression and rights to due process and equality before the law. However, assertions of rights such as these remain ideals for which to strive; in no country are the goals yet completely realized. In some cases governments set limits. In other cases social and economic situations or traditional cultural values impede the full realization of civil and political rights. The very idea that there are political and civil rights which should be respected and exercised is meaningful only if individuals know that such rights exist. In addition to being aware of those rights, individuals also must possess the means and the will to exercise their rights. Political education is the process by which individuals can acquire knowledge of their rights and the desire and abilities to exercise them.

While no UN document specifies that human beings have a right to a political education, it is still appropriate to include a chapter on political education in this book because it is through political education that young people will become prepared—or not prepared—to turn the ideals of political and civil rights into reality. The concern of this chapter is political education which fosters the realization of universal political participation and respect for everyone's civil rights.

Before beginning an exploration of political education, it is necessary to distinguish among political socialization, political education in a general sense, and political education which successfully fosters human rights. Political socialization is the totality of experiences through which one develops cognitive understandings and attitudes toward the political world. Both formal and nonformal educational experiences contribute to political socialization.

Political education consists of those aspects of education which are planned particularly to develop students' competencies in thinking about and acting in political arenas. Political education can be thought of as

173

developing four dimensions—information, values, inquiry skills and participation (Gillespie, 1981). Political education most often conveys information
about the structure and function of government, the rights and responsibilities of citizens, and how the political process works. Political education may
attempt to develop values of national loyalty and concern for justice,
equality and freedom.

This chapter focusses on political education which fosters—or has the
potential to foster—the exercise and respect of universal political and civil
rights. The chapter will describe goals for such a political education and it
will draw on the experience of educators in two countries to analyze the
difficulties in achieving those goals. Finally, future directions will be suggested so that schools can better contribute to the realization of both
dimensions of political rights—the rights to political participation and to
respect of individual civil liberties.

A limitation of this chapter is that two national case studies are not representative of all countries. To date there is not a sufficient research base to
form generalizations about political education which apply across boundaries of East and West, North and South. For the most part, comparative
education researchers have not given priority to political education and
political education researchers have not given priority to cross-national
studies. In fact, only one study has come close to addressing this need; the
International Association for the Evaluation of Educational Achievement
(IEA) measured students' political knowledge and attitudes in nine nations
(Torney, Oppenheim, & Farnen, 1975). But even in that study, socialist
countries were underrepresented and Third World or developing countries
were not included.

Some researchers have studied political education in countries concerned
with building a new nationalism or new commitments to political ideologies.
The experiences of nations such as Cuba, China, Nigeria, Japan and West
Germany have been reported. Other scholars have compiled country
reports on social studies education suggesting similarities and differences in
the political aspects of social studies programs (Becker & Mehlinger, 1968;
Gross & Dufty, 1977). This chapter attempts to contribute to the emerging
area of political education by drawing on the experiences of the United
Kingdom and the United States—two countries with long histories of
guaranteeing civil and political rights to their citizens and of providing
universal education.

The Goals

The UN Charter proclaims that all citizens shall be guaranteed fundamental freedoms and human rights. The *Universal Declaration of Human Rights*
and the *UN Covenants on Civil and Political Rights* spell out what those
rights are in the arena of civic and political life.[1]

[1] International documents cited in this section are summarized in the appendix to this volume.

The international documents also assert that every human being shall be guaranteed a set of civil liberties which includes the right to freedom of thought, conscience and religion, freedom of expression and the right of peaceful assembly. Further, everyone is guaranteed the right to equality before the law and due process in the courts.

Professor Ian Lister (1981) of the University of York has identified three dimensions of human rights education: teaching *about* human rights; teaching *for* (the securing and maintenance of) human rights; and teaching *in* human rights (i.e., teaching in institutions which themselves are characterized by an acceptance of, and a respect for human rights (Lister, 1981). In that context schools should, in particular, educate young people *about* political and civil rights, *for* the universal respect of political rights, and *in* the spirit of political rights by recognizing the dignity and worth of individual students in the climate of the classroom and the school environment.

There is wide agreement in the international community that to ensure the full exercise of political and civil rights some education is necessary. But no existing approach has yet proved to be adequate in achieving the goal of producing a citizenry that both fully respects and universally exercises political and civil rights. That is the case even in countries where individuals are guaranteed rights in constitutions or laws. Understanding the difficulties present in such settings is perhaps a necessary step before addressing problems of political education in countries with relatively recent or faltering commitments to citizens exercising their rights.

Political Education—Two Nations' Experiences

The United States and the United Kingdom are nations with distinctly different approaches to political education. In the United States, citizenship education is seen as a primary purpose of schooling. In the United Kingdom, on the other hand, until recently there has been very little deliberate political education.

In the United States curriculum guides for grades 1–12 (ages 6–17) almost always list some objectives which would fall into the category of "citizenship" or "political" education. Elementary school social studies textbooks (Goldstein, 1972) and textbooks used in high school history, government and economics courses contain much content relating to the political system and guarantees of rights. Textbooks are a good indication of what is taught since studies repeatedly conclude that most instruction in the United States is tied to a textbook (Shaver, Davis and Helburn, 1979).

Even though each local school system establishes its own curriculum and selects its own textbooks within guidelines established by each state government, the expectations for citizenship education are so similar across the country that most American children are exposed to similar information about the political world. Almost all states require a daily pledge of allegiance to the American flag and 120 minutes of social studies instruction per week in elementary schools. In practice, these mandates are often not implemented, however. Courses in civics or government and in US history are usually mandated by states and implemented by secondary schools. The typical pattern is for primary grade children to learn several patriotic songs and to celebrate national holidays such as George Washington's and Abraham Lincoln's birthdays or Thanksgiving (which is sometimes tied to the concept of religious freedom). Daily flag salutes are not as universal as they once were. Primary grade children usually study about "community helpers" such as the police and firefighters and about the need for rules and laws. In upper elementary grades, children are introduced to US history and the basic principles contained in the Bill of Rights to the US Constitution. Virtually every high school student takes a course in national history (often an 11th grade course covers the same events studied in the 5th and the 8th grades) and almost all secondary students take a course in government (Superka, Hawke and Morrisett, 1980). Instruction about the rights and responsibilities of citizens in the national context is thus assured. This is further reinforced by the messages of the hidden curriculum. A poster showing the presidents of the United States is a frequent sight in history and government classes and an American flag is usually flying in front of the high school. In recent years, the Law Related Education movement has had an influence in increasing the amount of instruction which students receive about the law, including that related to civil liberties and to students' rights (Hahn, 1985).

The strong tradition of overt political or citizenship education in the United States is usually explained in terms of the historical need to develop a cohesive community out of a nation of immigrants, and of the influence of leaders like Thomas Jefferson and John Dewey who argued that young people should be educated for their role as citizens in a democracy. Regular current events discussions and students reporting on current events are pervasive practices today which may be attributed to the Progressive era.

Political education occurs through what is omitted from the curriculum as well as through what is included. For example, in public schools in the United States the value of separation of Church and State is conveyed by not having courses in religious education, prayers in school or school assemblies with religious themes even at Christmas or Easter. History courses teach about world religions, but to protect religious freedom no part of the public school (as an agency of the state) may engage students in religious practice. This principle is currently being challenged by some groups who want to amend the US Constitution to permit school prayers. The cultural norm to keep religion out of the schools and to put much citizenship education into schools in the United States is quite the reverse of the British experience.

In Great Britain the tradition has been "to keep politics out of the schools" in the belief that political education is inherently indoctrinating and partisan. Until recently political concepts were taught incidentally through history, which most students took, and to some extent in religious education, which is a mandatory course. In some schools, humanities, English, or social education courses referred to political ideas. There were only a very few university-bound students who took courses in the British Constitution. For the most part, however, British youth were not taught political or citizenship education in a deliberate and planned manner through the school curriculum. Rather, most young people "caught" their political knowledge, attitudes and misinformation from the media, their parents, and the hidden curriculum of the school.

Some writers noted that even without explicit forms of political education in British schools, students were in fact being prepared for political life. They learned about Britain's greatness through history lessons, celebrations of Empire Day and a chauvinistic treatment of the English language (Lister, 1985). Even today the history to which students are exposed throughout their schooling is British history and English-centered world history. While the flag and pictures of the prime ministers are not displayed, charts depicting the chronology of the monarchy are a ubiquitous sight in second-ary history classrooms and in junior schools. Current events are rarely discussed.

Dissatisfaction with incidental political education grew in Britain in the 1960s and 1970s. When the legal age for voting was lowered to 18, many people recognized the need to better inform soon-to-be voters. Politicians were particularly concerned that many young voters were not joining the three main political parties and that extremist groups were appealing to young people. Advocates for planned political education cited surveys of student knowledge and opinion polls of the adult electorate, which showed most people in Britain lacked basic information about the political process (Stradling, 1975).

The Hansard Society for Parliamentary Government and the Politics Association proposed a Programme for Political Literacy to ensure that all students, regardless of social class, or academic stream would acquire an understanding of political concepts, an awareness of major political issues and the skills to analyze issues, make judgments, and take actions as citizens.

The calls for political education seem to have had some effect. A 1981 survey found that only 13 percent of the secondary schools did not then provide some form of political studies, and even many of those said that they were in the process of examining the non-examination parts of their curriculum and they expected that those elements would include some political objectives in the future (Stradling and Noctor, 1981). Twenty-two percent of the middle and secondary schools surveyed offered distinct political units or modules within general courses such as social education or general studies. The average length of a module was one hour per week for 12 weeks. Most of the remaining schools said they had integrated political education objectives into courses such as history or social studies. Even so, the amount of deliberate political education received by British youth is minor compared with that received by American students.

Finally, in both countries young people's understanding of civil rights is most often limited to the national context and to reciting abstract principles. And most importantly, regardless of whether students take distinct courses in civics and government or whether they acquire political ideas incidentally through history courses, they are not acquiring the knowledge, skills and attitudes necessary to fully exercise and respect political and civil rights.

Problems Encountered in Implementation

Several problems have been encountered in the United States and the United Kingdom which serve as barriers to the realization of universal political rights.

Nationalistic Bias

The first problem encountered in educating about, for, and in civil and political rights in the United States and the United Kingdom is that most students do not learn that such rights are international. Because of the nationalistic orientation of most history and civics courses, students in the two countries study about their nation's legal and political history and the evolution of the principles in their national constitution (although Britain's constitution is unwritten it is presented as a powerful and enforceable tradition). Students are not likely to have studied about the international documents.

Knowledge and Attitudes Lacking

The second problem is that often students do not acquire knowledge or develop attitudes which would lead them to exercise their rights as active participating citizens. In the United States the National Assessment of Educational Progress (NAEP) conducted nationwide studies of students' political knowledge and attitudes in 1970, 1972, and 1976. Over the time period studied, American youth declined in their knowledge of the structure and function of government, in their understanding of the political process, and in their comprehension of the meaning of democracy (National Assessment, 1978).

Similarly, one study of 15-year-olds in England and Wales for the same time period concluded that only about one-third of the students could be said to be politically knowledgeable (Stradling, 1975). Only a few students had a realistic idea of how the political system actually works and most were ignorant of where political parties stood on the main issues of the day.

But lack of knowledge is only part of the problem. Perhaps more important to the realization of political rights are citizens' attitudes; individuals must possess the will and the desire to participate. Studies of adults in the United States find that people with a high sense of political efficacy (belief that citizen participation can influence decisions) are most likely to vote and to undertake other political activities (Campbell, Converse, Miller and Stokes, 1960). The evidence in regard to young people's sense of political efficacy in the United States and the United Kingdom is not very encouraging. In national surveys of adolescents in the two countries, responses to the statement "politics is too complicated to understand" are troubling. Only 29 percent of the British and 41 percent of the American youth disagreed; the majority in both countries felt that political issues are incomprehensible (Jennings and Niemi, 1968; Stradling, 1975).

Political cynicism as well as a low level of political efficacy is of concern. Twenty-nine percent of the 15- to 17-year-old English students surveyed in another study (Dennis, Lindberg and McCrone, 1971) agreed with the statement that "government usually does more harm than good" but only 3 percent of the Americans surveyed agreed with that idea.

The rights of one particular group—women—are singled out with specific international documents assuring their right to participate in the affairs of state. This was done because in much of the world women were not permitted to vote or run for public office. Although for almost three quarters of a century women in the United States and the United Kingdom have been eligible to vote and to hold office, still today very few women in those countries run for public office.

Problems related to both knowledge and attitudes encountered in the school years serve as obstacles later to females' full political participation. A classic nine-nation study of civic education found that both young females and males in the United States were less supportive of women holding political office than youth in any of the other nations studied. However, in all countries studied, adolescent females were more favorable toward women's participation in politics than were males (Torney *et al.*, 1975). The hesitancy on the part of future voters, particularly males, to support women candidates is compounded by the fact that few girls show an interest in running for office nor are they inclined toward acquiring political information.

Studies in both the United States and the United Kingdom have found that young males tend to be more knowledgeable about politics than females (Dowse and Hughes, 1971b; Easton and Dennis, 1969; Greenstein, 1965; Jennings and Niemi, 1968; National Assessment, 1978; Nossiter, 1969; Merelman, 1971; Stradling, 1975; Torney *et al.*, 1975). Further, boys report much more than girls—89 percent as compared to 25 percent—that they watch the news on TV or listen to the news on the radio (81 percent and 25 percent) (Dowse and Hughes, 1971b).

Civil Liberties Undervalued

Other problems are associated with ensuring civil liberties for all. Children, like adults, say they believe in free speech for all. However, those same children (again, like adults) are not willing to apply the abstract principle to concrete situations when they do not like the dissenting group. For example, 60 percent of 11-year-olds in one California community said that they believed in free speech for all, but only 26 percent of the students were willing to allow a Communist Party member to make a speech in their city (Zellman, 1975; Zellman and Sears, 1971).

Studies of adults similarly find a lack of support for specific applications of civil liberties. One American study which used a national probability sample of almost 2500 adults from the 48 contiguous states came to such a conclusion. One-third of the sample said that newspapers should not be allowed to criticize the police, and over half said that people should not be able to publish books attacking the system of government or make speeches against God (Wilson, 1975). The British are only slightly less tolerant than Americans of individuals who publicly criticize government (Kramer, 1982, as cited in Torney-Purta, 1984).

Barriers to the full realization of international political rights apparently exist not only in countries with political, economic, and cultural system constraints on civic participation. They exist also in countries wih greater encouragement for participation; many youths are not aware of the international guarantees of political and civil rights, many young people lack knowledge which would facilitate their own active involvement in political decision making, and many children and adolescents are not willing to extend political rights to groups with which they disagree. These barriers, however, are not insurmountable.

Attempted Solutions

In the United States and in the United Kingdom there have been recent efforts to promote education about political rights and other human rights at both the national and international levels. The National Council for the Social Studies (NCSS), in the United States published a bulletin on International Human Rights (Branson and Torney-Purta, 1982) and devoted an issue of its journal *Social Education* to the topic *International Human Rights* (1985).

In the United Kingdom there have been teacher conferences on human rights education and a number of curriculum development projects have produced units on teaching about human rights. Examples of such units would be the curriculum units produced by the Jordanhill College Project in International Understanding, which are used in Modern Studies courses in Scotland, and the teaching unit produced by the UK chapter of Amnesty International, which is used in many social education courses (Amnesty, 1985).

Increasing Knowledge and Developing Participant Attitudes

The citizenship education movement in the United States and the political education movement in the United Kingdom have shown that courses can slightly increase students' knowledge of the political world (Mercer, 1974; Patrick, 1977; Stradling, 1975). But additional courses have little or no effect on political attitudes (Ehman, 1980; Mercer, 1974; Patrick, 1972, 1977; Stradling, 1975). The variables that have been found to relate to attitudes which support citizenship participation are an open classroom climate in which students feel free to discuss controversial issues, opportunities for students to participate in decision-making activities and a democratic school climate. The consistency of the findings is impressive.

In the cross-national study of civic learning which surveyed more than 30,000 students, the authors concluded that students are more politically knowledgeable, more politically interested, and less authoritarian if they regularly participate in classroom discussions in which they are encouraged to express their opinions. Students who receive most of their civics instruction by way of lectures and recitation and through patriotic rituals are less interested in politics, less knowledgeable about politics, and tend to be more authoritarian (Torney *et al.*, 1975).

A number of British scholars have advocated the use of open discussion in secondary schools. Bridges (1978) and Entwistle (1971) emphasize that since the time of the Greek city states, discussion has been essential to democracy because it is the best method for discovering the things people need to know in order to govern themselves (Entwistle, 1971). Further, Entwistle insists that the crucial activity for the democratic citizen is "this method of seeking the truth by seeking the opinion of all concerned, not simply seeking consent to cut and dried measures" (1971, p. 72).

In regard to political education in particular, Crick and Lister (1979) proposed a model for the discussion of public policy issues in the United Kingdom in which students would identify the issues and different positions on the issues. The students would consider the effects of alternatives on other people and on themselves. After carrying out their investigation and making a judgment, students would finally consider how they could persuade others to their position. This is based on the belief that in order to be effective participants, citizens must understand the issues, and be skillful in influencing decisions.

The Social Education Project, based at Nottingham University in the

United Kingdom, gave students practice in diagnosing community problems, examining possible solutions, and deciding what action, if any, was needed. Such experiences when children are young are believed to contribute to their desire to exercise participant political rights as adults. Unfortunately, we do not have the empirical data to verify that.

There have been several studies in the United States which show that students who participate in school activities, such as student government or clubs, show more predisposition toward citizenship participation (Ehman, 1980; Hess and Torney, 1967). Eyler's use of path analysis suggests, however, that it is students with predispositions toward participation who join clubs and run for student government offices, rather than the other way around (Eyler, 1982). Nonetheless, most secondary schools in the United States have student councils to give youth experience in quasi-governmental decision making. In contrast, only 37 percent of the secondary schools sampled in England and Wales reported that they had student councils (Stradling and Noctor, 1981).

Some critics would argue that no amount of student activities or classroom discussion can have much effect on student political attitudes as long as the context in which schooling takes place is authoritarian. Unfortunately, the researchers who have pursued this line of inquiry have used different indicators of open, participant environments and they have examined different dependent variables, making it difficult to generalize across studies. Since most of the research has found positive student attitudes associated with more participatory schools (Ehman, 1980; Hepburn, 1984; Siegel, 1977), this is an area worth further study. From John Dewey to contemporary critics of bureaucratic school environments, there have been calls in both the United States and the United Kingdom to democracticize the schools. Many people believe that only when students experience participant political rights will they become active participating adults in public affairs. This line of thinking is particularly potent for research on student attitudes in nations where the total society is subject to authoritarian rule.

The special political needs of women have been mentioned earlier. To overcome existing problems and to encourage women to participate in the political arena, both British and American feminists insist that young boys and girls see more women exercising their rights to participation. Textbooks need to be revised to show more females participating in policy making and attempting to influence decisions at the local, national and international levels (MacLeod and Silverman, 1973). When schools have women administrators as frequently as they have male administrators, and when more women seek political office, such behavior will become part of students' expectations.

Internalizing Civil Libertarian Values

We turn now from solutions for increasing the likelihood that participant political rights will be exercised to solutions for promoting the respect of the civil liberties guaranteed in the international documents. In both the United States and the United Kingdom, there have been curriculum projects and teacher education programs aimed at promoting more law studies in the schools. Most of those programs include units on civil liberties which use the case study approach. For example, in the United States elementary school-children using the *Law in a Free Society* program read simplified versions of the landmark Supreme Court cases dealing with free speech, the freedom to assemble, freedom of religion, and the procedural due process issues relating to arrest, detention and trials. In the United Kingdom, one curriculum unit uses European Court for Human Rights cases which involve British citizens raising questions about international civil rights (Grainger, 1983).

While there have been these few attempts in both the United States and Great Britain to expose students to the international dimensions of political and civil rights and to develop in youth both respect for such rights and the capacity to exercise their rights, for the most part political education has fallen short in this area.

Present Status

Reformers who call for greater attention to human rights from an international perspective, who argue for open discussion of controversial issues, and who advocate students inquiring into the continuing dilemmas associated with civil rights issues have raised the consciousness of some educators. And, those who emphasize the importance of young people seeing women as effective political actors have been consciousness-raisers. But all indications are that so far practice has changed very little. Most curriculum guides, syllabuses, textbooks, and examinations still emphasize descriptions of national governmental and political institutions and elite political actors (mostly male). Studies repeatedly find that controversial issues are avoided in most classrooms in the United States (Hahn, 1985; Massialas, 1972, pp. 7–8). And while topics related to sexuality (contraception, abortion, homosexuality), religion, and Third World or North/South issues are often part of the curriculum in British schools (Stradling, Noctor and Baines, 1984), students rarely explore local political issues or issues such as national security and disarmament. Nor are they encouraged to openly articulate diverse opinions about other issues perceived to be "political."

The picture in regard to presenting women as political leaders and decision makers is similarly dismal. The future offers much potential for improvement in this area, as well as in the other areas related to the full implementation of civil and political rights.

Future Plans and Prospects

In the United Kingdom currently there is ferment around reforming the examination system and revising related syllabuses. There is widespread concern about the appropriate educational experiences for the 16-year-old school leavers during a period of economic decline and increasing discontent. The time is right to reconsider the contribution that education can make to preparing citizens to exercise effectively their international political and civil rights.

In the United States, school systems are celebrating the bicentennial of the *US Constitution*, followed by the bicentennial of the Bill of Rights. That offers an excellent opportunity for students to study the underlying ideals of those documents in both a national and an international context. And recognizing the power of television on young people's political awareness, the media were encouraged to set their special bicentennial programs in an international context.

Political education about, for, and in the spirit of human rights can and should begin early and continue throughout the school years. Developmental researchers emphasize that even young children bring political ideas with them to school; they are not *tabula rasas* (Connell, 1971; Hess and Torney, 1967; Stevens, 1982). Even some 7-year-olds watch television news with interest and 9-year-olds enjoy discussing political and social issues when they are given the opportunity (Stevens, 1982). Since children begin by first focussing on political personalities, then understanding institutions and finally comprehending that alternative policies address complex issues, political education programs should proceed according to that sequence. On the other hand, political educators should keep in mind warnings from cross-national research: reliance on printed drill, facts and patriotic rituals is, if anything, counterproductive to civic education (Torney *et al.*, 1975).

Perhaps most importantly, students need to be able to openly investigate and express their opinions on controversial issues. Clearly, that is necessary if we want citizens to develop the increased levels of political interest, political efficacy and tolerance of dissent which is needed to maximize citizen participation in public affairs. Discussion of controversial issues in secondary school classrooms is the one variable that has been found to correlate with student support of civil liberties (Goldenson, 1978). Further, one line of research suggests that frequent discussion of moral dilemmas can increase students' level of moral reasoning (Leming, 1985) and that individuals who reason at higher levels are the most likely to apply abstract principles like free speech, freedom of the press, and freedom to assemble, to specific concrete cases and they are the most likely to become active participating citizens.

Further, national policies should encourage practices at the school level which reflect the spirit of human rights. Schools can model respect of freedom of expression in student publications and assemblies. Students should have the opportunity to vote and to run for school offices which have real influence in the school community. And secondary students who are only a few years away from voting should be encouraged to participate in community social action projects, to work for candidates, and to join political interest groups. The question is not whether to offer political education. (Regardless of the planned curricular objectives, students are developing attitudes and acquiring information (or misinformation) which affects political rights.) The more important questions to address are: Does the existing political education produce obedient and compliant or alienated citizens who let an elite rule and do not themselves exercise their rights to participate in public policy decision making? Does the existing approach produce citizens who repeat the rhetoric of "rights for all" but who are not supportive of those rights in concrete situations? Or will young people grow up respecting international human rights both at home and abroad and possessing the knowledge, skills, and attitudes that will lead them into active citizen participation? The evidence that we have from two countries suggests that there is much yet to be done before we can feel satisfied that schools have fulfilled their potential to adequately educate about, for, and in respect of fundamental freedoms and basic political and civil rights.

References

Amnesty International British Section (1985) *Teaching and learning about human rights.* London: Amnesty International.

Becker, J. M. and Mehlinger, H. D. (Eds.) (1968) *International dimensions of the social studies.* Washington, DC: National Council for the Social Studies.

Branson, M. and Torney-Purta, J. (Eds.) (1982) *International human rights, society, and the schools.* Washington DC: National Council for the Social Studies.

Bridges, D. (1978) *Education, democracy and discussion.* Oxford: NFER Publishing Company.

Campbell, D., Converse, P., Miller, W. and Stokes, D. (1960) *The American voter.* New York: John Wiley and Sons.

Connell, R. W. (1971) *The child's construction of politics.* Carleton, Victoria: Melbourne University Press.

Crick, B. and Lister, I (1979) Political literacy: The centrality of the concept. *International Journal of Political Education*, **2**, 83–92.

Dennis, J., Lindberg, L. and McCrone, E. (1971). Support for nation and government among English children. *British Journal of Political Science*, **1**, 25–48.

Dowse, R. E. and Hughes, J. A. (1971a) The family, the school, and the political socialization process. *Sociology*, **5**, 21–45.

Dowse, R. E. and Hughes, J. A. (1971b) Girls, boys and politics. *British Journal of Sociology*, **22**, 53–67.

Easton, D. and Dennis, J. (1969) *Children in the political system: Origins of political legitimacy.* New York: McGraw-Hill.

Ehman, L. H. (1980) The American school in the political socialization process. *Review of Educational Research*, **50**, 99–119.

Entwistle, H. (1971) *Political education in a democracy.* London: Routledge and Kegan Paul.

Eyler, J. (1982) A test of a model relating political attitudes to participation in high school activities. *Theory and Research in Social Education*, **10**, 43–62.

Gillespie, J. A. (1981) Introduction. In D. Heater and J. A. Gillespie (Eds.), *Political education in flux.* London: Sage Publications.

Goldenson, D. (1978) An alternative view about the role of the secondary school in political socialization. *Theory and Research in Social Education*, **6**, 44–72.

Goldstein, R. J. (1972) The elementary school curriculum and political socialization. In B. G. Massialas (Ed.), *Political youth, traditional schools: National and international perspectives.* Englewood Cliffs, NJ: Prentice-Hall.

Grainger, N. R. (1983) *Law teaching and contemporary human rights.* Unpublished paper. York, UK: University of York, Department of Education, Political Research Unit.

Greenstein, F. I. (1965) *Children and politics.* New Haven, CT: Yale University Press.

Gross, R. E. and Dufty, D. (1977) *Toward a world view of the social studies.* Boulder, CO: Social Science Education Consortium.

Hahn, C. L. (1985) The status of the social studies in the public schools of the United States: Another look. *Social Education*, **49**, 220–223.

Hahn, C. L. and Avery, P. G. (1985) Value analysis, political attitudes, and reading comprehension. *Theory and Research in Social Education*, **13**, 47–60.

Hepburn, M. A. (1984) Democratic schooling: Five perspectives from research in the United States. *International Journal of Political Education*, **6**, 245–262.

Hess, R. D. and Torney, J. V. (1967) *The development of political attitudes in children.* Chicago: Aldine Press.

International human rights education [Special issue]. (1985) *Social Education*, September. **49**, 444–538.

Jennings, M. K. and Niemi, R. G. (1968) Patterns of political learning. *Harvard Educational Review*, **38**, 443–467.

Leming, J. S. (1985) Reserearch on social studies curriculum and instruction: Interventions and outcomes in the socio-moral domain. In W. B. Stanley (Ed.), *Review of Research in Social Studies Education* (pp. 123–133). Washington, DC: National Council for the Social Studies.

Lister, I. (1981) *Reflections on the Council of Europe's seminar on human rights education held at Bergen, Norway.* Unpublished paper. York, UK: University of York, Department of Education.

Lister, I. (1985) *Political education in England: 1974–1984.* A paper presented to the Global Education Center, University of Minnesota. York, UK: University of York, Department of Education.

MacLeod, J. S. and Silverman, S. T. (1973) *You won't do: What textbooks on U.S. government teach high school girls.* Pittsburgh, PA: Know, Inc. (ERIC Document Reproduction Service No. ED 081 255).

Massialas, B. G. (1972) The inquiring activist: Citizenship objectives for the 70's. In B. G. Massialas (Ed.), *Political youth, traditional schools: National and international perspectives* (pp. 243–264). Englewood Cliffs, NJ: Prentice-Hall.

Mercer, G. (1974) Are we being fair to political education in the schools? *Research in Education*, **11**, 51–67.

Merelman, R. M. (1971) *Political socialization and educational climates: A study of two school districts.* New York: Holt, Rinehart and Winston.

National Assessment for Educational Progress (1978) *Changes in political knowledge and attitudes, 1969–76* (Citizenship/Social Studies Report No. 07, CS2). Denver, CO: Education Commission of the States.

Nossiter, T. (1969) How children learn about politics. *New Society*, July 31, **14**, 166–167.

Patrick, J. J. (1972) The impact of an experimental course, "American Political Behavior" on the knowledge, skills, and attitudes of secondary school students. *Social Education*, **36**, 168–179.

Patrick, J. J. (1977) Political socialization and political education in schools. In S. A. Renshon (Ed.), *Handbook of political socialization.* New York: The Free Press.

Shaver, J., Davis, O. L., Jr., and Helburn, S. W. (1979) The status of social studies education: Impressions from three NSF studies. *Social Education*, **43**, 150–153.

Siegel, M. E. (1977) Citizenship education in five Massachusetts high schools. *Theory and Research in Social Education*, **5**, 31–55.

Stevens, O. (1982) *Children talking politics: Political learning in childhood*. Oxford: Martin Robertson.

Stradling, R. (1975) *The political awareness of the school leaver*. London: The Hansard Society.

Stradling, R. and Noctor, M. (1981). *The provision of political education in schools: A national survey*. Unpublished paper. York, UK: University of York, Department of Education.

Stradling, R., Noctor, M. and Baines, B. (1984) *Teaching controversial issues*. London: Edward Arnold.

Superka, D., Hawke, S. and Morrisett, I. (1980) The current and future status of social studies, *Social Education*, **44**, 362–369.

Torney, J. V., Oppenheim, A, N. and Farnen, R. T. (1975) *Civic education in ten countries*. New York: John Wiley and Sons.

Torney-Purta, J. (1984) Political socialization and policy: The United States in a cross-national perspective. In H. W. Stevenson and A. E. Siegel (Eds.), *Child development research and social policy* (pp. 471–523). Chicago: University of Chicago Press.

Wilson, W. C. (1975) Belief in freedom of speech and press. *Journal of Social Issues*, **31**, 69–76.

Zellman, G. L. (1975) Antidemocratic beliefs: A survey and some explanations. *Journal of Social Issues*, **31**, 31–53.

Zellman, G. L. and Sears, D. O. (1971) Childhood origins of tolerance for dissent. *Journal of Social Issues*, **27**, 109–136.

PART 2

Education about Human Rights

CHAPTER 11

Human Rights Education in Schools

Susanne M. Shafer
Arizona State University

"Freedom of choice is like hitching a
Ride on a cloud to go change the future."
Leaysha Watson
Cactus Wren Poetry book '85
Washington Elementary District
Phoenix, Arizona

Schooling provides not only basic education, but under the best of circumstances it aids a child to explore the world and to express ideas, ask questions, and puzzle out answers. According to the *Universal Declaration of Human Rights* (Article 26, 1948), schooling is a human right. That assurance logically must be accompanied by education about human rights if individuals are to comprehend what rights accrue to them, their responsibility toward others, and the boundaries of state power set in the various human rights agreements. Particularly teachers must be familiar with human rights if they are to effectively help their students to respect these rights and to recognize any flagrant violations in the world.

In this chapter education about human rights is described as it has been advocated in different parts of the world. In some instances such instruction has been tangential to other parts of the curriculum, Zimbabwe and many American schools being examples. To what extent teachers then bring up the subject in class appears to vary widely. There are places, however, where the syllabi specifically set human rights education as a goal. In this chapter, the agreements chiseled out by the 21 Western and Southern European countries that belong to the Council of Europe are placed side by side with efforts to further human rights education in the United States as well as in the Federal Republic of Germany (FRG) and the German Democratic Republic (GDR). The Council of Europe documents, American practices, and West German instructional materials speak of the preservation of the rights of individuals while the latter, the GDR, illustrates a collectivist approach. How human rights education is linked to embuing students with a sense of social responsibility emerges from the discussion. We can then draw conclusions about the status of human rights education, ways of incorporating it into the school curriculum, and problems being encountered in doing so.

Conceptualization of Human Rights Education

To deal with human rights in schools requires clarification of the concept, the outcomes sought in teaching about human rights, the means to be used, and the relationship to other educational goals. Human rights education has been tried both directly and indirectly. Students in their history class may learn how the concept gained its legal definition over time. In an elementary classroom they may reason together as to what rights and responsibility they have toward one another. From a brief survey of where in the curriculum of the schools human rights education has been included we can deduce its broad definition and reasons for its presence.

Purpose of Human Rights Education

Three particular components of many a school curriculum contain human rights education as an explicit or implicit goal. These are global education, a somewhat recent construct, moral education, one of the most ancient, and social and civic education, which begins informally during early childhood at home and then is extended formally in schools.

Global education

A more comprehensive topic than human rights education, global education focuses broadly on ". . . people as individuals and as a society and how they relate to the world's physical conditions, human institutions, social and economic systems, and interconnecting world problems and developments" (US Commissioner of Education, 1979, p. 4). It is to ". . . contribute to the development of mutual respect for the human dignity of all peoples, cultures, and civilizations, at home and abroad" (US Commissioner of Education, 1979, p. 4). Global education thus incorporates multicultural education and peace education. Education for global perspectives also addresses such transnational concerns as the environment and energy resources and the examination of related critical ecological problems which demonstrate the interdependence of the world's people (US Commissioner of Education, 1979, pp. 4–5).

The issue of human rights pertains to global education in more than one respect. The *Universal Declaration of Human Rights* begins, "All human beings are born free and equal in dignity and rights" (*Universal Declaration*, Art. 1). The Declaration in subsequent articles mentions, among others, legal rights, rights of persons including freedom of movement (Art. 13), right to employment (Art. 23), to a family (Art. 16, #1), to practice religious beliefs (Art. 18), and to adequate health (Art. 25). These examples are congruent with the purpose of global education which is intended to create a sensitivity to human concerns around the globe.

Moral education

Human rights education may also be related to moral education. The latter is formalized in Koranic schools in many countries as well as in the formal school curriculum of different nations in the subject religion. In England, for example, students spend time comparing and contrasting the major religious faiths in the world represented among the nation's multi-racial society (Hampshire Education Authority, 1978). In West Germany where religion is also a school subject a similar exploration is conducted in classrooms (Etzold, 1984, p. 11). *The Religious and Moral Education Syllabus* for Zimbabwe's Junior Certificate speaks of students learning to accept responsibility and to help others in the community (Zimbabwe, Ministry of Education and Culture, 1984b). In other words, moral education as well as religious education introduces the learner to the moral principles or ideals and related formalized codes of conduct which have been incorporated into tribal and societal law. Human rights agreements belong with these codes.

Social and civic education

Human rights education, according to other educators, is effectively introduced as preparation for citizenship and social responsibility. Whether it is a distinct unit or woven into the total social studies curriculum varies. In the British Hansard Society's instructional guide on "Political Dilemmas", students are asked to consider *power* and *authority* as used by the state and also the use of violence as compared with peaceful means of influencing governments or persons (Stradling, 1980). In the United States the *US Constitution*, including the *Bill of Rights* or first ten amendments, is studied both in the required US History Class (grade 11) and American Government Class (grade 12). Holocaust studies have been included in World History and US History courses.

In the German Democratic Republic civic education or *Staatsbürgerkunde*, is to convey ideals related to human rights. "Youth forges its own future by accepting the rights and duties of the socialist society, by participating in that human society, and by accepting social responsibility" (Schmitt, 1980, p. 64).

In Zimbabwe, the new government has introduced history syllabi and textbooks which are African centered. They introduce students to the purposes of the former African slave trades (Sibanda, *et al.*, 1982, p. 118) and to South Africa's apartheid policy (Zimbabwe, Ministry of Education and Culture, 1984a).

Historical Basis of Human Rights

While human rights education may receive its definition as it is embedded in global education, moral education, or civic and social education, its specificity is further refined as students look at the international agreements from the *Universal Declaration of Human Rights* to the *Helsinki Accords* and the follow-up conference reports. As students inspect the Universal Declaration, they are reminded of both the *American Declaration of Independence* (1776) and the *United States Constitution* (1789). The former contains that powerful statement "We hold these truths to be self-evident, that all men are created equal, that they are endowed by their Creator with certain unalienable rights, that among these are life, liberty, and the pursuit of happiness. . . ."

Any historical approach to the derivation of human rights also introduces students to France's *Declaration of the Rights of Man* (1791) which stated that "men are born free . . ."; to the inhumanity of the African slave trade; to examples of the forced migration of peoples such as Indian tribes in North America; to the perpetration of genocide in the case of the Armenians at the hands of the Turks in 1915, the Jews during the Third Reich, and Cambodians in the 1970s; to the post-World War II independence movements in Africa, Asia, and the Caribbean; and to the plight of political refugees whether from Hitler Germany, Afghanistan, or El Salvador.

Legal Basis of Human Rights

A further means of defining human rights education is to study the major contemporary human rights agreements from the Universal Declaration onward. Many of them serve to implement in detail what is stated more generally in the different articles of that document. Examples are the *Convention on the Political Rights of Women* (1952), the *International Convention on the Elimination of All Forms of Racial Discrimination* (1965) and the *Convention Relating to the Status of Refugees* (1951).[1] These and others gain importance in the eyes of students as they at the same time study the violations of human rights which induced nations to reach these agreements.

Violations of Human Rights

The stark incidences of terrorism, torture, and other acts of violence around the globe which confront students and teachers alike today also give definition to human rights education. The list of such violations dramatically corroborates the excesses of human cruelty toward other human beings.

---

[1] See Appendices for summaries of relevant documents.

Human Rights Advocacy

The groups which by peaceful means systematically seek strict adherence to human rights agreements provide another important dimension to human rights education. The organization which systematically verifies accusations of human rights violations is Amnesty International. It focusses on "prisoners of conscience", people who are persecuted and imprisoned because of their convictions, that is, whose political and civil rights have been removed. Through letter-writing and publicity campaigns, sending missions and trial observers, and publishing special reports, Amnesty International, an independent worldwide movement, works to gain the freedom of Prisoners of Conscience and seeks humane treatment for all prisoners and detainees.

Living the Idea

As students are confronted with the violations of human rights and the historic efforts to preserve freedom for humankind, their response reveals that affective and cognitive learning around this topic are inextricably linked. To demonstrate the importance of human rights, teachers show students how to implement these rights in their own classrooms. Not only student-student relations but teacher-student as well as administrator-student relations must conform to the principles of human rights if students are to accept the validity of the concept.

Implementation by the Council of Europe

One body that has engaged in curriculum development centered on human rights education is the Council of Europe. Founded in 1949, the Council is a direct outgrowth of the lessons drawn by Western Europe from the interwar years and World War II itself. The 21 member nations, that is the democratic countries of Western and Southern Europe, together have stressed the importance of human rights beginning with their *Convention for the Protection of Human Rights and Fundamental Freedoms* (Council of Europe, 1953). Through the Council of Europe's Council for Cultural Cooperation (CDCC), education about human rights has developed into a major project in order ". . . to give young people knowledge and understanding of the concepts [of democracy and freedom], but—more importantly—also some real experience of them so as to create a deeper personal appreciation of their importance" (Council of Europe, 1984, p. 10).

In the course of the Council of Europe's meetings on human rights education, primary and secondary teachers emphasized this very point. They agreed that the teaching about human rights is important but to be meaningful must be accompanied in secondary schools ". . . by greater democratization of school life and of relationships between pupils and the administration and teachers" (Council of Europe, 1981, p. 36). "The school's social milieu should encourage pupils to recognize the right of other people to express their personalities and to tolerate other people's ideas and conceptions—that is, to practice human rights" (Council of Europe, 1981, p. 24).

Secondary Curricula

Project No. 1, *Preparation for Life*, began as a series of meetings of educators from the member states who came together over several years to address the problems involved in preparing teenagers for life in a democracy, working life, cultural participation, personal development, and extension of their education (Council of Europe, 1980, p. 2). Classroom teachers, principals, and officials from the different ministries of education listed among the areas of social education, or preparation for life, "a moral commitment to human rights and human dignity, a personal commitment to fundamental values and norms such as tolerance, understanding, cooperation, democracy, and justice, the readiness to defend human rights and to display social and civic responsibility. . . ." (Starkey, 1982, p. 16). Human rights was to be a specific topic in the curriculum.

The concern for human rights spawned another series of seminars for teachers and other educators (1980, 1981, 1983, 1984, and 1985) who addressed the ways to introduce human rights into the school curriculum. Participants arrived at what amounts to a set of guidelines for human rights education at the secondary level.

1. The teaching of human rights should begin in primary schools and be continued thereafter (Perotti, 1984, p. 9).
2. It should ". . . go hand in hand with a greater democratization of school life and be supplemented by a broad range of extracurricular activities" (Perotti, 1984, p. 9).
3. Human rights, to be taught effectively calls for participatory teaching and learning which leads to the acquisition of human rights skills (Perotti, 1984, p. 9).
4. "Human rights education should deal with economics, social, and cultural rights as well as civil and political rights, and any program of human rights education should also have a historical dimension" (Perotti, 1984, p. 10). The history of democracy should be included (Perotti, 1984, p. 10). The human record to secure human rights should constitute an identifiable part of what is taught (Starkey, 1984, p. 20).
5. Feelings are touched upon in the course of human rights education (Perotti, 1984, p. 10).
6. Human rights teaching requires a certain independence on the part of

the teachers involved (Mariet, 1981, p. 38). They need to feel free to deal with politically controversial issues. "Governments and education authorities have a role to play in dispelling fears about the nature of human rights education and in giving legitimacy to human rights as an appropriate topic for study in schools" (Starkey, 1985, p. 18).
7. All forms of international exchanges, among pupils and teachers alike, make for international understanding and mutual information; such contacts should be encouraged" (Mariet, 1981, p. 38).

Elementary Curricular Arrangements

Several teachers' seminars and other conferences for educators, sponsored by the Council of Europe, centered on human rights education in elementary schools. In general, "primary education . . . has to help children to acquire and practice democratic values of tolerance, participation, responsibility and respect for the rights of others" (Starkey, 1984, p. 3).

Primary teachers are in a position to introduce children to cultural differences which may characterize even people in their own community. An acceptance of others who differ in ethnicity, language, religion, or race can be taught as part of human rights education (Council of Europe, 1985, Group II).

American Approaches

While the United States is a democracy similar to those that belong to the Council of Europe, human rights education is shaped by America's past as well as by certain educational practices. The history of slavery, of subjugation of Indian tribes, and of discrimination based on religious ethnicity or sex (female) vividly exemplifies denials of human rights. How these forms of discrimination against segments of the American people have haltingly been abrogated also is part of the historical record. Starting with the Civil Rights Movement of the late 1950s, the formerly disadvantaged groups have established their legal and social equality. That discrimination based on race, religion, sex, ethnicity, or country of origin is wrong has gained broad cultural acceptance. The struggles by which this change in attitude has come about and the remaining economic and political issues both are included in the social studies curriculum.

It is in the social studies that human rights education can be most readily identified. Although the elementary classrooms, as well as classes in secondary schools, particularly science and English, lend themselves to human rights education, the social studies curriculum deals directly or tangentially with human rights. Teachers of American History or American Government classes are expected to introduce students to the institutions and principles which support human rights.

World History teachers deal with the French Revolution and the subsequent *Declaration of the Rights of Man*, with dictatorships and wars that make a mockery of basic human rights, and with people of different cultures. The last are also discussed in geography classes and elementary classrooms as students learn about other parts of the world and meet the people who live there. Global education, a new name given to this effort on the part of teachers, may well include a reference to human rights.

The topic of human rights internationally still occupies a minor role in the social studies curriculum. If the international agreements on human rights are mentioned at all, they are given only a short passage in textbooks. Still, the drama of contemporary world events may catapult the social studies teacher into human rights education. Interest or pressure groups working nationally or in a state or community may have a similar effect. Jewish community leaders have in the past called for an expanded treatment of the Holocaust. Hispanics have demanded bilingual education, i.e., the opportunity for students whose primary language is Spanish, to systematically and continuously study their language in school. (See Article 2.2, *International Covenant on Economic, Social, and Cultural Rights*.) Hoping to strengthen the quality of their children's education, Blacks have asked for integration of schools by means of busing, in keeping with the 1954 US Supreme Court decision of *Brown v Board of Education* of Topeka, Kansas, and with Article 26, #2 of the *Universal Declaration of Human Rights*. Environmentalist groups have urged that toxic waste clean-ups be carried out by government or by industries responsible for pollution. Among women's groups, family planning advocates have worked for sex education, family studies, and counseling, while most "Right to Life" groups oppose such provisions.

To encourage social studies teachers to accept responsibility for human rights education, the National Council for the Social Studies sponsored the publication of *International Human Rights, Society, and the Schools* (Branson and Torney-Purta, 1982). Also, the September, 1985, issue of its journal *Social Education* was wholly devoted to "International Human Rights Education" (Totten, 1985). Here teachers can find information on the holocaust, genocide, and apartheid, reflections on the history of human rights legislation, methods of introducing human rights education into classrooms, suggested instructional materials to be used, and an annotated bibliography for use by teachers themselves as well as their students. The purpose is "to assist teachers in introducing their students to many of the major human rights issues facing the world today; to delineate some of the complexities inherent in solving international human rights problems; and to encourage both teachers and students to ponder the implications of these issues" (Totten, 1985, p. 445).

The extent to which social studies teachers avail themselves of these and other material varies. As is true for teachers in Western Europe, American teachers differ in their eagerness to inject human rights education into the curriculum, in their knowledge of the requisite content and suitable methodology, and in their skill of creating a classroom atmosphere in which human rights concepts are understood and honored.

Two Germanys, Two Interpretations of Human Rights Education

From 1871 until the end of World War II, there existed only one Germany. Its division into two nations thereafter, first and foremost must be attributed to its National Socialist leader during the Third Reich, 1933–1945, Adolf Hitler. He was a dictator whose many aggressions brought together the nations that were repulsed by his demagoguery. In the postwar years they framed the meaning of human rights out of their experiences during the Hitler era. Hitler's unprovoked attacks on other nations, his curtailment of personal and political freedom in Germany, his destruction of the judicial system during his Third Reich, the concentration camps and his genocide of Jews in Europe, and the forced labor camps during World War II, all these became the offenses against humanity which were condemned in the subsequent human rights agreements.

For Germans, whether now in the Federal Republic of Germany or the German Democratic Republic, that part of German history remains identical. Their present conception of government, however, is quite different. The Federal Republic has allied itself with the Western democracies and is a member of the Council of Europe, while the German Democratic Republic is a socialist nation first shaped by and still closely linked with the Soviet Union. As might be expected, their respective interpretations of human rights differs and the implementation in schools therefore represents a noticeable contrast. Both, though, give attention to the topic in the curriculum.

The Federal Republic of Germany

Few countries have shown as much concern for human rights in our time as the Federal Republic of Germany. Since the 1959 Swastika painting episodes, the holocaust has been part of the content to be taught in history classes. Periodically a new impetus is given to this charge, such as when the American TV movie "The Holocaust" was shown on West German television, when US President Ronald Reagan visited the Bitburg cemetery in West Germany in 1985, or when the death in South America of Dr Joseph Mengele, the infamous Ausschwitz concentration camp doctor, was confirmed, that same year.

Human rights also are kept before the West German public, including students, because of the status of human rights in Eastern Europe. The

Soviet Union operationalizes human rights from a posture which places the welfare of the state ahead of individual freedoms. The Soviet leaders expect the GDR, Poland, and the other Warsaw Pact nations of Eastern Europe to place the same interpretation on human rights as they do.

To guide that facet of the curriculum, the Bundeszentrale für Politische Bildung (Central Office for Political Education) in Bonn, the West German capital, devoted some of its pamphlets to human rights (Bundeszentrale, 1978). The series of regularly published pamphlets, *Informationen*, are to aid teachers of political education, or social studies, geography, or history. Photographs illustrate dramatically the need for human rights agreements and instances where they have been violated. Teachers are also given suggestions for incorporating these materials into their curriculum, making the pamphlet a comprehensive and therefore invaluable resource for human rights education (Bundeszentrale, 1978c). Besides a more visually oriented and contemporary treatment of human rights in the *Zeitlupe 8: Menschenrechte* (Bundeszentrale, 1978) and a pamphlet explaining what the Council of Europe does to guard human rights (Bundeszentrale, 1978b), a further resource is the volume on human rights, *Die Menschenrechte—eine Herausforderung der Erziehung*, also published by the Bundeszentrale für Politische Bildung (Schmidt-Sinns and Dallinger, 1981). Based on conference papers and protocols of the working groups at a 1980 conference on human rights education, it implements the recommendation agreed to by the West German states' (*Länder*) ministers of education that ". . . the students should be ready to use the question of the realization of human rights as an important measure for judging political conditions at home and in other countries. Included in that readiness is that of being prepared to insist on the human rights of others" (Schmidt-Sinns and Dallinger, 1981, p. 7).

The book *Die Menschenrechte—eine Herausforderung der Erziehung* offers teachers a stimulating series of articles which reflect the political interpretations of the concept of human rights, as well as didactic approaches to human rights education in schools. Professor Wolfgang Hilligen urges the inclusion of the history of the events which gave rise to human rights agreements in order to engage students in discussing the conditions and difficulties that form part of that record.

Hilligen proposes four essential instructional elements for successful human rights education:

1. Systematic use of open communication within the classroom.
2. Group work and partner work.
3. Learning of analytical or investigative procedures and skills to permit students individually to dissect specific cases or problems.
4. Use of students' own questions and interests as starting points (Hilligen, 1981, p. 58).

These same ideas were found essential by the working groups at this particular human rights conference. Sponsored by the Bundeszentrale für Politische Bildung and the West German UNESCO Commission, it included in its agenda a report of a Bundeszentrale sponsored contest on innovative ways of teaching about human rights. One of the winners, a class of 10th grade students in Hamburg, had studied torture with the help of their civics (political education) and art teacher. They read, discussed, drew, and wrote about who uses torture, for what reasons, what it feels like, and the political conditions which lead to its use and those which prevent its occurrence. The class watched films and studied the work of Amnesty International. Their final topic was what each person can do to join the fight against the use of torture. In addition to becoming a member of Amnesty International, the students listed military operations, writing letters or campaigning to end torture, and informing fellow students about human rights (Kersten, 1980).

Another winner in the contest was a UNESCO model secondary school in West Berlin. Here the goal was to show the discrepancies between the *Declaration of the Rights of the Child* and the reality of everyday life for many children in the world.

While the contest of the Bundeszentrale encouraged West German teachers and students to plunge into human rights education, the curriculum guides of the eleven West German states ask that teachers regularly deal with certain aspects of human rights.

In the Federal Republic of Germany, as in the Council of Europe, any concern with human rights education soon gives recognition to the need for (1) teachers to be formally prepared to deal with human rights, (2) research to identify effective ways of introducing human rights principles, and (3) instructional materials for all age groups.

The German Democratic Republic

According to Otto Grotewohl, the German Democratic Republic's first prime minister, "fundamental human rights are an illusion if they are not matched by the political and economic realities which facilitate their implementation" (Grönert, 1985, p. 36). It is the government's responsibility to ensure that political and economic conditions are such that human rights exist in practice. In the German Democratic Republic (GDR), a socialist society, the constitution and subsequent legislation provide the following fundamental rights:

> The right to life in peace, to work, to economic security, to education, to democratic involvement in the affairs of society, and equal rights for women (Grönert, 1985, p. 37).

In reference to the first, the right to a life in peace, the GDR in 1950 enacted the Protection of Peace Act, which ". . . prescribes heavy penalties for any form of war propaganda, revanchism, and the incitement of racial hatred" (Grönert, 1985, p. 37). The East Germans had, after all, inherited the same yoke of guilt for the crimes of National Socialism as the West Germans.

Peace education in the GDR seems to be two-pronged. On the one hand ". . . a large proportion of teaching time at the 10-year polytechnical school is devoted to the idea of peace, international friendship and solidarity" (Grönert, 1985, p. 37). Elementary readers, the major textbook used in the early grades, attest to this objective. The primer, for example, features a poem entitled, "The Sun Shines on Everyone." It goes on to say that all children want peace, that peace means happiness and play, both of which all children want whether their parents are black, yellow, or white. Therefore, you must guard peace to let children everywhere be happy. (Krowicki, 1982). In a poem in the second grade reader children learn that the first of May, a Socialist holiday, should serve as a warning for all time to seek peace and friendship (Gruse, 1971, p. 58). In the fourth grade reader an entire section is labelled "For peace, friendship around the world and socialism— for a happy life for all peace-loving persons" (German Democratic Republic, *Lesebuch, Klasse 4*, 1972, p. 3).

The third grade social studies text echoes the other approach to peace education. That a defense posture is the means to maintain peace is conveyed here and in other textbooks by means of pictures of the *Volksarmee*, the GDR army which guards the nation's borders (Drefenstedt, 1976). "Imperialists," including the United States, are painted as the enemies of peace. According to an official in the Ministry of Defense, educators can have no higher calling than to prepare youth to be ready and able to defend their country. To do one's military service is a means of preserving peace.

The readiness to participate in defense is fostered in the GDR from kindergarten on, not only by means of stories that glorify soldiering, but also by children's visits to military posts, military displays on every national holiday, and an actual introduction to military skills in the upper grades of the school. (Wensierski, 1983). In grade 9 and 10 (when students are between 15 and 17 years of age), defense education is a required subject for four hours per week. For boys, military training is introduced, and for girls, civil defense is the focus (Zimmermann, 1985, (2)).

GDR youth know well that their rights include those of completing their education to the level where they can meet their peers' competition, of being included in the labor force, and making a living wage, and, if they are female, of possessing legal equality with males. That they experience discrimination should they opt out of participating in the FDJ (*Freie Deutsche Jugend*), a youth organization, or be active in the peace movement is known to many. While their right of access to knowledge is circumscribed in schools, universities, and the GDR's own media, youth and their elders can and do watch West German television without official interference. As a window to the West, the Federal Republic's telecasts, which include American, British, and other continental programs, may reshape East German youth's perception of human rights. What is significant in the case of the GDR is that human rights are viewed as the collective rights of citizens of the state, while in the FRG, as in other Western democracies, the state is charged with the preservation of individual rights, i.e., human rights. Human rights education in schools varies accordingly. In Third World countries, such as Zimbabwe, a fusion between the collectivist and the individualist approach to human rights education has not yet occurred.

Determinants of Education about Human Rights

The inclusion of human rights education in the curriculum of schools is a derivative of a series of factors, as these case studies indicate. First, the definition of human rights education varies. There is the legal definition which is drawn from the international documents that many nations have signed over the years. Some of the socialist nations offer their own political definition, which functions like a codicil attached to the international agreements. More important, teachers' and administrators' definitions of human rights education often include only those human rights which they think can be accommodated in their curriculum and classrooms.

A second determinant of human rights education is the general sense of the importance the society attaches to human rights. Where there is a genuine commitment or sense of urgency, an effort is made to include them in the curriculum. Such is the case in the Federal Republic of Germany. Human rights education receives support publicly and privately. The memory of the gross violations of human rights during the Third Reich remains. In reverse, where human rights are repeatedly curtailed, such as has been the case in Uganda and Argentina in the past, human rights education has been absent from the curriculum.

In the case of the Federal Republic of Germany, Ministry of Education guidelines state directly that human rights education is a part of the curriculum. The member states of the Council of Europe and some school districts in the United States fall into this category. In that case, teachers may well receive suggestions on how to engage in human rights education.

Human rights education is far more likely to be pursued in schools where teachers have been involved in workshops or seminars on the subject. For example, those teachers who have had the opportunity to do so under the umbrella of the Council of Europe have become convinced that human rights education can be included effectively in their classrooms. They have weighed the advantage of interspersing the topic throughout the subjects they cover in their classes against making a separate subject or topic out of it.

The persuasiveness with which teachers approach the subject may depend on their own involvement in Amnesty International or other formal organizations or information groups that show a deep concern for the maintenance of human rights around the world.

Human rights education, furthermore, is shaped by the opportunities teachers have to inform themselves about the subject and to discuss with others how it may be dealt with in their classes to evoke a caring response from their students. These issues clearly are more easily resolved when teachers either produce themselves or are provided with instructional materials which reflect the several aspects of human rights education that may be included in the curriculum.

The final determinant very likely is the teacher's own conviction that human rights can be effected in one's classroom. That same teacher's skill to do so becomes a critical factor. A democratic classroom where each student is respected by all others, where there reigns a caring atmosphere among students and teacher, and where the teacher designs the instructional plan with the students, and all participate in its execution, appear to be the ingredients of a classroom environment in which human rights are ever present. That kind of classroom forms a credible basis for human rights education.

References

Amnesty International (1985) *Today* July 1 National Broadcasting Corporation.

Amnesty International (1984) Amnesty International (Pamphlet).

Branson, M. S. and Torney-Purta, J. V. (1982) *International human rights, society, and the schools*. Washington, DC: National Council for the Social Studies.

Bundeszentrale für Politische Bildung (1978a) *Zeitlupe 8: Menschenrechte* [Focus on today: human rights]. Bonn: Bundeszentrale für Politische Bildung.

Bundeszentrale für Politische Bildung (1978b) *Was tut der Europarat zum Schutz der Menschenrechte?* [What does the European Parliament do for the protection of human rights?] Bonn: Bundeszentrale für Politische Bildung.

Bundeszentrale für Politische Bildung (1978c) *Die Menschenrechte: Informationen zur Politischen Bildung*. [Human rights: Information for political education] 129. Bonn: Bundeszentrale für Politische Bildung.

Council of Europe (1953) *Convention for the protection of human rights and fundamental freedoms*. Strasbourg: Council of Europe, European Treaty Series, No. 5, entered into force on September 3, 1953.

Council of Europe (1980) *Project No. 1—Preparation for life*. Strasbourg: Council of Europe, Council for Cultural Cooperation.

Council of Europe (1981). *The teaching of human rights*. Report on the Eighth European Seminar of Teachers in Member States. Donaueschingen, Federal Republic of Germany, May 19–23, 1980. Strasbourg: Council for Cultural Cooperation.

Council of Europe (1984) *Learning for life*. Strasbourg: Directorate of Press and Information of the Council of Europe.

Council of Europe (1985) *Human rights education in primary schools*. Reports of Working Groups I, II, and III. Twenty-eighth European Teachers' Seminar, Donaueschingen, Federal Republic of Germany.

Drefenstedt, B. (Ed.) (1976) *Heimatkunde, Klasse 3* [Community study, geography, and social studies, 3rd grade]. Berlin: Volk und Wissen Volkseigener Verlag.

Etzold, S. (1984) Religion at school: Success "is being not meaningless". Kölner Stadt-Anzeiger, in *The German Tribune* (Hamburg, January 9, 1984), 1115, p. 11.

German Democratic Republic (1972) *Lesebuch Klasse 4* [Reader, Grade 4]. Berlin: Volk und Wissen Volkseigener Verlag.

Grönert, B. (1985) Human rights: Words and deeds. *Prisma*, **3**(85), 36–41.

Gruse, A. (1971) *Unser Kampftag—unser Feiertag, Lesebuch Klasse 2* [Our fighting day—Our holiday, reader, grade 2] (A. Gruse, Ed.). Berlin: Volk und Wissen Volkseigener Verlag.

Hampshire Education Authority (1978) Agreed syllabus for religious education. Winchester, UK: Author.

Hilligen, W. (1981) Die Menschenrechte in Erziehung und Unterricht [Human rights in education]. In D. Schmidt-Sinns and G. Dallinger (Eds.), *Die Menschenrechte: Eine Herausforderung der Erziehung* [Human rights: A challenge to education] Vol. 181. Bonn: Bundeszentrale für Politische Bildung, pp. 41–65.

Kersten, M. (1980) *Torture—Report to the Conference on Human Rights Education*. Hamburg: Haus Riessen.

Krowicki, M. (1982) *Unsere Fibel* [Our primer] (9th ed.). Berlin: Volk und Wissen Volkseigener Verlag.

Mariet, F. (1981) *The teaching of human rights*. Eighth European Seminar, Donaueschingen, Federal Republic of Germany, May 19–23, 1980. Strasbourg: Council of Europe.

Perotti, A. (1984) *Action to combat intolerance and xenophobia*. Strasbourg: Council of Europe.

Schmidt-Sinns, D. and Dallinger, G. (Eds.) (1981) *Die Menschenrechte: Eine Herausforderung der Erziehung* [Human rights: A challenge to education], Vol. 181, p. 7. Bonn: Bundeszentrale für Politische Bildung.

Schmitt, K. (1980) *Politische Erziehung in der DDR* [Political education in the German Democratic Republic]. Paderborn: Schoningh.

Sibanda, M., Moyana, H. and Gumbo, D. S. (1982) *The African heritage: History for junior secondary school*, book 1. Harare, Zimbabwe: Zimbabwe Educational Books.

Starkey, H. (1982) Social education for teenagers: Aims, issues, and problems. Report on Council for Cultural Cooperation Project No. 1, *Preparation for life*. Solna, Sweden, September 15–19, 1980. Strasbourg: Council of Europe.

Starkey, H. (1984) *Human rights education in schools in Western Europe*. Symposium, Vienna, Austria, May 17–20, 1983. Strasbourg: Council of Europe.

Starkey, H. (1985) Teachers' course on teaching and learning about human rights in schools. Strasbourg: Council of Europe.

Stradling, R. (1980) *Political Dilemmas*. London: Hansard Society for Parliamentary Government.

Totten, S. (1985) International human rights education. *Social Education*, **49**, 444–543.

United States. Commissioner of Education (1979) *Task force on global education*. Washington, DC: Author.

Wensierski, P. (1983) Friedensbewegung in der DDR [Peace movement in the German Democratic Republic]. *Aus Politik und Zeitgeschichte*, April 30, pp. 5–14.

Zimbabwe. Ministry of Education and Culture (1984a) *History syllabus: Zimbawe Junior Certificate Forms I and II, first examination, 1984*. Harare, Zimbabwe: Curriculum Development Unit.

Zimbabwe. Ministry of Education and Culture (1984b) *Religious and moral education syllabus: Zimbabwe Junior Certificate, first examination, 1984*. Harare, Zimbabwe: Curriculum Development Unit.

Zimmerman, H. (Ed.) (1985) *DDR Handbuch* [German Democratic Republic almanac] (3rd ed). Bonn: Bundesministerium für Innerdeutsche Beziehungen: Cologne: Verlag Wissenschaft und Politik.

CHAPTER 12

Education About Human Rights: Teacher Preparation

Kim Sebaly
Kent State University, USA

Introduction

Since the adoption of the *UN Charter* (1945) and the *Universal Declaration of Human Rights* (1948), there has been no shortage of recommendations that teachers should be better prepared to develop human rights perspectives and skills among their students. The increasing recognition of the universal right to learn about human rights is making human rights education a vital part of international education activities throughout the world. Publications, seminars and international conferences have supported teacher educators in their attempts to discover how to include more teaching about human rights in their programs. They have also given guideposts to educators exploring the meaning of schooling and teacher education in the rapidly emerging "global village."

This chapter presents a survey of efforts by different nations, largely through the UN system, to introduce human rights in the education of prospective and inservice teachers, and highlights some of the conceptual and procedural issues that have emerged from them. It also examines some of these issues from the perspective of the author's experience of using human rights as a central theme in a graduate course in comparative education at his university. The chapter concludes with reflections on different meanings international human rights have in the civic learning of teachers in different countries, and explores possible implications for teacher education reforms.

Issues in Teacher Education for Human Rights

Preparing teachers in all fields to teach for international understanding has been a predominant theme in the activities of the UN Educational Scientific and Cultural Organization (UNESCO) since its inception in 1946 (UNESCO, 1949; Willcock, 1962; Serden, 1962; Domnitz, 1965; Scotney, 1967; Lawson, 1969, UNESCO, 1970; Montandon, 1983). For four decades

UNESCO has provided a forum for Member States to express and share contrasting concepts of international education and information about programs and achievements. Although peripheral in most national teacher education efforts, how to prepare teachers to understand and appreciate other cultures in a human rights context has been central in UNESCO programs.

To help close the gaps between various UNESCO initiatives and activities undertaken by its Member States, UNESCO adopted an integrative instrument on education for international understanding in 1974: *Recommendation Concerning Education for International Understanding, Cooperation and Peace and Education Relating to Human Rights and Fundamental Freedoms*. Adopted during a period of increasing awareness of conclusive international economic and social changes, it reflected shifting emphases in interpretations and conceptual linkages between traditional civil and political rights and the economic, social and cultural rights (UNESCO, 1973). The 1974 Recommendation established the first international criteria and priorities for teaching about human rights that would activate international, regional and national efforts to accomplish them.

"Teacher preparation," Section VII of the Recommendation, reveals its scope and the comprehensive range of tasks it is thought that teacher education institutions need to undertake to achieve the goals noted in the long title. Besides teaching preservice teachers to commit themselves to the ethic of human rights and the aim of changing society toward more complete fulfillment of human rights goals, preparation programs would help future teachers learn to:

—appreciate the fundamental unity of mankind; to instill in others an appreciation of the riches of diverse cultures.
—acquire a basic interdisciplinary knowledge of world problems and problems of international cooperation, and how to work in solving them.
—take active part in devising international education programs, educational equipment and materials.
—comprise experiments in the use of active methods of education and techniques of evaluation.
—develop aptitudes and skill to continue their training; experience teamwork and interdisciplinary studies, and knowledge of group dynamics.

Preservice teachers would also study different experiments in international education, especially those in other countries, and have opportunities for direct contact with foreign teachers. The Recommendation also addressed the need for inservice education for admininstrators and other school personnel.

Within this context UNESCO led or co-sponsored a series of activities to promote the implementation of the Recommendation. Among the publications which resulted from these and other UNESCO meetings, and which have particular relevance to teacher educators, are the *UNESCO Handbook for the Teaching of Social Studies* (Mehlinger, 1981); *Frontiers of Human Rights Education* (Eide and Thee, 1983); and *Teaching for International Understanding, Peace and Human rights* (Graves, Dunlop, Torney-Purta, 1984). Although of less direct relevance to professional educators, UNESCO's college-level text on human rights, *The International Dimensions of Human Rights* (Vasak, 1982) is of interest for the analysis it provides on the way human rights are viewed from African, Latin American, Asian, and Eastern European perspectives. Human rights traditions and problems in teaching about human rights are also explored in numerous regional and national reports (Australian National Advisory Committee for UNESCO, 1972; O'Conner, 1980; Tay, 1981; Haavelsrud, 1983; Dougherty, 1984; Lister, 1984; Starkey, 1984, 1985).

In both UNESCO and national reports, the most frequently noted shortcoming in efforts to advance human rights teaching, at all levels and in all fields, is the lack of well-qualified teachers. The following profiles of issues and prescriptions for successful human rights teaching reveal some of the basic challenges teacher education institutions in any culture would face if the promotion of international human rights were to become a primary goal in their work.

Different Concepts of Human Rights

Each region, if not each country in the world, has its own way of defining human rights and interpreting human rights questions (Georgeoff, 1968; Charmant, 1979; Margocsy, 1979; Dinsdale, 1980; Donnelly, 1982; Pollis, 1982; Coomarswamy, 1982; Kovalenko, 1982; Kartashkin, 1982; Eide and Thee, 1983; Eide, 1983; Senarclens, 1983; Tomasevski, 1983; Tchakarov, 1982; Yamane, 1983; Welch and Meltzer, 1984). Each country presently views the current pattern of human rights teaching outside of its region as "subversive" (Yamane, 1983; Eide, 1983). Developing nations tend to view human rights teaching as subversive when objectives do not emphasize peoples' rights, indigenous values and institutions, and barriers to economic growth caused by their dependencies on western democratic or Marxist-Socialist nations. Socialist nations stress the importance of economic, social and cultural rights standards and the duties of individuals inherent in state actions to protect rights in these areas. The failure of human rights teaching to emphasize the fundamental inalienable character of civil rights, and the perceived shift to a consideration of "people's" rights under UNESCO leadership, has led the United States and Great Britain to withdraw from the organization altogether, and to encourage other Western states to follow their lead.

The Content of Human Rights Teaching

Closely related to issues that result from different interpretations of human rights are questions about what constitutes the cognitive and affective content of human rights that prospective teachers should learn. One approach, influenced by the lead taken by faculties of law throughout the world, emphasizes the juridical basis of human rights. The documents, resolutions and the interpretations given to them in the context of the historical, philosophical, and legal traditions of different societies are emphasized.

The social science approach to human rights content draws relationships between rights statements and major contemporary problems and international events. Teaching about human rights is closely associated with development, peace and disarmament education and specific topics of human rights violations; e.g., apartheid, racism, colonialism, terrorism, and poverty and starvation (UNESCO, 1978; UNESCO, 1982; UNESCO, 1983).

Emphasis in successful programs is also given to affective content. Tolerance, mutual respect, commitment to the proposed new international economic order, special empathy with the most desperate victims of human rights violations, yearning for human rights, objective "human-centered concern" are but a few of the affective objectives that different projects recommend that students should learn (Churchill and Omari, 1981).

Methods of Human Rights Teaching

In addition to acquiring the skills to foster critical thinking, beginning teachers would need to learn numerous methods thought to be critical in human rights teaching. They should learn how to lead and participate in open discussion; involve students in the creation of curricula; establish classroom climates conducive to equal participation by all students; encourage expression of opinions about social and economic problems and government's actions to resolve them; emphasize student opportunities to exercise judgments and solve problems (Kidd, 1968; Leming, 1982; Torney-Purta, 1983).

Teachers would learn about the need for a staged introduction of human rights concepts from preschool through adulthood; and how at each stage to connect them with personal situations and experiences.

Organizational Support for Human Rights Teaching

Most observers have pointed out that human rights teaching is usually limited to one specialist or enthusiast. To enlist more primary and secondary teachers in the effort, several organizational issues require resolution.

Participation and cooperation must pervade the climate of the school and teachers must be given the freedom to teach. Appropriate materials, books and opportunities for foreign study must be available to all teachers (Graves, Dunlop, Torney-Purta, 1984).

Research Issues and Human Rights Teaching

Not only should teachers learn how to share their experiences of human rights teaching, including evaluated classroom experiences, but they should also know how to conduct studies that would lead to a better understanding of the relationship between different categories of human rights, economic development, disarmament and peace. Through their researches, they should also be able to help understand how catastrophic social, economic and political events affect their teaching; e.g., terrorism, refugees, unemployment (Yamane, 1983).

Human Rights in a Comparative Study of Education

The course described below evolved in response to the renewed challenge to appraise the meaning of citizenship in American life, to devise a new conception of the civic mission of American education and to establish pilot programs for developing new models of teacher education (Jones, 1985). The project was also undertaken to stimulate faculty and student awareness of the human rights movement since 1948, and to consider its potential contribution in the effort to make civic values central in the education of teachers (Butts, 1982).

The participants were experienced teachers, administrators, counselors, and educators in various non-school settings. Two of the classes met once a week for ninety minutes, for fifteen weeks, and one met for twenty sessions during a five-week summer term. The course evolved in a somewhat different manner each time, but in each class students worked to overcome an initial indifference to the study of human rights, acquired knowledge of basic human rights documents and their educational provisions, formulated education rights questions and applied them in different case studies. The readings and course materials outlined in Appendix A were essentially the same for each group.

Images of the "global village" provided the starting point for the classes. It was assumed that if we are living in a global society, then human rights are a plausible and perhaps necessary framework from which to evaluate the educational performance of different nations. Most of the examples of contemporary global linkages and dependencies were drawn from the teachers' experiences. Films and tapes also reinforced the connections that were drawn, and introduced the human rights issues that were implied. "Remember Me," produced for the International Year of the Child (1979) focussed on the lost educational opportunities of twelve children from different regions of the world and the consequent loss of talent and creativity to their families and communities. Roger Rosenblatt's brief television essay on the death of strangers near and far was useful in considering questions about the limits of responsibility for human rights violations in places physically and psychologically distant from one's culture. The essay, originally broadcast at the end of a nightly news hour, probed the meaning of human rights through deaths in Nazi concentration camps, the suffering of homeless people in Washington, DC, famine victims in Ethiopian and Sudanese villages and refugees in numerous societies. "One Word of Truth," a dramatization of Alexander Solzhenitsen's Nobel Prize speech, explored similar themes and examined the role of artists and writers in revealing the unity of human values.

Charles Humana's *World Human Rights Guide* (1984) provided the class with an indispensable starting point for discussing formal human rights documents and the theoretical issues of universality and indivisibility of rights. In the initial version of the *Guide* (1984) seventy-five countries are ranked on their adherence to fifty human rights standards, and summary ratings for thirty-two others are included in Humana's classification. The ratings and background data on each ranked country are provided on two facing pages of text. His survey of the limitation of his classification, which is based solely on the Civic and Political Covenant, introduced students to the distinction between the two UN Covenants and the background of their adoption.

Humana's rankings encouraged teachers to raise questions about human rights formulations, when and how they were devised, and how they related to one another. The study of regional accords, especially those sections that detail various aspects of education as a right, led members of the groups to discuss the way rights are variously defined by countries with different political and social priorities. Conditions which led to the proposal and adoption of particular education rights and records of which nations had signed, ratified or voiced support for the general agreements were also appraised.

The *Universal Declaration of Human Rights* and both UN Covenants provided the basis for devising criteria by which to compare and judge the educational performance of different nations. Categories of education rights, established to clarify what they meant in the context of educational systems, are outlined in Appendix B. The three major categories were, the *rights of access* to a country's educational system; the *freedom to learn* certain things in the formal system; and the *right to control* the process of education under certain conditions. Qualifications, similar in form to those used by Humana, were devised to test the common standards for vulnerable groups or different subjects.

By the middle of the term students began to focus their study of education rights in different country settings, working in some cases individually and in others as members of a team exploring the background of a single nation. Western-democratic, Marxist-socialist and non-aligned nations were represented in both individual and group efforts. Collectively students drafted questions they thought should be asked to determine the education rights performance of a country. In drafting the questions, students were instructed to consider possible rankings of the countries studied, using a format similar to that adopted by Humana. More films on the countries selected for study were shown to the entire class.

The questionnaire (see Appendix B) devised by the classes generated the most discussion of any procedure in the course. After using it to organize information about the educational systems being studied, students criticized the questionnaire's tendency to reflect the more cognitive aspects of education rights. They did not think the questions they had devised revealed what actually occurred in schools, what opportunities were given, what concepts were learned, and what students, parents and teachers thought about their educational rights.

The process of drawing up the questionnaire did focus attention on each education right and the almost limitless number of questions that could be raised about how education occurred under these descriptions. It also led students to a more thorough search of source material about education in different societies. UN documents, UNESCO reports, World Bank Studies and the reports of numerous regional educational organizations helped students to become aware of discrepancies in various encyclopedic surveys of education and in some monographic literature as well. Feelings of inadequacy in responding to questions about countries for which they had little knowledge and appreciation also increased their desire to meet people from or to visit the countries they were studying.

Observations on Education Rights and Teaching Human Rights

Evidence that knowledge about human rights increased as a result of the course was apparent from the personal statements prepared at the end of it. All students felt that they had been inadequately prepared to study other cultures and were generally unaware that there were explicit statements of international human rights. Their initial resistance to study human rights in light of their present occupational commitments and professional specialisms was overcome mainly through the elaboration of the educational rights questionnaire. Many discovered in the process that the ultimate rationale for many of the duties they regularly performed could be traced to various human rights provisions.

Several students resisted relinquishing the stereotypes they held of other countries and their educational systems, even after their analyses. This was particularly so in the cases of the Soviet Union, which received relatively high rankings by students; Japan, which received numerous critical comments; and India, which was discovered to be among the leading industrial nations in the world with a complex modern system of education in most urban regions. There was reluctance on the part of most students to be critical of the US educational performance on different rights questions. This became a central issue in one class when a foreign student selected the United States for study and presented some of her findings.

Perhaps the most difficult question for participants in the comparative class was caused by the discovery that human rights are variously defined according to different political and economic traditions in the modern world. Recognition that different nations have had shifting perspectives on human rights during the past 40 years underscored what some accepted as the dynamic character of human rights.

Five tentative conclusions about teaching human rights through comparative education might be useful in a consideration of some of the broader issues of teacher education reform outlined in the first part of this chapter.

—Carefully structured sessions to explore the concept of the "global village" in light of personal local experiences, are prerequisites to making the study of broad human rights concepts believable and worthwhile to experienced educators, pursuing rigidly structured degree programs.

—Examination of human rights documents and interpretations of human rights traditions in different societies is required, especially if balanced interpretations of education and other rights are to be compiled. The comparison of education rights performance reveals as many differences within nations as between them.

—The use of a valid comprehensive human rights ranking system is an effective means to introduce human rights and stimulate questions about their meaning in different societies. The compilation of a ranking system for education rights may be a critical pedagogical tool.

—Human rights may be an essential element of professional education, especially in institutions where students are trained for specialization in such diverse areas as health, mental retardation, vocational education, media, administration, adult education and reading. It may be unethical *not* to have human rights education for teachers.

—Human rights performance in one area (e.g., education) may increase or decrease the observance of human rights in other areas (e.g. political participation and health services). The determination of course syllabi and teaching methods for human rights should focus on the conceptual framework of the particular discipline, but it should also lead students to see connections with other domains of human rights inquiry.

References

Australian National Advisory Committee for UNESCO (1972) Seminar on education for international understanding. Adelaide, Australia, October 9–10, 1970 (ERIC Document Reproduction Service No. ED 070 721).

Butts, R. (1982) International human rights and civic education. In M. Branson and J. Torney-Purta (Eds.), *International human rights, society and the schools* (pp. 23–33).

Charmant, H. (1979) An international conference on political socialization: Some reflections on the Eastern European approach. *International Journal of Political Education*, **2**, 375–382.

Churchill, S. and Omari, I (1981) Evaluation of UNESCO Associated Schools Project in education for international cooperation and peace. (ERIC Document Reproduction Service No. ED 110 214).

Coomaraswamy, R. (1982) A third world view of human rights. *The UNESCO Courier*, August–September, pp. 49–52.

Dinsdale, J. (1980) Teaching and education to promote the respect of human rights: The Council of Europe's recent efforts to promote teaching, education and research in the field of human rights. *International Journal of Political Education*, **2**, 163–175.

Domnitz, M. (Ed.) (1965) *Educational techniques for combating prejudice and discrimination and for promoting better intergroup understanding*. Hamburg: UNESCO Institute for Education.

Donnelly, J. (1982) Human rights and foreign policy. *World Politics*, **34**(4), 576–595.

Dougherty, J. (1984) *Materials for teaching human rights in secondary schools*. Strasbourg: International Institute of Human Rights.

Eide, A. (1983) Dynamics of human rights and the role of the educator. *Bulletin of Peace Proposals*, **14**(1), 105–114.

Eide, A. and Thee, M. (Eds.) (1983) *Frontiers of human rights education*. Oslo: Universitetsforlagat.

Georgeoff, P. (1968) *The social education of Bulgarian youth*. Minneapolis, MN: University of Minnesota Press.

Graves, N. J., Dunlop, O. J. and Torney-Purta, J. V. (Eds.) (1984) *Teaching for international understanding, peace and human rights*. Paris: UNESCO.

Haavelsrud, M. (1983) Report on the UNESCO meeting on the teaching of human rights. *International Journal of Political Education*, **6**(1), 87–92.

Humana, C. (1984/1985) *World human rights guide*. London: Hutchinson. (*Guide mondial des droits de l'homme*. Paris: Buchet/Chastel).

Jones, E. (Ed.) (1985) *Civic learning for teachers: Capstone for educational reform*. Ann Arbor, MI: Prakken.

Kartashkin, V. (1982) The socialist countries and human rights. In K. Vasek (Ed.) *The international dimensions of human rights*, pp. 631–650. Westport, CT: Greenwood Press.

Kidd, S. (1968) *Some suggestions on teaching about human rights*. Paris: UNESCO.

Kovalenko, Y. I. (1982) International education in schools in the Union of Soviet Socialist Republics. *UNESCO, International Understanding at School* (Circular No. 43).

Lawson, T. (Ed.) (1969) *Education for international understanding*. Hamburg: UNESCO Institute for Education.

Leming, J. S. (1982) Civic learning, schooling and the dynamics of normative socialization. Paper presented at the Annual Meeting of the American Educational Research Association, March 19–23. (ERIC Document Reproduction Service No. ED 218 210).

Lister, I. (1984) *Teaching and learning about human rights*. Strasbourg: Council of Europe.

Margocsy, J. (1979) Education for peace and international understanding in the training of teachers. *Prospects: Quarterly Review of Education*, **9**(2), 197–202.

Montandon, E. (1983) Education for international understanding, peace and human rights. *Educational Documentation and Information* #266. Geneva: International Bureau of Education.

O'Conner, E. (1980) *World studies in the European classroom*. Strasbourg: Council of Europe.

Pollis, A. (1982) Liberal, socialist and third world perspectives of human rights. In A. Pollis and P. Schwab (Eds.), *Toward a human rights framework* (pp. 2–26). New York: Praeger.

Scotney, G. (Ed.). (1967) *The Associated Schools Project at the primary level—Study of other countries and other cultures in promoting education for international understanding.* Hamburg: UNESCO Institute for Education.

Senarclens, P. de (1983) Research and teaching of human rights: Introductory remarks. *Bulletin of Peace Proposals*, **14**(1) 7–14.

Serden, H. (Ed.) (1962) *Education for international understanding under conditions of tension.* Hamburg: UNESCO Institute for Education.

Starkey, H. (Ed.) (1984) *Human rights education in schools in western Europe.* Symposium, Vienna, Austria, May 17–20, 1983. Strasbourg: Council of Europe.

Starkey, H. (Ed.) (1985) *Teaching and learning about human rights in schools.* Teachers' course, Livry-Gargan, France, May 28–30, 1984. Strasbourg: Council of Europe.

Tay, A. (Ed.) (1981) *Teaching about Human Rights: An Australian symposium.* Canberra: Australian Government Publishing Service.

Tchakarov, N. (1983) Education for peace and international understanding in the People's Republic of Bulgaria. *International Review of Education*, **29**(3), 409–413.

Tomasevski, K. (1983) Approaches to human rights in the socio-economic and cultural context of eastern Europe. *Bulletin of Peace Proposals*, **14**(1), 97–102.

Torney-Purta, J. (1983) Psychological perspectives on enhancing civic education through the education of teachers. *Journal of Teacher Education*, **346**(6), 30–34.

UNESCO (1970) *Education for international understanding and peace, with special reference to moral and civic education.* Paris: UNESCO. (ERIC Document Reproduction Service No. ED 053 054).

UNESCO (1973) *Preliminary report on education for international understanding, cooperation and education relating to human rights and fundamental freedoms* (UNESCO Document No. ED/MD/27). Paris: UNESCO.

UNESCO (1978) *Proceedings of the International Congress on the Teaching of Human Rights.* Vienna: UNESCO.

UNESCO (1982) *Experts' meeting on the teaching of human rights* (UNESCO Document No. SS-82/Conf. 401/24). Strasbourg: International Institute of Human Rights.

UNESCO (1983) *Synthesis of member states reports on the application of the recommendation concerning education for international understanding, cooperation and peace and education relating to human rights and fundamental freedoms* (UNESCO Document ED 83/Conf. 214/2). Intergovernmental Conference on Education and International Understanding, Cooperation and Peace and Education Relating to Human Rights and Fundamental Freedoms, with a View to Developing a Climate of Opinion Favourable to the Strengthening of Security and Disarmament. Paris: UNESCO.

Vasak, K. (1982) *The international dimensions of human rights* (Vol. 2). Westport, CT: Greenwood Press.

Welch, C. and Meltzer, R. (Eds.) (1984) *Human rights and development in Africa.* New York: State University of New York Press.

Willcock, J. (1962) *Preparing teachers for education for international understanding.* Hamburg: UNESCO Institute for Education.

Yamane, H. (1983) Development of human rights teaching and research in Asia: Toward a de-ideologization through information. *Bulletin of Peace Proposals*, **14**(1), 45–52.

APPENDIX A

Comparative Education

Basic readings

Faure, E. *et al.* (1972) *Learning to be.* Paris: UNESCO.
Pollis, A. (1982) Liberal, socialist and third world perspectives of human rights. In A. Pollis and
P. Schwab., *Toward a human rights framework.* New York: Praeger.
Streeten, P. (1981) Basic needs and human rights. In P. Streeten, et al., *First things first:
Meeting basic human needs in developing countries.* Washington, DC: World Bank.
Humana, C. (1984) *World human rights guide.* London: Hutchinson.
Excerpts from various human rights documents (4 pp.)
Films:
"Future" [three scenarios]
"Any Man's Death Diminishes Me" [R. Rosenblatt Essay—MacNeil/Lehrer, 12/5/84]
"Remember Me" [International Year of the Child, 1979]
"Letters" [Brazil—Adult Literacy]
"The Soviet Union: A New Look" [1979]
"One Word of Truth" [A. Solzhenitsen's Nobel Prize Speech]
"Keep Fit, Study Well, Work Hard" [China, 1974]
"Children of the Tribe" [Japan]
"Transition Generation" [Afghanistan, 1973]

Recommended Readings

Bay, Christian. Self-respect as a human right: Thoughts on the dialects of wants and needs in
the struggle for human community. *Human Rights Quarterly, 4,* No. 1 (1982), pp. 53–75.
Benjamin, Harold. *Under their own command: Observations on the nature of a people's
education for war and peace.* New York: Macmillan, 1947.
Branson, Margaret and Torney-Purta, J. (eds.) *International human rights, society, and
schools.* Washington, DC: National Council for the Social Studies, 1982, pp. 23–33.
Buergenthal, T. and Torney, J. *International human rights and international education.*
Washington, DC: US National Commission for UNESCO, 1976.
Claude, R. P. (ed.) *Comparative human rights.* Baltimore: The Johns Hopkins University
Press, 1976.
Deminguez, J. I., Nigel, S., Wood, B. and Falk, R. *Enhancing global human rights.* New York:
McGraw-Hill, 1979.
Fischer, D. H. *Historians' fallacies: Toward a logic of historical thought.* New York: Harper &
Row, 1970.
Frank, T. M. *Nation against nation: What happened to the U.N. dream and what the U.S. can do
about it.* New York: Oxford University Press, 1985.
Gladwin, T. N. and Walter, I. *Multinationals under fire: Lessons on the management of conflict.*
New York: John Wiley & Sons, 1980. (see especially Ch. 5, "Human rights—the issues,"
pp. 131–166).
Gotesky, Rubin and Laszlo, Ervin (eds.) *Human dignity: This century and the next.* New York:
Gordon and Breach, 1970.
Hughes, Barry B. *World futures: A critical analysis of alternatives.* Baltimore: The Johns
Hopkins University Press, 1985.
Human rights, *Daedalus,* Fall, 1983. (A special issue of *Daedalus* based on the symposium
Rethinking human rights, sponsored by Emory University, 1982).
Lane, David. Human rights under state socialism. *Political Studies, 23* (September, 1984), pp.
349–368.
Levin, Leah. *Human rights: Questions and answers.* Paris: UNESCO, 1981.
Nelson, Jack L. and Green, V. M. (eds.) *International human rights: Contemporary issues.*
Stanfordville, NY: Human Rights Publishing Group, 1980.

Rights and responsibilities: International, social and individual dimensions. Los Angeles: University of Southern California Press, 1980. (See especially, David Mathews, Shifting values in higher education: From the individual to the ecological. (pp. 247–259).

Scott, A. *The Dynamics of interdependence.* Chapel Hill: The University of North Carolina Press, 1982.

United Nations. *Human rights: A compilation of international instruments.* New York: UN Sales No. 4 83, **14**(1), 1983.

Welch, C. E. and Meltzer, R. I. (eds.) *Human rights and development in Africa.* Albany, NY: State University of New York Press, 1984.

Woito, R. (ed.) *International human rights kit.* Chicago: World Without War Council, 1977.

APPENDIX B

International Education Rights Questionnaire
(Preliminary Draft)

1. *The Right to Free and Compulsory Primary Education*
   1.1   What constitutional or legal provision is made for primary education (including child labor laws)?
   1.2   What primary school age is designated or customary?
   1.3   What is the total female and male population for this age cohort?
   1.4   How many females with the following characteristics attend primary school on a regular basis without financial hardship?
   —urban
   —rural
   —religious, ethnic or minority group
   —high social class groups (upper social groups)
   —middle to lower social groups
   —physically challenged
   —mentally retarded
   1.5   How many males with the following characteristics attend primary school on a regular basis without financial hardship?
   —(same characteristics as above)
   1.6   What arrangements are made for preschool education?
   1.7   Are there procedures for enforcement of compulsory attendance?
   1.8   Is adequate transportation supplied without cost?
   1.9   Are adequate numbers of teachers trained to teach primary students?
   1.10 Are adequate buildings and facilities available?
   1.11 Do school personnel maintain contact with parents of students to encourage attendance and completion of school activities?
   1.12 Are health and medical measures taken (including free meals and counseling) to assure healthy students?

2. *The Right to Secondary Education in Its Different Forms (including technical and vocational) by All Appropriate Means*
   2.1   What constitutional or legal provision is made for secondary education?
   2.2   What secondary school age(s) is (are) designated or customary?
   2.3   What is the female and male population for this (these) age cohort(s)?
   2.4   How many females with the following characteristics attend secondary schools on a regular basis without financial hardship?
   —(same characteristics as above)
   2.5   How many males with the following characteristics attend secondary school on a regular basis without financial hardship?
   —(same characteristics as above)
   2.6   (see questions 8–12 under right to primary education above)
   2.7   What entrance requirements exist for different forms of secondary education?

2.8 Are selection examinations given at different stages of secondary schools to regulate entry and progress in different programs?

2.9 Is effective multiple language teaching available where student's language and medium of instruction are different?

2.10 Are scholarships provided for private secondary education?

3. *The Right to Equal Access to Higher Education*

3.1 What constitutional or legal provision is made for post-secondary education?

3.2 How many post-secondary places are available each year in different types of institutions; e.g.
   —part-time courses (including correspondence)
   —technical institute
   —first degree
   —post-graduate degree
   —foreign undergraduate
   —foreign graduate

3.3 How many students with the following characteristics are enrolled in each type of post-secondary institution without financial hardship?
   —male
   —female
   —upper social groups
   —middle to lower social groups
   —physically challenged
   —minority language background
   —minority religious background

3.4 Are admissions quotas for lower social groups reserved in university level institutions?

3.5 Are scholarships or grants provided for those qualified but without the means to study in post-secondary institutions?

3.6 Are selection and merit examinations fairly administered to guarantee equal access to professional studies?

3.7 Do students participate in meaningful ways in institutional governance?

3.8 Are adequate residential facilities (including student services and barrier free designs) provided?

4. *The Right to Acquire Fundamental Literacy*

4.1 What is the total female population of the country?

4.2 What is the estimated total number of female literates in each of the following categories?
   —(same characteristics as in 1.4)
   —different age cohorts (especially 15–35)

4.3 What is the total male population of the country?

4.4 What is the estimated total number of male literates in each of the following categories?
   —(same characteristics as in 1.4)
   —different age cohorts (especially 15–35)

4.5 What proportion of the effort to help citizens acquire fundamental literacy has been devoted to each of the following?
   —private volunteer
   —government sponsored targeted literacy projects
   —government sponsored mass literacy campaigns (including mass communication)

5. *The Right to Learn the Values and Customs of One's Group*

5.1 Is instruction (teachers, texts, materials, examinations) at the primary level provided in the languages of the students who attend?

5.2 What provision is made for students eligible to attend secondary schools to learn the national or official or other significant language if different from their own?

5.3 Does the instructional program of the dominant culture include materials that accurately portray the heritage (history, literature, art, world view) of minority group students?

5.4 Does the primary and secondary school allow for the observance of religious holidays of different groups of students?

5.5 Does the curriculum of the schools teach about the influences different cultures had on the formation of the existing dominant culture?

5.6 Is the concept and practice of citizenship education in the system one of cultural pluralism or cultural assimilation?

5.7 Can parents who would seek to establish their own school to teach their religious values do so?

6. *The Right to Obtain Vocational Guidance*

6.1 What laws govern the establishment of vocational guidance procedures and their relation to vocational training institutions?

6.2 Are diagnostic test instruments in the student's language available for vocational guidance in secondary institutions?

6.3 What test instruments or counseling procedures for vocational guidance and career placement are available in post-secondary institutions?

6.4 Are provisions made in academic institutions and work settings to facilitate career changes?

6.5 What is the status of the vocational counseling and personnel management professions? (societies, journals)

6.6 Is vocational guidance available to males and females on an equal basis?

6.7 Do licensing procedures discriminate unfairly against any groups seeking to enter vocations?

7. *The Right to Learn about Human Rights*

7.1 Has the government signed or ratified the basic human rights covenants?

7.2 To what extent is the constitution of the country based on principles explicitly stated in human rights covenants and other declarations?

7.3 What do citizens know about basic human rights?

7.4 Are units of instruction on the United Nations and its human rights activities developed sequentially during formal education?

7.5 Do students learn about procedures for filing complaints for violations of human rights provisions?

7.6 Does the content of citizenship education include instruction on international human rights?

7.7 Do scholars in different fields participate in international human rights research and organizations?

7.8 To what extent have policies for educational institutions such as the following been formulated from a human rights perspective?

—the rights of females to teach; to participate in sports and physical education; to receive scholarships and study grants

—the elimination of all forms of racial discrimination (except affirmative action)

—the availability of therapy and care for mentally retarded persons

8. *The Right of Parents to Choose the Kind of Education That Will Be Given to Their Children*

8.1 Can parents withhold their children from school attendance if a satisfactory alternative can be provided at home?

8.2 Can religious minorities establish schools to teach their religion?

8.3 Do parents participate in the process of selecting teachers and administrators?

8.4 Can parents make recommendations to alter the curriculum or the examination pattern of the school system?

8.5 Are parents part of the selection process where students are selected for different types of secondary schools?

8.6 Are scholarships available for study in private primary and secondary schools when parents wish to but cannot afford to send their children to them?

8.7 Can parents sit with teachers and school administrators to discuss the educational plan for their children?

9. *The Right to Freedom of Thought, Conscience and Religion*

   9.1   Is there separation of religious establishment in state controlled schools?

   9.2   Are religious and other groups permitted to establish their own schools?

   9.3   Does instruction on social issues and citizenship encourage divergent as well as convergent thinking about moral and political issues?

   9.4   Does instruction at all levels in the educational system encourage student initiated questions about the content covered and the conclusions implied in lessons?

   9.5   Is human rights perceived as a moral issue?

   9.6   Are teachers required to take loyalty oaths or are their social and political beliefs used to judge suitability for teaching?

   9.7   To what extent does instruction encourage problem solving and reflective thinking rather than only transmission of cultural values and skills?

CHAPTER 13

Human Rights and Education Viewed in a Comparative Framework: Synthesis and Conclusions

Judith Torney-Purta
University of Maryland at College Park
USA

Introduction

Human rights is a topic more often associated with lawyers than with educators. The specialists in comparative education and social science who have contributed to this volume bring a fresh yet discipline-based view to the subject, giving satisfying answers to some familiar questions but also raising new questions about the relation between education and human rights. A special strength of this book is that it melds the comparative and the international perspectives. Although these terms are often used synonymously, they have slightly different meanings. One can conduct a *comparison* of the domestic human rights policy or practice of different nations; one can also examine the human rights which are recognized in the *international* system, through international organizations and their declarations or other instruments. This volume takes internationally recognized human rights as a starting point and makes between-country comparisons of implementation, giving a welcome coherence of organization to a very diverse topic. This concluding chapter will do three things: first, suggest a context of general assumptions in which the other chapters should be viewed; second, delineate six thematic questions, each of which is addressed by several of the chapters; third, suggest some directions for further study of human rights by specialists in comparative education.

The volume makes a contribution quite different from that which would be made by one authored by legal experts. Nevertheless, it must include the perspective of international law on human rights as part of its background assumptions. Otherwise a major context for understanding educational rights issues will be missing. Some of the distinctions made by international lawyers concerning human rights are of particular importance. For example, clear differentiations between *basic rights* (such as the right not to be tortured), *civil and political rights* (such as the right to participate in one's

223

government), and *social, economic and cultural rights* (such as the right to an adequate standard of living for oneself and one's family) are at the core of most discussions of international human rights. Although respect for educational rights is usually considered as a part of social, economic, and cultural rights, provisions for education also have a role to play in ensuring that citizens are aware of and able to exercise civil and political rights. Legal specialists and those who must make policy decisions regarding human rights are regularly occupied with questions such as the relative importance of civil and political as compared with social, economic and cultural rights, or whether human rights violations practiced by different types of governments should be judged differently. Although these issues are not specifically considered in this volume, they are a necessary part of the context for any serious human rights discussion.

Human rights activists form a second group which regularly participates in debate about these issues. This volume differs from one which might be written by that group in the relative absence of a focus on violations of human rights or on passionate commitment to change. This may be because rights relating to education are not as likely to inspire the same kind of passion as does the right not to be tortured, or the right to leave one's country and return to it. Deprivations of educational rights are more likely to have their impact on the quality of an individual's life in the future, provoking less concern than a human rights violation with a more immediate visible impact. However, in countries where educational rights are seriously restricted, there is more passion on the subject than may be apparent to observers from countries where education is widely available and even taken for granted. Another reason for the more subdued approach may be that the authors of these chapters believe that educational policy makers will be amenable to rational argument—in contrast, perhaps, to military leaders or others who are regularly addressed by human rights activists. However, in the desire to be rational about education as a human right and education about human rights, it is important not to forget the motivating force of passionate concern entirely. Human rights are those entitlements which are basic to being human and not connected to the accident of being born in a certain country or with skin of a particular color. The universality and depth of the core concern which has been enunciated in international documents should not be underestimated. Human rights is a powerful concept, one which mobilizes both careful scholarly study and great feelings of concern and commitment in some individuals.

The depth of this concern can be understood by looking at the historical context, especially during the period when the *UN Charter* and the *Universal Declaration of Human Rights* were drafted. After World War II both political leaders and people in general wanted to enunciate basic human rights principles that would stand the test of time. That meant rights which would not be made obsolescent by computer technology or by genetic engineering or by advances in understanding human cognitive processes or by political developments—rights that might in fact become more important as technological and social changes took place. The human rights enunciated in these documents were addressed to fundamental structures of human experience, aspirations that were part of the character of human beings in the majority, if not all, human societies. They were intended not only to be translated into the languages of the world, but to be a manifestation of the experience and aspirations of the peoples of the world. This does not mean that these rights have been adequately recognized or implemented by all, or even most, governments. There is evidence, however, that they are aspirations of individuals everywhere in the world. Scholars can and should debate the influence of the social, economic or cultural context on human rights, detailing ways in which national constitutions enumerate rights and courts adjudicate them. But it is important not to lose sight of the basic core of universally agreed upon human rights, which in some sense exists without reference to cultures or constitutions.

The right to education is in some respects the pivotal human right precisely because it is so essential to socializing the younger generation into understanding the culture, the society and the polity. Although the school cannot solve all the social problems it is asked to address, it is an institution with enormous potential for improving the future quality of life for members of the society. Further, it is through education that individuals learn about their civil and political rights and about how to effectively ensure continuing respect for them. Human rights, in summary, are more than a convenient but arbitrary set of pegs on which to hang this program or that curriculum plan. The breadth of societies addressed in this volume where human rights is a vital issue gives an index of that. Keeping these points in mind, let us look at the major themes covered in the chapters. No attempt will be made to resolve contradictions between the diversity of views represented or to argue for one view as opposed to another. The aim is rather to seek overall themes illustrated in several chapters and to look to the future of human rights research in comparative education in light of these themes.

Thematic Questions Emerging from this Analysis of Human Rights and Education

Although the chapters are quite varied, they can be thought of as addressing six questions dealing with educational rights and their implementation. These questions provide a prototype analytic model for considering these rights in a comparative context and for identifying significant gaps in the base of knowledge. In other words, one way to make the comparative view of human rights more comprehensive is to consider a potential framework for analysis of human rights and education in different countries.

The first thematic question is *education for whom?* The first several chapters deal in considerable detail with the issues of adequacy of wide-spread access to education and nondiscrimination, which are vital and basic human rights issues in all countries. To examine implementation in this area analytically requires trustworthy national statistics, preferably including rates of completion for various levels of education and figures concerning the provision of schooling relative to population growth, not merely raw frequencies indicating how many enter school or enroll in a given trade. Stress is usually placed on access to primary education continuing to the level at which literacy is thought to be attained, since this is the most basic educational right. However, it is important to note that access means more than a school with an open door and an empty place. There are a variety of forces which determine whether a student will remain in school, and those who drop out are constrained in many ways from returning.

A number of authors pay special attention to groups which are often denied the right to education—females, minority group members and the mentally or physically handicapped, for example. It is recognized at several places in the book that rural students, though they may not be obviously discriminated against in their access to schooling, nevertheless suffer in the quality of education they receive. Likewise, the definition of the populations for whom exceptional educational services are provided may differ widely. A certain level of educational development in a country appears to be required before there is much concern about educational access for students who do not possess at least average abilities.

Asking "education for whom?", is also asking whether education is available across the life span, to adults as well as young people. In one sense that is the distinction between formal and non-formal education, but at another level it includes concern with whether education is an attractive option tailored to adults' special needs and demands. In some countries it is important to consider the gap created when the younger generation has a much wider access to education than the parent generation had.

The second thematic question is *education with what goals and content?* Several of the chapters deal either explicitly or implicitly with this issue. Education may be aimed toward providing technically trained manpower or toward promoting universal literacy or toward ensuring cultural trans-mission (or toward a combination of these). Further questions may be raised with respect to these goals. For example, is attention given to supporting literacy beyond the point of basic skill acquisition, especially in countries with diverse language groups. The human rights question regarding goals and content can be phrased in another way as well—education to prepare the individual for what kind of adult roles? An education may prepare an individual for a role as a worker, or as a religious participant, or as a citizen able to participate in political decisions, or as a parent able to read materials on childrearing to aid in the educational process of the young. The emphasis on these roles differs across societies, and each role has particular human rights implications. Plotting backwards from the kind of adult roles which are valued in a society to the goals of schooling is a way of assessing the reality of the implementation of educational rights. One chapter highlights the problem which arises when the primary school concentrates on preparing students for further schooling aimed toward a limited number of elite roles, rather than concentrating on skills which prepare even school dropouts for adult roles which are widely available in the society.

A consideration of the goals and content of education would not be complete without attention to the content of human rights education. One chapter argues that it includes teaching about human rights (in a descriptive sense), teaching for human rights (in the sense of action to promote human rights), and teaching in educational institutions where human rights are respected.This raises the important issue of the degree to which the content of human rights teaching is explicit and intended and the extent to which implicit and unintended education are important.

The third thematic question addressed by the chapters is *education responsive to what social, cultural, political, or economic context?* A number of instances are discussed in which the form of education is influenced by the social and political context, often in ways with implications for the implementation of human rights. For example, some authors discuss the extent to which the education system fosters the maintenance of mother tongue skills in immigrants and/or established ethnic groups. Another important question is whether the maintenance of culture, a recognized human right, is respected. Several of the chapters deal with limitations in the implementation of recognized human rights resulting from prevailing cultural and religious views regarding, for example, the status of women and the authoritative role of parents in education. The prevailing view of national identity and interest may also influence education. Note for example, the linkage of human rights education with defense education in some countries. There are also more subtle ideologies influencing educational rights in other nations.

Several authors deal with the reluctance of those holding political power to acknowledge deprivations of educational rights, apparently in the hope that cultural minorities or illiterates will not organize to demand redress. There is also a tendency for authorities to seek to place the responsibility for promoting some educational rights on to private groups as their humanitarian duty.

Examining the political context can also indicate positive directions. Some authors suggest that it is possible to mobilize political will to implement provisions for equality—for example, to tackle problems of illiteracy, or access to education for rural populations and the handicapped, or the democratization of education. Sometimes there is a surge of public commitment to providing education for students with less than average ability or to advancement for society as a whole, even at some cost to individual achievement. Analysis of these situations may contribute to understanding how to mobilize similar political will in other situations to benefit the implementation of educational rights.

The economic context also has a tremendous impact, often in a kind of vicious circle. For example, illiteracy is both a consequence and a cause of nations' poverty. The linkage of poor economic circumstances to malnutrition and inadequate health care to poor learning abilities is also a problem which replicates itself across generations. One author also notes that the worsening worldwide economic situation, coupled with the ideology which has guided some literacy programs, leads to a pessimistic view concerning the possibility in the near future of commitment on the part of industrialized countries to universal literacy.

The influence of the socio-economic structure and its associated ideology is noted by several authors. To take one example, the socio-economic position occupied by cultural minorities is vital in understanding their human rights status. To take another example, in some countries those preparing for university education are also required to acquire technical education and experience in the work force. Although the bias toward white collar occupations is strong and tenacious, in some developed countries small pay differentials between occupational strata have reduced that preference, at least with respect to occupations requiring long training. In developing countries, however, it remains a problem that an educated civil servant who is earning twelve times the average per capita wage is unlikely to be motivated to substantially broaden access to the educated elite.

The fourth thematic question is *education given by teachers with what preparation and experiencing what freedom of expression?* The question of the rights, status and training of teachers has been of tremendous interest to many international organizations, because of the assumption that the educational system cannot adequately provide an education in human rights without attention to such issues. According to this view, education conducted by teachers who do not have the right to deal with controversial issues through free discussion in their classrooms is in danger of being little more than indoctrination. There is clear evidence presented in this volume of the importance of an open climate for discussion in the classroom for achieving the major aims of political education and human rights education. More generally, there is increasing interest in the rights of teachers as professionals, especially given the power of school authorities and the absence in many countries of legal precedents concretizing teacher rights.

The chapters raise specific questions about what is included in teacher training as well. Preparation for teaching which would contribute to a climate respectful of human rights includes a wide variety of skills. Are teachers educated appropriately to implement vocational education, including experience in the world of work? Are they prepared to deal with conflicting views about how children with special handicaps should be educated? Is there attention to the special needs of adult learners in programs for those who will instruct them? How sensitive are teachers to areas of possible discrimination in educational opportunity and to ways of enhancing respect for the human rights of diverse cultural groups inside and outside the school's formal curriculum?

The fifth thematic question is *education organized within what decision making structure?* Since the chapters cover more than a dozen countries, they give examples of traditions both of codified and of common law, as well as illustrating differences in the balance between national and local educational decision making. Difficult issues such as an educational bureaucracy with little accountability, as well as both deliberate and unintentional mismanagement are considered for their impact on educational effectiveness. The problem of implementing broadly based multicultural education when decision-making power is vested in the hands of one or two ethnic or linguistic groups is also important.

In some countries, parents have a great deal of power, while in others they have very little to say about the schooling their children receive. These factors have an enormous influence on the way in which educational rights are viewed and implemented, as well as on the content of teaching about human rights. An example was given of the participation of labor unions in decisions regarding vocational education. Declines in economic productivity have resulted in business groups seeking to directly or indirectly influence curriculum reform in many countries. Perhaps most important, several chapters note that those who wish to improve the situation in education must take a different direction according to the decision-making structure which characterizes the politics of education in a given nation.

The sixth and final question addressed by the chapters is *education judged by what criteria of overall success?* The comparative view reminds us that some countries judge success by proportion of an age cohort enrolled, while others consider scores on tests of achievement of the greatest importance. In some countries it is only the achievement of the average majority that is important, while in others the achievement of handicapped students or those with special educational needs is considered. Whether one takes a view of education rooted in the liberal arts or in vocational preparation makes an enormous difference in how successful an educational system is judged to be. In some countries no matter how excellent the test scores, the educational system would be judged as deficient if it did not respect the rights of parents and other members of the community to control education. The observation of children interacting on the playground with those from other cultural groups or of youth willing to educate others in their community about their rights would be a sign of success for some kinds of human rights education. An appropriate balance between citizens' awareness of their rights and responsibilities or the acceptance by a majority of policy designed to foster multiculturalism would be signs of the success of education in many countries.

These thematic questions considered in a comparative framework, can raise awareness about many dimensions along which variations in the implementation of human rights take place across countries, without adopting a cultural relativism which would deny the importance of human rights. Such a framework for examining implementation can also provide the impetus for a conceptualization model of the role of education in human rights and the role of human rights in education. It would be useful not only as an analytic view of the past but as a guide to further analysis in the future. It could serve as a way to move beyond the recognition of the human rights dimension of education to the full study of its implementation.

Recommendations for the Involvement of Comparative Education Specialists in the Study of Human Rights

The authors of the chapters in this book have written from their perspective as specialists in comparative education and not as lawyers or human rights activists. There have not been many volumes written from this perspective on this subject. Thus, a number of gaps in the analysis and understanding of education as a human right and education about human rights have been identified by this rich international overview. Future work by comparative education specialists could contribute to filling some of these gaps. The field in general, and the volume in particular, suffer from some inconsistencies in the level of analysis used to examine different types of rights. The development of an analytic model which could be applied across the different types of rights might be a step forward. The thematic questions suggested here were used as a framework for synthesizing a diverse set of contributions; these questions had not been set out in advance and thus were not addressed in a comprehensive way in the volume. Although extended examples of a number of countries were included, a further contribution would be made by an analysis of policy and implementation in the area of educational rights in national case studies—each organized around a common set of thematic questions. This would allow comparisons between types of educational rights as well as between countries. Such comparisons might also lend themselves to generalizations about human rights in education in different national settings.

An alternative way of organizing further work on these issues would be to consider three major themes: policy, behavioral and social research, and curriculum, all of which are touched on in the book.

A more comprehensive analysis of the formation of policy, its implementation, and how public opinion supports progress in respect for human rights, is needed both internationally and in national settings. Within the analysis of policy, there are several important issues which could benefit from comparative educators' attention. One chapter suggests two independent continua for analysis—commitment to policy and commitment to implementation. That chapter also classifies several countries along these continua with respect to education for the handicapped. The same analytic framework might be applied to other human rights policy areas, especially multicultural education and political education.

To take another example, experience in some settings suggests that it is only in the face of blatant anti-democratic actions that human rights policy regarding education is confronted and measurably strengthened. Comparative educators could contribute to understanding how to raise the awareness of policy makers about the need for attention to human rights as a way of preventing crises rather than responding to them.

Looking at policy and implementation historically can also provide interesting insights. There was a confluence of interest in human rights, especially in relation to education, about 10 years ago. UNESCO issued its *Recommendation on Education for International Understanding, Cooperation and Peace and Education relating to Human Rights and Fundamental Freedoms* in 1974. For the first time in an educational document, the specifics of respect for human rights and knowledge of international instruments protecting them was added to the relatively vague idea of promoting understanding between peoples. This document guided not only the international activities of UNESCO but also the educational programs of many member states. UNESCO also put into place procedures through which educators, artists, social scientists and those in related fields could file complaints about violations of their human rights. During the same period, human rights took on a new importance in the foreign policy formation of some nations. Although there is great division of opinion regarding how successful these foreign policy initiatives were, the debate in the press has created a new level of awareness in the public mind of human rights and their meaning in the democratic tradition (domestically and internationally). Among scholars, there has also been a new interest in these issues, with new journals and publications in many regions of the world. The Bicentennial of the *US Constitution* provides a new impetus for scholars and citizens to attend to these issues. Enhanced Canadian interest in human rights has been indicated by the recent *Charter of Rights and Freedoms*. Interesting insights could be gained from a close study of this instrument and its implementation. The Council of Europe has a comprehensive program of human rights education which has been used in a diversity of national settings. This program might be examined as a kind of model.

Several chapters highlighted the diversity of approaches to human rights issues by considering differing models for reaching a single goal–enhanced adult literacy or education for the handicapped. These comparisons suggest new parameters for study of other human rights problems as well. There are some factors which have been found to make a positive contribution in several areas (such as the active participation of learners in program design); there are other relatively universal problems (such as expectation for short-term results) which could be highlighted.

Understanding how the public will can be mobilized to bring issues of educational rights to attention on the national agenda is of special interest in many countries. For example, what are the major political interest groups on these issues? In particular, what role is played by parents and students in assuring their own rights and seeing them in the context of the community's or the nation's interest? Professional groups such as educators and administrators of aid programs also have recognizeable interests in this process, as do members of the business community. How well organized are these interest groups and how much is their influence recognized? What impact does conflict between the rights claimed by these groups have on education? What role is played by presentations of violations of rights in the media? How does policy regarding the provision of life-long learning programs or materials supporting literacy influence adults' awareness of human rights interests? Policy analysis in a comparative context can play a vital role in understanding these issues in countries with varying patterns of human rights implementation—with the aim of reducing the gap between policy and practice.

Second, comparative education can make a contribution to this field through social and behavioral research. Although the summary statistics contained in the chapters on the participation of various groups in education are very useful, they should be supplemented by studies at the micro-level of the realization of educational rights in the classroom, on the playground, and in the community. We need carefully designed studies on a regular basis about literacy as a school achievement and a culturally valued skill, in order to know how the achievement of literacy influences the individual's view of society and other human rights. We need better understanding of intelligence and its measurement to more effectively provide opportunities for both handicapped and gifted students. We need a clear delineation of the benefits for all to be derived from education in multicultural settings, and ways of assessing particular programs' effectiveness. Research is needed on female student's patterns of vocational choice, especially in countries where the occupational stucture has been rigidly sex stereotyped.

We also need a better understanding of how individuals in different nations and at different levels of education think about their civil and political rights. How does political education or education about human rights contribute to those values and to individuals' willingness to be active participants in a democratic political system? Landmark changes in the protection of human rights, such as the Canadian Charter, should be thoroughly studied for their impact on attitudes and values. Although extensive research has been conducted by psychologists on moral development, many of the potential links with concepts of human rights have not been explored because of a tendency for behavioral scientists to ignore the social and political context. Comparative educators have already made tremendous contributions to understanding the character of common aspirations for education in societies across the world, but have yet to link these ideas fully with human rights.

Finally, comparative educators have a contribution to make to school curricula and educational programs. How should human rights be presented within the context of a national heritage or identity as well as in an international context? In particular, how can one promote interest and motivation on the part of students to contribute to enhancing educational opportunities? A curriculum limited to memorizing provisions of national constitutions or of international standard-setting documents will be counter-productive for adults as well as young people. There is considerable evidence from research that simulations of actual decision making and active participation in classroom discussion are approporiate and effective methods. The value of teaching students to generate alternative positions and make critical judgements about them is another consistent theme relating to educational success. Special attention needs to be given to teacher training, however, since such methods are difficult to implement and must build on a basic level of knowledge in both teachers and students. Further study of ways to evaluate a human rights education program's effectiveness with different groups is also necessary. Such evaluation would allow programs found to be effective in promoting human rights in one national setting to be modified for use elsewhere. These are also issues to which study by comparative educators could make a valuable contribution.

The authors of these chapters have presented studies of both the gap between human rights policy and practice in a variety of national settings and of achievements which have substantially lessened that gap. The volume presents a long and rich agenda for the further work of comparative educators in examining the right to education and education about human rights. It is a challenging and important area which deserves careful analysis and research.

Epilogue

It is clear, from the preceding chapters, that human rights are intrinsically important. They are an essential part, the *sine qua non*, of the democratic process, and life would be hardly worth living without them. It is becoming more and more apparent every day, however, that they are much more than that, because, in the nuclear age in which we live, our very lives and those of our children may well depend upon whether we can devise better mechanisms for their respect. There is a very close relationship between respect for human rights and the peace of nations. We must, if our planet is to have any future as a place where men and women can live, enshrine what lawyers call the rule of law at the international level, and as part of that process, ensure respect for human rights everywhere. The *UN Charter* was the direct consequence of the worst war yet known by mankind, a war brought about largely by the denial of human rights and fought to vindicate them.

Human rights, then, are of paramount importance. What does this mean for teachers? Other things being equal, human rights are more apt to be respected in countries where the public knows what these rights are and what they mean than in countries where this is not the case. But it is at the international level that the role of education in the matter of human rights is especially important. Given the relative weakness of existing mechanisms for the implementation of international law, an educated world public opinion is then the ultimate sanction of human rights.

There exists an international law of human rights. A law, as that term is understood by lawyers, does not however necessarily tell you, as do the laws of physical science, what will happen. It only tells you what should or ought to happen. And the same is true of sanctions. The law prohibits murder, but murders occur and murderers do not always suffer the prescribed penalty.

The international law of human rights is in force at the world level that confers certain rights on individual men and women. It hardly existed before World War II. Traditional international law was, as the prefix "inter" indicates, law that governed the relations of states only. It was a law *between* states. Only states had what lawyers call international legal personality, the capacity, that is to say, to possess rights and to owe duties. Individual men and women could be the objects of the law, just as animals are, but they were not subjects of the law. What is meant by that kind of lawyers' language? Simply this: that, while the ultimate beneficiaries of the law might be individuals, in traditional international law, the rights belonged not to them, but to states; and individuals had no guarantee that their governments would act on their behalf. Human rights moreover fell within the exclusive jurisdiction of states: what a state did to its citizens was its own business and beyond the reach of international law. All that has now changed, and, if lawyers were as logical as they pretend to be, they would call the discipline not international, but world law.

What are the sanctions that support this new international law of human rights? Such sanctions rarely exist and when they do, they are more theoretical than real. They do not, moreover, include the threat or application of coercive measures of the kind that support most national laws. Provision may be made in a treaty for a finding that there has been a violation of the law, but that is about all. Of what use then are they? The answer is that they help educate world public opinion. And public opinion is something to which even authoritarian governments are sensitive. Why otherwise would they be at such pains to control the press and other information media? And why otherwise would they bother defending their conduct before international tribunals that have no power to impose the application of coercive sanctions?

Education is one such sanction. As the world organization and individual states move to guarantee the right to education, teachers have an important role to play. Not only is it their duty, in the words of the *Universal Declaration of Human Rights*, to direct education to the full development of the human personality and the sense of its dignity and to strengthen respect for human rights and fundamental freedoms, but also to further the dissemination of information regarding the human rights activities of the United Nations, its specialized agencies and other international organizations.

Conferences such as the recent one at Long Beach, California on Human Rights and Education, and this book that has emerged from that conference, are thus extremely important. For, it is clear that *education* is, after all, the ultimate sanction of *Human Rights*.

JOHN P. HUMPHREY
Professor of Law
McGill University

Appendix 1

UN Human Rights Documents
(Summaries of Education Provisions)

UN Charter (1945):

Reaffirms "faith in fundamental human rights, in the dignity and worth of the human person, in the equal rights of men and women and of nations large and small. . ."

Article 1: (Chapter 1.3) suggests that the United Nations promote and encourage respect for human rights and for fundamental freedoms for all without distinction as to race, sex, language, or religion.

Article 2: (Chapter 1.7) cautions against the United Nations intervening in matters which are essentially within the domestic jurisdiction of any State with Chapter VII allowing for application of enforcement measures.

Article 13: (Chapter 1) authorizes the General Assembly to assist ". . . in the realization of human rights and fundamental freedoms for all without distinction as to race, sex, language, or religion."

Article 55: (Chapter IX) suggests that the United Nations promote "universal respect for, and observance of, human rights and fundamental freedoms for all without distinction as to race, sex, language, or religion."

Article 73: (Chapter XI) regarding non self-governing territories under the administration of member States, requires "due respect for the culture of the peoples concerned, their polititical, economic, social and educational advancement, their just treatment, and their protection against abuses."

Article 76: (Chapter XII) regarding international trusteeship system, encourages "respect for human rights and for fundamental freedoms for all without distinction as to race, sex, language, or religion," and encourages "recognition of the interdependence of the peoples of the world . . ."

Universal Declaration of Human Rights (1948):

Article 26 (1) "Everyone has the right to education. Education shall be free, at least in the elementary and fundamental stages. Elementary education shall be compulsory. Technical and professional education shall be made generally available and higher education shall be equally accessible to all on the basis of merit.

(2) Education shall be directed to the full development of the human personality and to the strengthening of respect for human rights and

fundamental freedoms. It shall promote understanding, tolerance and friendship among all nations, racial or religious groups, and shall further the activities of the United Nations for the maintenance of peace.

Parents have a prior right to choose the kind of education that shall be given to their children."

Convention Relating to the Status of Refugees (1951):

Article 22 (1) "The Contracting States shall accord to refugees the same treatment as is accorded to nationals with respect to elementary education.

(2) The Contracting States shall accord to refugees treatment as favourable as possible, and, in any event, not less favourable than that accorded to aliens generally in the same circumstances, with respect to education other than elementary education, and, in particular, as regards access to studies, the recognition of foreign school certificates, diplomas and degrees, the remission of fees and charges and the award of scholarships."

Convention Relating to the Status of Stateless Persons (1954):

(Stateless persons are defined as those who are not considered as nationals by any State under the operation of its law.)

Article 22 (1) "The Contracting States shall accord to stateless persons the same treatment as is accorded to nationals with respect to elementary education.

(2) The Contracting States shall accord to stateless persons treatment as favourable as possible and, in any event, not less favourable than that accorded to aliens generally in the same circumstances, with respect to education other than elementary education and, in particular, as regards access to studies, the recognition of foreign school certificates, diplomas and degrees, the remission of fees and charges and the award of scholarships."

Delaration of the Rights of the Child (1959):

Reaffirms Universal Declaration of Human Rights. Sets out 10 principles:

Principle (1) "The child shall enjoy all the rights set forth in this Declaration. Every child, without any exception whatsoever, shall be entitled to these rights."

Principle (2) "The child shall enjoy special protection, and shall be given opportunities and facilities, by law and by other means, to enable him to develop physically, mentally, morally, spiritually and socially in a healthy and normal manner and in conditions of freedom and dignity . . ."

Principle (4) ". . . special care and protection shall be provided both to him and to his mother. . ."

Principle (5) "The child who is physically, mentally or socially handicapped shall be given the special treatment, education and care required by his particular condition."

Principle (7) "The child is entitled to receive education, which shall be free and compulsory, at least in the elementary stages. He shall be given an education which will promote his general culture and enable him, on a basis of equal opportunity, to develop his abilities, his individual judgment, and his sense of moral and social responsibility, and to become a useful member of society.

The best interests of the child shall be the guiding principle of those responsible for his education and guidance; that responsibility lies in the first place with his parents.

The child shall have full opportunity for play and recreation, which should be directed to the same purposes as education; society and the public authorities shall endeavour to promote the enjoyment of this right."

Principle (9) ". . . He shall not be the subject of traffic, in any form. The child shall not be admitted to employment before an appropriate minimum age; he shall in no case be caused or permitted to engage in any ocupation or employment which would prejudice his health or education, or interfere with his physical, mental or moral development."

Principle (10) "The child shall be protected from practices which may foster racial, religious and any other form of discrimination. He shall be brought up in a spirit of understanding, tolerance, friendship among peoples, peace and universal brotherhood, and in full consciousness that his energy and talents should be devoted to the service of his fellow men."

Convention Against Discrimination in Education (1960):

Reaffirms Universal Declaration's assertion of the principle of non-discrimination and the right of every person to an education.

Article 2 indicates that the establishment of separate education systems by sex shall not be deemed discriminatory if there is equivalent access and quality. Separate educational systems for religious or linguistic reasons shall not be deemed discriminatory if in keeping with wishes of parents, if they are optional, and conform to standard. The establishment of private educational institutions shall not be deemed discriminatory if they supplement public facilities.

Article 3 undertakes "to ensure, by legislation, where necessary, that there is no discrimination in the admission of pupils to educational institutions; not to allow any difference of treatment by the public authorities between nationals, except on the basis of merit or need, in the matter of school fees and the grant of scholarships . . . to give foreign nationals resident within their territory the same access to education as that given to their own nationals."

Article 4 agrees (a) "To make primary education free and compulsory;

make secondary education in its different forms generally available and accessible to all; make higher education equally accessible to all on the basis of individual capacity; assure compliance by all with the obligation to attend school prescribed by law;"

(b) "To ensure that the standards of education are equivalent in all public education institutions of the same level . . ."

(c) "To encourage . . . the education of persons who have not received any primary education . . ."

`(d) "To provide training for the teaching profession without discrimination."

Article 5 (b) "It is essential to respect the liberty of parents . . . to choose for their children institutions other than those maintained by the public authorities . . ."

(e) "It is essential to recognize the right of members of national minorities to carry on their own educational activities . . . the use or the teaching of their own language, provided however, that this right is not exercised in a manner which prevents the members of these minorities from understanding the culture and language of the community as a whole . . . that the standard of education is not lower than the general standard . . . that attendance at such schools is optional."

Protocol Instituting a Conciliation and Good Offices Commission to be Responsible for Seeking a Settlement of any Disputes Which May Arise Between States Parties to the Convention Against Discrimination in Education (1962):

Article 12 indicates that if one State considers that another State is not carrying out a provision of the convention, it may bring that to the attention of the latter in writing. The receiving State shall respond in writing within three months. If the matter is not adjusted to the satisfaction of both within six months, either State can refer the matter to the Commission.

Article 11 indicates that the Commission shall deal with a matter only after it has ascertained that all available domestic remedies have been exhausted.

Article 17 notes that the Commission seeks an amicable solution of the matter.

Article 18 points out that the Commission may seek an opinion from the International Court of Justice.

United Nations Declaration on the Elimination of all Forms of Racial Discrimination (1963):

Article 1 condemns discrimination on the grounds of race, colour or ethnic origin as denial of the principles of the *Charter of the United Nations* and the *Universal Declaration of Human Rights*.

Article 3 stresses efforts in education.

Article 8 "All effective steps shall be taken immediately in the fields of teaching, education and information, with a view to eliminating racial discrimination and prejudice and promoting understanding, tolerance and friendship among nations and racial groups, as well as to propagating the purposes and principles of the *Charter of the United Nations*, of the *Universal Declaration of Human Rights* and of the *Declaration on the Granting of Independence to Colonial Countries and Peoples.*"

International Convention on the Elimination of all Forms of Racial Discrimination (1965):

Article 7: "States Parties undertake to adopt immediate and effective measures, particularly in the fields of teaching, education, culture and information, with a view to combating prejudices which lead to racial discrimination and to promoting understanding, tolerance and friendship among nations and racial or ethnical groups, as well as to propagating the purposes and principles of the *Charter of the United Nations*, the *Universal Declaration of Human Rights*, the *United Nations Declaration on the Elimination of all Forms of Racial Discrimination*, and this Convention."

Declaration on the Promotion Among Youth of the Ideals of Peace, Mutual Respect and Understanding Between Peoples (1965):

Principle I "Young people shall be brought up in the spirit of peace, justice, freedom, mutual respect and understanding in order to promote equal rights for all human beings and all nations, economic and social progress, disarmament and the maintenance of international peace and security."

Principle II "All means of education . . . should foster . . . the ideals of peace, humanity, liberty and international solidarity . . ."

Principle III "Young people shall be brought up in the knowledge of the dignity and equality of all men, without distinction as to race, colour, ethnic origins or beliefs, and in respect for fundamental human rights and for the rights of peoples to self-determination."

Principle IV "Exchanges, travel, tourism, meetings, the study of foreign language, the twinning of towns and universities without discrimination . . . should be encouraged . . ."

Principle V "National and international associations of young people should be encouraged . . . Youth organizations . . . should take all appropriate measures . . . in order to make their contribution . . . to the work of educating the young generation in accordance with these ideals."

Principle VI stresses moral qualities and the family; responsibilities in the world.

Protocol Relating to the Status of Refugees (1967):

Extends provisions of 1951 Convention to new refugees.

International Covenant on Economic, Social and Cultural Rights (1966):

Article 3 ensures equal right of men and women to enjoyment of all economic, social and cultural rights set forth in the Covenant.

Article 6 includes provision for technical and vocational guidance.

Article 10 provides for protection of the family especially while it is responsible for the care and education of dependent children. Special protection is suggested for mothers. Children and young persons should be protected from economic and social exploitation. States should prohibit child labour below set age limits.

Article 13 (1) "The State Parties to the present Covenant recognize the right of everyone to education. They agree that education shall be directed to the full development of the human personality and the sense of its dignity, and shall strengthen the respect for human rights and fundamental freedoms. They further agree that education shall enable all persons to participate effectively in a free society, promote understanding, tolerance and friendship among all nations and all racial, ethnic or religious groups, and further the activities of the United Nations for the maintenance of peace."

(2) "The States Parties to the present Covenant recognize that, with a view to achieving the full realization of this right:

(a) Primary education shall be compulsory and available free to all;

(b) Secondary education in its different forms, including technical and vocational secondary education, shall be made generally available and accessible to all by every appropriate means, and in particular, by the progressive introduction of free education;

(c) Higher education shall be made equally accessible to all, on the basis of capacity, by every appropriate means, and in particular, by the progressive introduction of free education;

(d) Fundamental education shall be encouraged or intensified as far as possible for those persons who have not received or completed the whole period of their primary education;

(e) The development of a system of schools at all levels shall be actively pursued, an adequate fellowship system shall be established, and the material conditions of teaching staff shall be continuously improved."

(3) "The States Parties to the present Covenant undertake to have respect for the liberty of parents and, when applicable, legal guardians to choose for their children school, other than those established by the public authorities, which conform to such minimum educational standards as may be laid down

or approved by the State and to ensure the religious and moral education of their children in conformity with their own convictions."

(4) "No part of this article shall be construed so as to interfere wih the liberty of individuals and bodies to establish and direct educational institutions, subject always to the observance of the principles set forth in paragraph 1 of this article and to the requirement that the education given in such institutions shall conform to such minimum standards as may be laid down by the State."

International Covenant on Civil and Political Rights (1966):

Article 19 stresses freedom to seek, receive and impart information and ideas of all kinds.

Article 20 (1) "Any propaganda for war shall be prohibited by law."

(2) "Any advocacy of national, racial or religious hatred that constitutes incitement to discrimination, hostility or violence shall be prohibited by law."

Article 24 (1) "Every child shall have, without any discrimination as to race, colour, sex, language, religion, national or social origin, property or birth, the right to such measures of protection as are required by his status as a minor, on the part of his family, society and the State."

Article 27 "In those States in which ethnic, religious or linguistic minorities exist, persons belonging to such minorities shall not be denied the right, in community with the other members of their group, to enjoy their own culture, to profess and practice their own religion, or to use their own language."

Optional Protocol to the International Covenant on Civil and Political Rights (1966):

States that are party to this protocol recognize the Human Rights Committee's authority to receive and consider communications from those who consider themselves victims.

Declaration on the Elimination of Discrimination Against Women (1967):

Article 3 calls for appropriate measures to educate towards the eradication of prejudice based on the idea of the inferiority of women.

Article 9 calls for equal rights with men in education at all levels including:

(a) "equal conditions of access to, and study in, educational institutions of all types, including universities and vocational, technical and professional schools;

(b) the same choice of curricula, the same examinations, teaching staff with qualifications of the same standard, and school premises and equipment of the same quality, whether the institutions are co-educational or not;

(c) equal opportunities to benefit from scholarships and other study grants.

(d) equal opportunities for access to programmes of continuing education, including adult literacy programmes;

(e) access to educational information to help in ensuring the health and well-being of families."

Proclamation of Teheran (1968):

Proclaims that the *Universal Declaration* "constitutes an obligation for the members of the international community;" that States should conform to the *International Covenant on Civil and Political Rights*, the *Declaration on the Granting of Independence to Colonial Countries and Peoples*, and the *International Convention on the Elimination of All Forms of Racial Discrimination*.

Protests apartheid, racial discrimination, denials of human rights in armed conflicts. "International action aimed at eradicating illiteracy from the face of the earth and promoting education at all levels requires urgent attention. The discrimination of which women are still victims in various regions of the world must be eliminated. The protection of the family and of the child remains the concern of the international community."

Declaration on the Rights of Mentally Retarded Persons (1971):

"The mentally retarded person has a right to . . . such education, training, rehabilitation and guidance as will enable him to develop his ability and maximum potential."

International Convention on the Suppression and Punishment of the Crime of Apartheid (1973):

Article I decrees apartheid a crime against humanity. Declares criminal those who commit apartheid.

Article II (c) "Any legislative measures and other measures calculated to prevent a racial group or groups from participation in the political, social, economic and cultural life of the country and the deliberate creation of conditions preventing the full development of such a group or groups, in particular by denying to members of a racial group or groups basic human rights and freedoms, including the right to work, the right to form recognized trade unions, the right to education, the right to leave and to return to their country, the right to a nationality, the right to freedom of movement and residence, the right to freedom of opinion and expression, and the right to freedom of peaceful assembly and association" constitutes the crime of apartheid.

Article IV notes that States Parties to the present Convention undertake to adopt measures to prosecute and punish persons responsible for acts of apartheid.

Declaration on the Rights of Disabled Persons (1975):

Disabled persons have the same fundamental rights as their fellow citizens, the same political and civil rights, and are entitled to measures designed to enable them to become as self reliant as possible. Disabled persons have a right to . . . education, vocational training and rehabilitation, aid, counselling, placement services. They have a right to have their special needs taken into consideration at all stages of economic and social planning.

Declaration of the World Conference to Combat Racism and Racial Discrimination (1978):

(21) "Endorses the right of indigenous peoples to maintain their traditional structure of economy and culture, including their own language . . ."

(22) Calls for special efforts to eliminate the effects of racial discrimination on the status of women who are doubly discriminated against.

(23) Urges international bodies to consider the psychological and physical consequences for children who are victims of racial discrimination.

(24) Stresses the need to protect the rights of immigrants and migrant workers.

Declaration on the Elimination of all Forms of Intolerance and of Discrimination Based on Religion or Belief (1981):

Article 5 states that: (1) Parents or legal guardians have the right to organize family life and moral education in accordance with their religion or belief.

(2) No child shall be compelled to receive teaching on religion or belief against the wishes of parents or guardians.

(3) "The child shall be protected from any form of discrimination on the grounds of religion or belief. He shall be brought up in a spirit of understanding, tolerance, friendship among peoples, peace and universal brotherhood, respect for freedom of religion or belief of others, and in full consciousness that his energy and talents should be devoted to the service of his fellow men."

(4) If there is no parent or guardian, account shall be taken of the wishes of the child in the matter of religion or belief.

(5) Practices of religion or belief must not be injurious to the child's physical or mental health or full development.

Convention on the Elimination of all Forms of Discrimination Against Women (1981):

Article 4 proposes temporary affirmative action to accelerate de facto equality between men and women.

Article 10 states that, in the field of education, State Parties shall take all appropriate measures to ensure: the same conditions for career and vocational guidance, access to studies and earning of diplomas; access to the same curricula, teaching staff and standards; the elimination of stereotyped concepts of the role of men and women, the same opportunities for scholarships, the same access to continuing education, sports and physical education. The reduction of female student drop out rates and access to educational information on family and family planning is sought.

NBT

Appendix 2

UNESCO Human Rights Documents
(Summaries of Education Provisions)

Constitution 1945:

Preamble: ". . . the education of humanity for justice and liberty and peace are indispensable to the dignity of man and constitute a sacred duty. . .":

Article 1: Purpose of the organization is to contribute to peace and security by promoting collaboration among the nations through education, science and culture in order to further universal respect for justice, for the rule of law and for the human rights and fundamental freedoms which are affirmed for the peoples of the world, without distinction of race, language or religion by the *Charter of the United Nations.*"

Convention Against Discrimination in Education, 1960:

Reaffirms Universal Declaration's assertion of the principle of non-discrimination and the right of every person to an education.

Article 2: indicates that the establishment of separate educational systems by sex shall not be deemed discrimination if there is equivalent access and quality. Separate educational system for religious or linguistic reasons shall not be deemed discriminatory if it is in keeping with wishes of parents, it is optional, and it conforms to standards. The establishment of private educational institutions shall not be deemed discriminatory if they supplement public facilities.

Article 3: States parties to this Convention undertake "to ensure, by legislation where necessary, that there is no discrimination in the admission of pupils to educational institutions; not to allow any difference of treatment by the public authorities between nationals, except on the basis of merit or need, in the matter of school fees and the grant of scholarships . . . To give foreign nationals resident within their territory the same access to education as that given to their own nationals."

Article 4: The States Parties to this Convention agree: "(a) To make primary education free and compulsory; make secondary education in its different forms generally available and accessible to all; make higher education equally accessible to all on the basis of individual capacity; assure compliance by all with the obligation to attend school prescribed by law;

(b) To ensure that the standards of education are equivalent in all public education institutions of the same level . . .

(c) To encourage . . . the education of persons who have not received any primary education . . .

(d) To provide training for the teaching profession without discrimination."

Article 5: (b) "It is essential to respect the liberty of parents . . . to choose for their children institutions other than those maintained by the public authorities . . ."

(c) "It is essential to recognize the right of members of national minorities to carry on their own educational activities . . . the use or the teaching of their own language, provided however; that this right is not exercised in a manner which prevents the members of these minorities from understanding the culture and language of the community as a whole . . . that the standard of education is not lower than the general standard . . . that attendance at such schools is optional."

Protocol Instituting a Conciliation and Good Offices Commission to be Responsible for Seeking a Settlement of any Disputes Which May Arise Between States Parties to the Convention Against Discrimination in Education, 1962

Article 12: indicates that if one State considers that another State is not carrying out a provision of the convention, it may bring that to the attention of the latter in writing. The receiving State shall respond in writing within three months. If the matter is not adjusted to the satisfaction of both within six months, either State can refer the matter to the Commission.

Article 14: indicates that the Commission shall deal with a matter only after it has ascertained that all domestic remedies have been exhausted.

Article 18: indicates that the Commission may seek an opinion from the International Court of Justice.

Recommendation Concerning the Status of Teachers 1966:

Reaffirms "that the right to education is a fundamental human right." Reaffirms Article 26 of the *Universal Declaration*; Principles 5, 7, 10 of the *Declaration of the Rights of the Child*; and the *UN Declaration Concerning the Promotion among Youth of the Ideals of Peace, Mutual Respect and Understanding between Peoples*.

Guiding Principles: (1) "Education from the earliest school years should be directed to the all-around development of the human personality . . . to the inculcation of deep respect for human rights and fundamental freedoms."

(4) "Advance in education depends largely on the qualifications and ability of the teaching staff."

(6) Teaching is to be regarded as a profession.

(7) "All aspects of the preparation and employment of teachers should be free from any form of discrimination . . ."

(8) Establishes minimal working conditions.

(9) Suggests teachers' organizations should be recognized as a force which can contribute greatly to educational advance . . . and should be associated with the determination of educational policy.

Preparation of the profession: Deals with selection, teacher preparation programs, in service education.

Employment: Calls for probationary period, stability of employment and tenure, protection against arbitrary action; defines disciplinary measures; suggests protection for women with family responsibilities or in time of pregnancy and maternity leave.

Rights and Responsibilities: Defends teachers' rights to academic freedom, essential role in choice and adaptation of teaching materials, participation in development of new courses, teaching materials etc. Suggests systems of inspection or supervision designed to encourage and help teachers, objective and open assessment with right of appeal, protection against unfair interference by parents, protection against risk of having damages assessed, freedom to exercise all civic rights, appropriate machinery for dealing with settlement of disputes between teachers and their employers.

Conditions: Suggests limitations on class size, ancillary staff for non-teaching duties, teaching aides, hours established in consultation with teachers' organizations, time for in-service training, adequate annual vacation with pay, special leave for exchanges and multicultural experiences, sick leave, maternity leave, special provision for teachers in rural areas, salaries and benefits commensurate with status as professionals.

Revised Recommendation Concerning Technical and Vocational Education, 1974: adopted by General Conference at 18th session:

Education is a lifelong process. Reaffirms Articles 23 and 26 of *Universal Declaration* guaranteeing all the right to work and to education. Education should enable full participation in society. Reaffirms instruments of *International Labour Conference: Vocational Guidance Recommendation* of 1949, *Vocational Training Recommendation* of 1956, *Vocational Training Recommendation* of 1962.

Scope: Technical and vocational education refers to "those aspects of the educational process involving, in addition to general education, the study of technologies and related sciences and the acquisition of practical skills, attitudes, understanding and knowledge relating to occupations in various sectors of economic and social life." Defines technical and vocational education as an integral part of general education, a means of preparing for an occupational field, and an aspect of continuing education . . .

Objectives: To contribute to greater democratization, lead to understanding of technological aspects of contemporary civilization, be part of a system of lifelong education adapted to needs of each country, and part of general education; to begin with broad basic vocational education permitting articulation within system and eliminating discrimination.

Policy: To involve educational authorities as well as many other sectors, establish criteria and standards subject to periodic review and evaluation, foster research, provide material resources.

As Part of General Education: Initiation to technology and the world of work must be an essential component of general education.

As Preparation for an Occupational Field: Avoid premature specialization; make special provision for women, migrants, out-of-school youth, physically and mentally disadvantaged. Organize on national or regional level, consider means to deal with high cost of equipment, program content, guidance, and integration of theory and practice.

Staff: Recruitment and preparation of competent teachers with equal benefits based on *Recommendation on Status of Teachers.*

Recommendation Concerning Education for International Understanding, Cooperation and Peace and Education Relating to Human Rights and Fundamental Freedoms.
Adopted by the General Conference at its 18th session, Paris, 19 November, 1974

Guiding Principles:
Reaffirms *UN Charter, UNESCO Constitution* and *Universal Declaration.* Spells out objectives including: international dimension at all levels of education, understanding and respect for all peoples, awareness of increasing global interdependence, abilities to communicate with others, awareness of duties towards each other, understanding of necessity for international solidarity and cooperation, readiness to participate in solving the problems of community, nation and world.

National policy, planning and administration: Each Member state should formulate and apply policies to increase efficacy of education and to strengthen contribution to international understanding. They should take steps to foster cooperation between ministries and departments and carry out concerted programs of action in international education.

Ethical and civic aspects as well as the major problems of mankind should be studied from an interdisciplinary, problem oriented perspective. Examples from Associated Schools should be utilized.

Preschools are key to formation of attitudes on race. Special attention to the preparation of parents for their role in pre-school education is also recommended. Post-secondary and university education should also contribute to attainment of goals.

Teacher Preparation: Member states should improve preparation and certification of teachers, as well as supervisors, inspectors, principals, etc. for their role relevant to the objectives. Educational study abroad and exchanges of teachers should be encouraged.

Recommendation on the Development of Adult Education: 1976 (General Conference, 19th session):

Reaffirms Articles 26 and 27 of *Universal Declaration* and Articles 13 and 15 of *International Covenant on Economic, Social and Cultural Rights.*

Aims of Adult Education: Promote work for peace, international understanding and cooperation; develop understanding of social problems, emphasize relationship between people and environment, respect diversity of cultures, and develop aptitudes.

Principles: Based on needs of participants, confident of ability to make progress throughout lives; utilizing life experiences with highest priority to underprivileged; adapted to conditions of life and work, organized flexibly, involving learners in decision making.

Each member state should:
- recognize adult education as necessary component of education system,
- promote creation of structure, programs and methods to meet needs of all categories of adults without discrimination;
- not use as subtitute for adequate youth education,
- eliminate isolation of women from adult education,
- take measures to promote participation of underprivileged and illiterate population.

Declaration of Fundamental Principles Concerning the Contribution of the Mass Media to Strengthening Peace and International Understanding of the Promotion of Human Rights and to Countering Racialism, Apartheid and Incitement to War, adopted by the General Conference, 22 November, 1978.

Article IV: "The mass media have an essential part to play in the education of young peoples in a spirit of peace, justice, freedom, mutual respect and understanding, in order to promote human rights, equality of rights as between all human beings and all nations, and economic and social progress. Equally, they have an important role to play in making known the views and aspirations of the younger generation."

Declaration on Race and Racial Prejudice, adopted by the
General Conference, 27 November, 1978.

(2) "States . . . as well as . . . the entire teaching profession, have a responsibility to see that the educational resources of all countries are used to combat racism, more especially by ensuring that curricula and textbooks include scientific and ethical considerations concerning human unity and diversity and that no invidious distinctions are made with regard to any people; by training teachers to achieve these ends; by making the resources of the educational system available to all groups of the population without racial restriction or discrimination; and by taking appropriate steps to remedy the handicaps from which certain racial or ethnic groups suffer with regard to their level of education and standard of living and in particular to prevent such handicaps from being passed on to children."

(3) "The mass media . . . are urged—with due regard to the principles embodied in the *Universal Declaration of Human Rights*, particularly the principle of freedom of expression—to promote understanding, tolerance and friendship among individuals and groups and to contribute to the eradication of racism . . . by refraining from presenting a stereotyped, partial, unilateral or tendentious picture of individuals and of various human groups."

International Charter of Physical Education and Sport (1978)

Reaffirms *UN Charter* and *Universal Declaration*.

Article 1: The practice of physical education and sport is a fundamental right for all. States that this is essential for the full development of personality, intellectual, physical, and moral powers. The opportunity for attaining a level of achievement corresponding to one's gifts must be guaranteed within the educational system and in other aspects of social life. Special opportunities must be made available for preschool, aged and handicapped population.

Article 2: Physical education and sport are an essential element of lifelong education.

Article 3: Physical education and sport programs must meet individual needs with priority to requirements of disadvantaged groups.

Article 4: Provides for qualified personnel to teach, coach and administer.

Article 5: Provides for adequate facilities and equipment.

Article 6: Provides for research and evaluation.

Article 7: Provides for information and documentation efforts.

Article 8: Seeks positive influence of mass media.

Article 9: Involves national public authorities—enforcing of legislation providing fiscal support.

Article 10: Calls for international cooperation.

Second Medium Term Plan (1984–1989) Education For All
(4XC/4)

Main task is to "help pave the way for the widest participation by individuals and groups in the life of the societies to which they belong and in that of the world community" through three planks:

1. Access: "Development and renewal of primary education and total elimination of illiteracy",

2. Democratization of education: so it is available to all without any kind of discrimination,

3. Lifelong education: non-formal, continuing.

Six programs were approved for this 5 year period to work on these three planks:

1. Promotion of general access to education: development and renewal of primary education and intensification of the struggle against illiteracy.

Aimed at enrolling all children in school and intensifying literacy training of adults. Four subprograms to better understand the problem, to provide assistance, to train literacy personnel and to avoid relapse into illiteracy.

2. Democratization of education.

Four subprograms to establish standards and general measures, study aspects of problem, achieve coordination between formal and non-formal, promote early childhood education efforts.

3. Adult education.

Four subprograms—adult education and work, exercise of civic rights and responsibilities, leisure time, and later life.

4. Equality of educational opportunity for girls and women:

Four subprograms to identify obstacles to educational equality, to promote access, to further access to sciences and technical and vocational education and to consider educational role of women in society.

5. Extension and improvement of education in rural areas

Three subprograms to extend education, improve standard of education, and provide for contribution of education to development.

6. Promotion of the right to education of particular groups

Three subprograms to overcome obstacles on behalf of disabled, refugees, and migrant workers.

Education, Training and Society (Resolution 4XC/2/05)

Among the six programs is:

Program V.3: Education and the World of Work

To strengthen the linkage and ensure full development of human personality and preparation for active life and work. Includes three subprograms to promote interaction between education and productive work, to form relationships between education and employment, and to expand and improve technical and vocational education.

Elimination of Prejudice, Intolerance, Racism and Apartheid (Reslution 4XC/2/12)

Reaffirms *Universal Declaration* and various declarations on race and prejudice adopted by committees of experts convened by UNESCO (1950, 51, 64, and 67) and the Athens Appeal (1981).

Three programs:

1. *Studies and Research on Prejudice, Intolerance and Racism* include three subprograms to study theoretical and ideological bases of prejudice, concepts and models, policies, institutions and practices conducive to intolerance.

2. *Action Against Prejudice, Intolerance and Racism in the Fields of Education, Science, Culture and Communication* includes four subprograms all designed to take action in the fields of education, communication and culture.

3. *The Struggle Against Apartheid* includes studies on and action against apartheid, and cooperation with the national liberation movements recognized by the Organization of African Unity.

NBT

Appendix 3

Regional Human Rights Documents
(Summaries of Education Provisions)

American Declaration of the Rights and Duties of Man, adopted by the 9th International Conference of American States, Bogota, 1948

Article VII: Proclaims the right to special protection for women during pregnancy and nursing period and to children.

Article XII: "Every person has the right to an education, which should be based on the principles of liberty, morality and human solidarity.

Likewise, every person has the right to an education that will prepare him to attain a decent life, to raise his standard of living and to be a useful member of society.

The right to an education includes the right to equality of opportunity in every case, in accordance with natural talents, merit and the desire to utilize the resources that the state or the community is in a position to provide.

Every person has the right to receive, free, at least a primary education."

Convention for the Protection of Human Rights and Fundamental Freedoms, adopted by the Council of Europe, 4, November, 1950, Rome

Article 14: "The enjoyment of the rights and freedoms set forth in the Convention shall be secured without discrimination on any ground such as sex, race, colour, language, religion, political or other opinion, national or social origin, association with a national minority, property, birth or other status.

Article 19: To ensure the observance of the engagements undertaken by the High Contracting Parties in the present Convention, there shall be set up: (a) A European Commission of Human Rights . . . (b) A European Court of Human Rights."

Protocol to the Convention for the Protection of Human Rights and Fundamental Freedoms, adopted by the Council of Europe, Paris, 20, March, 1952.

Article 2: "No person shall be denied the right to education. In the exercise of any functions which it assumes in relation to education and to teaching, the State shall respect the right of parents to ensure such education and teaching in conformity with their own religious and philosophical convictions."

Conference on Security and Cooperation in Europe, Helsinki, 1975.

Article VII: Reiterates respect for human rights and fundamental freedoms including religious practice, equality before the law for minorities, and the right of the individual to know and act upon his rights.

Recommendation No. R(85)7, Committee of Ministers to Member States on Teaching and Learning About Human Rights in Schools, 1985.

Recommends that, within their national educational systems, the government of member states encourage teaching and learning about human rights according to suggestions provided, such as: inclusion of human rights education in the school curriculum, intellectual and social skills and knowledge to be acquired in the study of human rights, the climate of the school, teacher training, and observance of international human rights day.

Universal Islamic Declaration of Human Rights, adopted at Paris, 19 September, 1981

Forward: "Human rights in Islam are an integral part of the overall Islamic order and it is obligatory on all Muslim governments and organs of society to implement them in letter and in spirit within the framework of that order."

Preamble: Asserts the obligation to establish an Islamic order "wherein all human beings shall be equal and none shall enjoy a privilege or suffer a disadvantage or discrimination by reason of race, colour, sex, origin or language."

Article III: Right to Equality and Prohibition against impermissible discrimination: (a) "All persons are equal before the Law and are entitled to equal opportunities and protection of the Law."

Article X: Rights of Minorities: (b) "In a Muslim country religious minorities shall have the choice to be governed in respect of the civil and personal matters by Islamic Law, or by their own laws."

Article XIII: Right to Freedom of Religion: "Every person has the right to freedom of conscience and worship in accordance with his religious beliefs."

Article XVIII Right to Social Security: "Every person has the right to food, shelter, clothing, education and medical care consistent with the resources of the community."

Article XIX: Right to Found a Family and Related Matters: (a) "Every person is entitled to marry, to found a family and to bring up children in conformity with his religion, traditions and culture."

(d) "Every child has the right to be maintained and properly brought up by its parents, it being forbidden that children are made to work at an early age . . ."

Article XXI Right to Education: (a) "Every person is entitled to receive education in accordance with his natural capabilities."

Explanatory notes: The term "person" refers to both the male and female sexes. The term "Law" denotes the Sharī'ah.

Banjul Charter of Human and Peoples' Rights (adopted by the Organization of African Unity, Nairobi, Kenya, 1981.)

Introductory note makes clear that the commission established by the Charter does not have the authority to interfere with the internal affairs of member states and that "the Charter does not protect certain rights such as the right of independence and the rights of women and wives . . ."

Chapter 1, Article 2: "Every individual shall be entitled to the enjoyment of the rights and freedoms recognized and guaranteed in the present Charter without distinction of any kind such as race, ethnic group, color, sex, language, religion, political or any other opinion, national and social origin, fortune, birth or other status."

Article 9: Guarantees right to receive information.

Article 17: "Every individual shall have the right to education . . ." Also guarantees individual's right to freely take part in the cultural life of his community.

Article 18: "The State shall ensure the elimination of every discrimination against women and also ensure the protection of the rights of the woman and the child as stipulated in international declarations and conventions."

"The aged and the disabled shall also have the right to special measures of protection in keeping with their physical or moral needs."

Chapter II: Establishes mandate of African Commission on Human and Peoples' Rights to protect rights laid down by Charter.

Chapter IV: Directs Commission to draw inspiration from international law on human and peoples' rights—particularly the *UN Charter*, the *Charter of the Organization of African Unity* and the *Universal Declaration of Human Rights*.

NBT

Index